THE UNITARY EU PATENT SYSTEM

The purpose of this book is to explore the key substantive, methodological, and institutional issues raised by the proposed unitary EU patent system contained in EU Regulations 1257/2012 and 1260/2012, and the Unified Patent Court Agreement 2013. The originality of this work lies in its individual contributions and uniquely broad approach, taking six different (historical, constitutional, international, competition, institutional and forward-looking) perspectives on the proposed patent system. This means that the book offers a multi-authored and all round legal appraisal of the proposed unitary system from experts in patent law, EU constitutional law, private international law, and competition law, as well as leading figures from the worlds of legal practice, the bench, and the European Patent Office. The unitary patent system raises issues of foundational importance in the fields of patent and intellectual property law, EU law and legal harmonization, which it is the purpose of the book to engage with.

This is a work which will enjoy wide and enduring interest among academics, policy makers and decision makers/practitioners working in patent law, intellectual property law, legal harmonization, and EU law.

Volume 19 Studies of the Oxford Institute of European and Comparative Law

Studies of the Oxford Institute of European and Comparative Law

Editor
Professor Stefan Vogenauer

Recent titles in this Series

Volume 12: Article 82 EC: Reflections on its Recent Evolution
Edited by Ariel Ezrachi

Volume 13: Prohibition of Abuse of Law: A New General Principle of EU Law?
Edited by Rita de la Feria and Stefan Vogenauer

Volume 14: Constitutional Pluralism in the European Union and Beyond
Edited by Matej Avbelj and Jan Komárek

Volume 15: The Protection of Fundamental Rights in the EU After Lisbon
Edited by Sybe de Vries, Ulf Bernitz and Stephen Weatherill

Volume 16: The Involvement of EU Law in Private Law Relationships
Edited by Dorota Leczykiewicz and Stephen Weatherill

Volume 17: Current Problems in the Protection of Human Rights: Perspectives from Germany and the UK
Edited by Katja S Ziegler and Peter M Huber

Volume 18: Legal Challenges in the Global Financial Crisis: Bail-outs, the Euro and Regulation
Edited by Wolf-Georg Ringe and Peter M Huber

The Unitary EU Patent System

Edited by

Justine Pila and Christopher Wadlow

•HART•
PUBLISHING
OXFORD AND PORTLAND, OREGON
2017

Hart Publishing
An imprint of Bloomsbury Publishing Plc

Hart Publishing Ltd
Kemp House
Chawley Park
Cumnor Hill
Oxford OX2 9PH
UK

Bloomsbury Publishing Plc
50 Bedford Square
London
WC1B 3DP
UK

www.hartpub.co.uk
www.bloomsbury.com

Published in North America (US and Canada) by
Hart Publishing
c/o International Specialized Book Services
920 NE 58th Avenue, Suite 300
Portland, OR 97213-3786
USA

www.isbs.com

First published in hardback, 2015
Paperback edition, 2017

British Library Cataloguing-in-Publication Data
A catalogue record for this book is available from the British Library.

ISBN: PB: 978-1-50991-417-3
HB: 978-1-84946-619-6

Typeset by Compuscript Ltd, Shannon
Printed and bound in Great Britain by
Lightning Source UK Ltd

PREFACE

These are the collected papers of the Workshop on the Unitary (EU) Patent and Unified Patent Court, jointly organised by the University of Oxford (Institute of European and Comparative Law) and the University of East Anglia (ESRC Centre for Competition Policy), held at Jesus College, Oxford, on the 4th and 5th of October 2013.

The Unitary Patent Regulation[1] and the Agreement on the Unified Patent Court[2] represent the culmination of over 50 years of attempts to legislate for a system under which patents could be enforced within Europe on a supranational, and perhaps ultimately pan-European, basis. Although the Unified Patent Court Agreement is not yet in force (it has not yet received all necessary ratifications), preparations for the new regime are proceeding apace, and it is increasingly likely that the organs of the Unified Patent Court will be up and running in 2015 or 2016, initially to adjudicate the validity and infringement of existing European patents, the owners of which have not chosen to opt out of the system.

The 10 full papers published in this volume explore these two interlinked systems from the perspectives of their historical origins (Justine Pila and Christopher Wadlow), their relationship with the European Patent Office and the Court of Justice of the European Union (Stefan Luginbuehl and Angelos Dimopoulos), their place in the EU legal and constitutional order (Tuomas Mylly), their relationship to competition law (Stefan Enchelmaier and Steven Anderman), and to American law and private international law (Rochelle C Dreyfuss and Paul LC Torremans), and finally with regard to the expectations of likely users (Alan Johnson). Our thanks to all our speakers and contributors (and where appropriate to their institutions or firms) both for their participation, and for these published papers.

We are also particularly grateful to Sir David Kitchin for opening the Workshop and to Alison Brimelow CBE (herself a UEA alumna) for delivering the closing remarks.

At the time the Workshop was held, the legal situation regarding the Unitary Patent and Unified Patent Court was very fluid (as is the case even today) and some of the contributions may now need to be read in the light of more recent developments which it has not been possible to incorporate here.

[1] Regulation (EU) No 1257/2012 of the European Parliament and of the Council of 17 December 2012 implementing enhanced cooperation in the area of the creation of unitary patent protection, OJ L 361/1 (31 December 2012).

[2] Agreement on a Unified Patent Court, OJ C 175/1 (20 June 2013).

The Workshop was made possible by the generous financial support of the ESRC Centre for Competition Policy at the University of East Anglia and the Oxford Institute of European and Comparative Law at the University of Oxford.

Christopher Wadlow and Justine Pila
Norwich and Oxford
June 2014

CONTENTS

LIST OF ABBREVIATIONS

CJEU	Court of Justice of the European Union
EC	Consolidated Version of the Treaty Establishing the European Community, OJ C 325/33 (24 December 2002)
European Convention on Human Rights (ECHR)	European Convention for the Protection of Human Rights and Fundamental Freedoms, 4 November 1950, ETS 5
ECtHR	European Court of Human Rights
EU Charter	Charter of Fundamental Rights of the European Union, OJ C 364/1 (18 December 2000)
Paris Convention	Paris Convention for the Protection of Industrial Property (20 March 1883) 13 UST 1 (as revised)
SME	Small and medium sized enterprise
Supplementary Protection Certificate (SPC) Regulations	Regulation 1610/96/EC of 23 July 1996 concerning the creation of a supplementary protection certificate for plant protection products; Council Regulation (EC) 469/2009 of 6 May 2009 concerning the supplementary protection certificate for medicinal products
TEU	Consolidated Version of the Treaty on European Union, OJ C 83/13 (30 March 2010)
TFEU	Consolidated Version of the Treaty on the Functioning of the European Union, OJ C 83/01 (30 March 2010)
Treaty of Lisbon	Treaty of Lisbon amending the Treaty on European Union and the Treaty establishing the European Community, OJ C 306/1 (17 December 2007)
TRIPS	Agreement on Trade-Related Aspects of Intellectual Property Rights, Marrakesh Agreement Establishing the World Trade Organization, Annex 1C, Legal Instruments-Results of the Uruguay Round, vol 31 (15 April 1994) 33 ILM 81

LIST OF CONTRIBUTORS

Professor Steven Anderman is Emeritus Professor of Law at the University of Essex and Visiting Professor of European Law at the University of Stockholm.

Alison Brimelow CBE is former President of the European Patent Office.

Dr Angelos Dimopoulos is Lecturer in Law, Queen Mary University of London.

Rochelle C Dreyfuss is Pauline Newman Professor of Law at New York University School of Law.

Professor Stefan Enchelmaier is Professor of European and Comparative Law at the University of Oxford and a Fellow of Lincoln College, Oxford.

Alan Johnson is a Partner at Bristows LLP.

Sir David Kitchin is Lord Justice of Appeal, Court of Appeal of England and Wales.

Dr Stefan Luginbuehl is a lawyer in the Directorate International Legal Affairs at the European Patent Office.

Professor Tuomas Mylly is Professor of European Economic Law at the University of Turku.

Dr Justine Pila is University Lecturer in Intellectual Property Law at the University of Oxford, and Fellow of St Catherine's College, Oxford.

Professor Paul LC Torremans is Professor of Intellectual Property Law at the University of Nottingham.

Professor Christopher Wadlow is Emeritus Professor of Law at the University of East Anglia.

TABLE OF CASES

Australia

European Commission

Court of Justice of the European Union

European Court of Human Rights

European Patent Office

France

Germany

United Kingdom

United States of America

TABLE OF LEGISLATION

EUROPEAN UNION

Treaties, Conventions, Agreements

Directives

Regulations

NATIONAL LEGISLATION

Germany

United Kingdom

United States of America

TABLE OF INTERNATIONAL INSTRUMENTS

1

Introductory Remarks: A Judicial Perspective

SIR DAVID KITCHIN*

Over the past two years a curious thing has happened. Everyone has become interested in patents. Industry has spoken up and politicians have woken up. And as a result it seems most Member States are about to take another significant step in what has been a very long journey. Whether it is the right step or even a step in the right direction are matters to which consideration is given in the chapters which follow. So let me first set the scene and then mention a few of the issues to which I think the current proposals give rise, and I of course do so from my perspective as a judge of a national system.

As we know, the Convention on the Grant of European Patents of 5 October 1973 (EPC) as revised in 1991 and 2000 established the European Patent Office (EPO) and entrusted to it the task of granting European patents. The EPC system sits alongside national patent systems and permits an inventor to file a single application at the EPO and secure the grant of a European patent in each of the territories he has designated.

The EPC system has obvious advantages, at least as an alternative to the existing national systems. It allows an applicant to secure a bundle of national European patents off the back of a single application, and he need only file his application in one of the three official languages of the EPO. So, at least in theory, it provides a cheaper option, and there can be no doubt that it has been an enormous success. Each year the EPO publishes the number of direct European applications filed and the number of international applications (PCT) entering the European phase. In 2013, just under 265,700 filings were recorded, around 2.8 per cent more than in 2012.[1]

But the EPC system is also thought to have serious deficiencies. The patentee ends up with a bundle of national patents which he must enforce in the national courts of different Member States. This can be costly and result in inconsistent decisions. It may also fragment the market by allowing the erection of barriers to intra-Community trade.

* Lord Justice of Appeal, Court of Appeal of England and Wales.

[1] <http://www.epo.org/about-us/annual-reports-statistics/annual-report/2013.html>.

Nor is the granting procedure entirely straightforward. The patentee must file translations of the claims into the other two official languages of the EPO. Perhaps more significantly, the various Member States which he has designated may also have different validation requirements. So, for example, the patentee may have to pay a fee to the local patent office and also provide a translation of the patent in the official language of the state in which he seeks protection. All of this means that the cost of securing pan-European patent protection is still very substantial.

So the need for a unitary patent and unitary enforcement system has long been recognised. Among the now familiar milestones marking the endeavour to realise that aim, the Community Patent Convention was signed in Luxembourg in 1975; the European Commission made a proposal to create a Community patent in 2000; attempts to reach a final agreement failed in 2003; negotiations were launched once again in 2007; and then, in the light of what seemed to be insurmountable difficulties in reaching agreement on the language issue, 12 Member States wrote to the Commission in December 2010 indicating they wished to establish enhanced cooperation and asking the Commission to submit a proposal to the Council to that end. Soon afterwards 13 more Member States indicated they too wished to participate, bringing the total to 25.

The Council's response was swift. It authorised enhanced cooperation by its decision of 10 March 2011, paving the way for what the Commission calls 'the unitary patent package'. This package consists of three elements:

- Regulation 1257 of 17 December 2012 creating the unitary patent;[2]
- Regulation 1260 also of 17 December 2012 establishing a language regime applicable to this new patent;[3]
- And an agreement signed by participating Member States on 19 February 2013 to set up the Unified Patent Court or UPC.[4]

The aims and objectives of the package are indeed laudable. The Commission describes them as being, in the case of the patent: the creation of 'a unitary patent with uniform protection within the territory of the participating 25 Member States'.[5] And it says:

> The unitary patent will be available on a one-stop shop basis at affordable costs, as it will be centrally granted by the EPO and no further validation requirement needs to be fulfilled and applications can be filed in any language;[6]

[2] Regulation (EU) No 1257/2012 of the European Parliament and of the Council of 17 December 2012 implementing enhanced cooperation in the area of the creation of unitary patent protection, OJ L361/1 (31 December 2012) (Regulation 1257/2012).

[3] Regulation (EU) No 1260/2012 of 17 December 2012 implementing enhanced cooperation in the area of the creation of unitary patent protection with regard to the applicable translation arrangements, OJ L361/89 (31 December 2012).

[4] Agreement on a Unified Patent Court, OJ C175/1 (20 June 2013) (UPC Agreement).

[5] <http://ec.europa.eu/internal_market/indprop/patent/faqs/index_en.htm>.

[6] Ibid.

In the case of the court, the aim is:

> [The creation of] a unified and specialised jurisdiction in patent matters for the participating Member States, and thus avoid an unnecessary duplication of litigation cases before the various courts of the various Member States concerned, and enhance legal certainty.[7]

And generally:

> It [that is to say, the package] will ensure the dissemination of patent information in all languages of the European Union through high-quality machine translation services which will be online and free of charge.[8]

Not only are these aims laudable but the Commission seems confident they will be delivered. Indeed Vice-President Viviane Reding, the EU's Justice Commissioner said in July of 2013: 'In the event of a dispute companies will no longer have to launch actions before a number of courts in different countries'.[9] She continued:

> Removing bureaucratic obstacles, extra costs and the legal uncertainty of having 28 different and often contradictory systems makes the single market more attractive. This is a very good example of how justice policies can stimulate growth.[10]

In the same press release the Internal Market and Services Commissioner, Michel Barnier, told us:

> It is of crucial importance for Europe's competitiveness that innovators benefit as quickly as possible from the multiple benefits of the long awaited European unitary patent.

And the Commission declared that the figures speak for themselves. In the USA, in 2011, 224,000 patents were granted, in China 172,000 while in Europe only 62,000 patents were delivered. One reason for this, it sternly warned us, is the prohibitive cost and complexity of obtaining and enforcing patents throughout the single market. However, we are to be reassured because 'all this will change in the near future thanks to the unitary patent package'.[11]

I hope you will forgive my note of scepticism. But I think it manifest that these proclamations contain a good deal of hyperbole, although no doubt buoyed by good intentions. By way of example, it is hard to see what the *high quality machine translation services* have got to do with the package at all. They may be provided with it, but they could just as easily be provided without it. And the EPO is rightly proud of its partnership with Google which led to the launch last year of the free automatic translation service called Patent Translate.[12] This already offers what it

[7] Ibid.
[8] Ibid.
[9] European Commission Press Release, 'Justice for growth: Commission fills legal gaps for unitary patent protection' IP/13/750 (29 July 2013) <http://europa.eu/rapid/press-release_IP-13-750_en.htm?locale=FR>.
[10] Ibid.
[11] Ibid.
[12] See 'EPO and Google remove language barriers from patent documentation' (29 February 2012) <http://www.epo.org/news-issues/news/2012/20120229.html>.

calls on-the-fly translation between English and 13 European languages covering 95 per cent of all patents issued in Europe. It also includes an English–Chinese translation service and by 2014 is expected to cover 32 languages including Russian, Japanese and Korean.

So also, the notion that the discrepancy in patent filings between the USA and China, on the one hand, and Europe, on the other, is attributable to the costs of enforcement seems somewhat far-fetched when every day we hear of further instances of Europe falling behind its competitors in the global race to harness innovations. Just last summer we have read that the UK is investing £60m to develop graphene, a remarkable material which was first isolated in 2004 by two scientists working at Manchester University; work, I may say, for which they were awarded the Nobel Prize for physics in 2010. But where is the UK now? According to Cambridge IP, the world's top 10 graphene patent owners are all based in the USA, South Korea and China.[13] Filings from the UK relating to graphene comprise less than one per cent of the total. This particular illustration chimes with the general EPO statistics on all filings which show most have come from the USA and Japan, with China and the Republic of Korea high on the list. Germany is the only country which can match them, with France not far behind.

We must therefore view the package with a critical eye, and consider it holistically—for unitary patents will be of no use without an effective means of enforcement.We must also keep well in mind that these patents could operate as a wholly unjustified fetter on competition if businesses are denied an effective means of challenging them, or defending themselves against unjustified infringement allegations.

Looked at in this way, as part of the whole, what can we say of the unitary patent? As I began, there can be no doubting the soundness of the principle. But this patent has a number of features about which I do have concerns. First of all, it will only be available in those territories which ratify the agreement, and there need be no more than 13 of those. It will not be available in other EU Member States or other EPC Contracting States. Further, for those countries that do ratify the agreement, the unitary patent will sit alongside the other existing systems or, in other words, this patent will be an *alternative*. And further still, for at least seven years, patentees may opt to keep their European patents outside the scope of the Unified Patent Court system, where it is understood they will remain unless opted back in.

So what will be the effect of these alternatives? I fear the answer is that it will create an extremely complex landscape, and one which will enable patentees to develop their portfolios in such a way as to further their commercial interests by suppressing competition. Defendants may face claims for infringement of national patents, EP patents outside the scope of the UPC, EP patents within the

[13] See 'Commercial innovation league table for grapheme: The world's top 10 graphene patent owners' (14 February 2013) <http://www.cambridgenetwork.co.uk/news/worlds-top-10-graphene-patent-owners/>.

UPC and unitary patents—four different co-existing systems with different rules, a challenge for any business, let alone small and medium-sized enterprises(SMEs).

A more prosaic but nonetheless important question is: what is the unitary patent going to cost? This is a matter to which the authorities are giving anxious consideration, and rightly so, for studies and common sense indicate that uptake of this option and the level of renewals will depend on the fees. The Commission says that obtaining patent protection across all Member States costs about €36,000 but that under the new system these costs will fall to about €5,000, or perhaps a little more during the transitional period.[14] Should that prove to be the case it would certainly benefit applicants who currently file widely. But the EPO has stayed silent, save to indicate that it hopes to set the fees in the summer of 2014, and that it will do so having regard to such matters as the need to promote innovation and increase competitiveness; the size of the applicant and its location; the size of the market the unitary patent will protect; and the costs incurred by the EPO itself. And we must also remember that at the moment few find it necessary to file right across Europe, and many file only in a combination of Germany, France, the UK, the Netherlands and Italy.

There is also the significant question of renewal fees—something which is often overlooked in the debate but may have a significant effect on the uptake of the unitary patent. Under the existing system patentees often trim their portfolios geographically to reflect the commercial success of their inventions. But this will not be possible with the unitary patent. It is all or nothing and remains so for the whole of its life.

So that brings me to the court itself, an essential component of the package. Here too I have great concerns, and they start with its structure. As we know the court of first instance is divided into local or regional divisions and the central division, which itself has two regional sections, one in Munich and one in London. This, it is said, will provide patentees with better and more effective protection.

But I would like to focus for a moment on the defendant and take by way of example a small business located in the UK and with most but not all of its customers based here. Under the current UK system it would likely find itself sued in the Patents County Court (now the Intellectual Property Enterprise Court) with a procedure not unlike that of the UPC but with a cap on recoverable costs of £50,000, for a determination on liability, and no court fees. An equivalent business in Germany would expect to find itself in front of a similarly convenient court. But under the UPC system such a business may find itself before the local or regional division of any participating Member State into which its goods have been sold, and facing a pan-European injunction which will shut down its domestic manufacture and home market.

Now that, you may say, is a feature of any pan-European system. And so it is. But one would expect to find inherent in such a system an effective way of

14 <http://ec.europa.eu/internal_market/indprop/patent/faqs/index_en.htm>.

challenging the asserted right. Here lies the UPC's greatest structural vice—its inbuilt propensity for bifurcation. Let us return to our small or medium-sized trader who finds himself before a local or regional division in a territory other than his own. Suppose he decides to counterclaim. But instead of having his counterclaim dealt with by the local division, he may find himself sent to the central division, in whichever of the three centres is applicable to the subject matter of the invention. And if he loses in either the local division or the central division he must appeal. For that he must go to a third country, Luxembourg. So to protect his main UK business he must go to three jurisdictions. I ask: how many will have the means to do that?

You may also say, well, bifurcation is already a feature of the German system. And again you would be right. But I would respond with two points. First, bifurcation has been shown to provide a patentee with significant advantages: it allows him to argue for different constructions of his claims before different courts—Mario Franzosi's familiar Angora cat; but, more importantly, it allows him to secure his injunction before the patent's validity has ever been properly tested. This latter advantage is one which is compounded by the fact that in Germany it is not permissible to commence revocation proceedings until after the conclusion of proceedings before the EPO, often producing a substantial temporal gap—sometimes called 'the injunction gap'—between the grant of an injunction by the infringement court and an order for revocation by the Federal Patent Court.

Second, that temporal advantage has until now been one which a reasonably well-funded defendant could address by commencing revocation proceedings before another court, such as the High Court in England, which has been prepared to hear revocation proceedings early in the life of a patent and while EPO opposition proceedings are pending. An order for revocation of the UK equivalent has often raised sufficient doubt in the mind of the German first instance Regional Court or, on appeal, the Higher Regional Court to deter it from granting an injunction. Of course, under the UPC system this will not be an option.

An open letter of 26 September 2013 from a remarkable alliance of fierce competitors including Google, Yahoo, Microsoft, Apple, Samsung and BlackBerry showed these concerns are not solely the province of SMEs.[15] As they explained, the risk of injunctions granted at the request of unprincipled claimants suing on low quality patents whose validity has not been tested could drive them to relocate their factories elsewhere—so undermining rather than promoting innovation in Europe.

As I have argued before, bifurcation may have another important consequence. Some local divisions may adopt this practice more than others—perhaps because that is what the judges sitting in that division are used to doing—and we must remember that many local divisions and all regional divisions will have two local judges. If they do then naturally they will become popular with patentees and so

[15] <https://docs.google.com/file/d/0BwxyRPFduTN2NkpoN29UVm11OWc/edit?pli=1>.

reinforce the tendency of those courts to bifurcate. This will in turn encourage forum shopping. And I fear it will be forum shopping of a very dangerous kind for business—shopping for those courts most likely to grant pan-European injunctions on weak patents. I believe a much better solution would have been to have a single court without central or local divisions but to allow it to sit locally when convenient. Sadly that is not an option—so we must hope for a strong Court of Appeal which is prepared to issue clear guidance.

Now a word about the judges. Users commonly say that they will opt out of the UPC unless they have confidence in its judges. For example, inexperienced judges may be too ready to grant interim injunctions, another concern raised in the open letter of 26 September to which I have referred. This, it appears, is one of the features thought critical to the success of the court. Who are these judges going to be? We know there are going to have to be a good many because each panel of the local and regional divisions is to have three legally qualified judges—unless the parties agree otherwise. At the request of the parties or of the court there may also be a technically qualified judge. As for the panels of the central division, these are each to have two legally qualified judges and one technically qualified judge. The Court of Appeal is going to sit in panels of five: with three legally and two technically qualified judges—even, it seems, when the court is hearing appeals on points of law or procedure. All these judges are to be appointed by the Administrative Committee on the basis of a list prepared by the Advisory Committee. The composition of these committees is yet to be determined and the criteria for appointment to them are provided for only in the barest outline. As for the judges, we may be reassured that these are to be of 'the highest standards of competence' with 'proven experience',[16] and a training framework is to be established to ensure a 'broad geographic distribution'.[17] So the Administrative Committee is mandated to ensure 'the best legal and technical expertise' and a 'balanced composition … on as broad a geographical basis as possible'.[18] The challenge will be to secure judges of the appropriate calibre and experience whilst not allowing the court to be dominated by judges from a few nations. Nor is the task made easier by the absence of any published proposals for the terms of their engagement.

Cost is another critical element, not only for the success of the court in terms of attracting patentees, but also for defendants. The court is expected to be self-financing after seven years, and the fees and other revenues must be set accordingly. But at the same time there must be access to justice, including for SMEs and natural persons. Indeed, the system contemplates the provision of legal aid. How is this balance of fees and expenditure to be achieved? We have not been told—but I fear that the fees will necessarily be high absent substantial government support. This, it must be remembered, is the first of its kind: a self-standing court across many different territories dealing with validity and infringement of substantial

[16] UPC Agreement, Art 15.
[17] Ibid, Art 19.
[18] Ibid, Art 3(3).

property rights. It must be supported by an administration and IT systems, secure the use of premises for all of the local, regional and central divisions, and the Court of Appeal, and fund the cadre of judges to which I have referred, many of whom will have to travel away from their homes to meet the requirement for multi-national panels. In addition, there are the costs of the action itself. Upon whom will the burden of all these fees and costs fall? Plainly in part upon patentees, but in one way or another they can always opt out. Even after the transitional period, they can continue to file nationally. The defendants, on the other hand, have no choice. If they are sued in the UPC system then that is where they must stay. And if they wish to bring a counterclaim to secure the revocation of the patent then they too must pay an upfront fee. Is this something small businesses can really hope to shoulder—in addition to their own costs?

These are some of the issues. There are many others. For example, there are gaps in the package, as the Max Planck Institute has pointed out in its 'Twelve reasons for Concern'[19]—as they say, compulsory licensing is left to the national law. There will be difficulties for traders who wish to 'clear the path'; they may find that proceedings for revocation or declarations filed centrally are 'stalled' by the patentee launching infringement proceedings in a local division. We must expect patentees to try and 'game' the system—indeed, it would be naïve to suppose otherwise. They will divide their portfolios—file some applications nationally, file others for EP patents both within and without the UPC, and file yet others for unitary patents. They may try to require any counterclaim to be brought in the Central Division by ensuring actions are brought by exclusive licensees, and so forth.

So in conclusion, let me draw the threads together. I applaud the concept and aims of the unitary patent and the UPC. Major markets such as China and the USA have a single patent and a single legal system for its enforcement. We need the same. But the unitary patent package has structural deficiencies and in important respects remains opaque. Sitting, as it will, alongside the existing systems, it has the potential to favour patentees and to increase the cost and complexity of patent litigation. Should that prove to be the case, it may stifle innovation and competition, and even drive manufacturing businesses out of the EU. Delivery of a successful and fair system will, I think, require the constructive engagement of academics, practitioners and industry in the working up of the package, the continued financial support of participating Member States and, ultimately, a strong and determined judiciary.

[19] R Hilty et al, 'The Unitary Patent Package: Twelve Reasons for Concern' (2012) 10 *CIPA Journal* 553.

2

An Historical Perspective I: The Unitary Patent Package

JUSTINE PILA*

I. Introduction

The so-called unitary patent package of 2012 and 2013 (UPP)[1] invokes a sense of déjà vu: we seem to have been here, or somewhere close to here, before; the first time in the 1970s and 1980s with the Community Patent Convention 1975 and Luxembourg Agreement 1989,[2] and more recently in the 2000s with the Community Patent Regulations 2000–09 (CPR).[3] Given this, it is natural to ask how the UPP differs from these past initiatives, and what, if anything, its differences reflect about the changes in the European patent and general legal systems since the 1950s.[4] Does the UPP represent a case of *plus ça change* in European law *plus c'est la meme chose* in the unitary patent proposals of the European Union (EU) and its Member States, or is it a substantively new proposal for a new reality? And to what extent can any differences be justified?[5]

* BA/LLB Hons, PhD (Melbourne). University Lecturer in Intellectual Property Law, University of Oxford; Senior Law Tutor, St Catherine's College, Oxford; Research Fellow, Oxford Institute of European and Comparative Law.

[1] See Regulation (EU) No 1257/2012 of the European Parliament and of the Council of 17 December 2012 implementing enhanced cooperation in the area of the creation of unitary patent protection, OJ L361/1 (31 December 2012) (Regulation 1257/2012); Regulation (EU) No 1260/2012 of 17 December 2012 implementing enhanced cooperation in the area of the creation of unitary patent protection with regard to the applicable translation arrangements, OJ L361/89 (31 December 2012); Agreement on a Unified Patent Court, OJ C175/1 (20 June 2013) (UPC Agreement).

[2] Convention for the European Patent for the Common Market 76/76/EEC (15 December 1975) (CPC); Agreement relating to Community patents 89/695/EEC (15 December 1989), OJ L401/1 (30 December 1989) (Luxembourg Agreement). By Art 1(4) of the 1989 Agreement, it was to replace the 1975 Convention upon taking effect.

[3] See especially Proposal for a Council Regulation on the Community patent, COM(2000) 412 final OJ C337 E (28 November 2000) 278–90; Proposal for a Council Regulation on the European Union Patent, Council Doc 16113/09 ADD 1 (27 November 2009).

[4] When work began on the CPC. For a more detailed account of its origins see J Pila, 'The European Patent: An Old and Vexing Problem' (2013) 62 *ICLQ* 917.

[5] For other views on this question see, eg R Hilty et al, 'The Unitary Patent Package: Twelve Reasons for Concern' (2012) 10 *CIPA Journal* 553.

Considering these questions is the initial aim of the current chapter. It will be shown that the UPP *is* substantively different from its predecessors, primarily in the degree and form of its European-ness. In particular, the UPP is—or has the potential to be—less *communitaire* than each of the CPC, Luxembourg and CPR proposals, due to it being less supportive of EU autonomy and of the integration of general EU law and policy into the European patent field. It will also be suggested that while this may be explicable with reference to changes in the legal and political context in which it was concluded, including the widespread dissatisfaction with the EU and its contribution to patent law to date, it cannot be justified, whether from an EU single market or a substantive patent law perspective. Among other things, this is because of the risk that it will ignore, and thereby undermine, the deep connections between patent law and social and economic rights and freedoms.

II. The UPP in the Light of Prior Unitary (EU) Patent Initiatives

A. Prior Unitary (EU) Patent Initiatives

The UPP is the most recent in a line of proposals to create a unitary patent system for Europe. While the earliest date back to the eighteenth century, the first EU initiative was launched in the late 1950s, and culminated in the conclusion of the Community Patent Convention in 1975.[6] Working alongside the drafters of the supranational European Patent Convention of 1973 (EPC),[7] the then six members of the European Economic Community (EEC) sought to achieve three legal ends by means of the CPC.[8] The first was to create a second and autonomous species of European patent to supplement the European 'bundle' patent created by the EPC in the form of a 'Community patent'.[9] While the Community patent was also to be granted by the EPO applying the patentability provisions of the EPC, it was to differ from the bundle patent in conferring unitary protection throughout the entire EEC territory,[10] rather than, as conferred by bundle patents, a set of national grants for two or more (EEC and non-EEC) Contracting States designated for protection by the patentee and requiring separate validation, translation, renewal and enforcement in each designated country. The second aim of the CPC was to extend the code of substantive patent law already contained in the Council

[6] See Pila (n 4).
[7] Convention on the Grant of European Patents (5 October 1973) 13 ILM 268.
[8] On their wider aims see Pila (n 4).
[9] See CPC, Art 2(3).
[10] See CPC, Arts 1(2) and 2.

of Europe's Strasbourg Patent Convention 1963 (SPC)[11] and the supranational EPC (covering patentability and aspects of patent scope) by introducing a new European law governing the effects of Community patents more generally.[12] And the third and last of the CPC's aims was to lay the foundations for supranational patent litigation and compulsory licensing arrangements by committing EEC Member States to commence work on creating such arrangements as soon as the CPC entered into force, and to adopt certain (albeit excludable) rules on compulsory licensing in the interim.[13] Until then the enforcement of Community patents was to be left to the national courts of Member States, supported by the EPO exercising jurisdiction in respect of patent revocation applications,[14] and the European Court of Justice (ECJ) exercising appellate jurisdiction in respect of EPO revocation decisions[15] and hearing preliminary referrals from national courts in respect of all aspects of substantive patent law.[16] So too compulsory licensing was to be left to Member States, with the effect of any licences granted confined to the territory of the granting state, consistent with their aim of protecting local social and economic interests, including public health.[17]

At the time the CPC was concluded, there was no suggestion that the EEC had competence to create a new patent title, and so it was that this earliest initiative was concluded as an international agreement rather than an EEC instrument. By express provision of Article 94, it depended on the ratification of all EEC Member States to take effect, which for some required a national referendum and constitutional amendment. The onerousness of this process, combined with the fact that all future Member States would have needed to enter a new agreement to accede, might explain why the Convention never took effect. However, there were likely other reasons for its failure as well.[18] One was its burdensome language regime, which required that patent claims be translated into the languages of all Member States, and permitted individual states to reserve the right to demand also that specifications be translated into their own language for the patent to take effect in their territory.[19] Another related reason was its uncertain economic impact, due in part to its bifurcation of validity and infringement proceedings, and the concerns that it would discriminate against small and medium-sized enterprises (SMEs) particularly. And a third was the all-or-nothing protection it offered patentees,

[11] Convention on the Unification of Certain Points of Substantive Law on Patents for Inventions (Strasbourg, 27 November 1963) ETS 47.

[12] See CPC, Ch II.

[13] See CPC, Arts 46–48, 69(4), 82 and 89; Resolution on Common Rules on the Granting of Compulsory Licences in Respect of Community Patents.

[14] See CPC, Arts 9 and 10.

[15] See CPC, Art 63.

[16] See CPC, Art 73.

[17] See n 13.

[18] See Pila (n 4); also 'Promoting Innovation through Patents: Green Paper on the Community Patent and the Patent System in Europe' COM(97) 314 (24 June 1997) (Commission Green Paper 1997).

[19] See CPC, Arts 14, 33 and 88.

and the nervousness among some at the prospect of having their monopolies invalidated or enforced for the entire EEC by a single proceeding before the EPO or a national court of another country. Given that the EPC had itself only recently been introduced, and that the availability of Community patents would not have precluded the grant of European bundle patents designating one or more EEC Member States,[20] the CPC could be said to have offered too little too soon to be worth the trouble of ratifying.[21]

So too, it seems, for the Luxembourg Agreement of 1989. According to the prevailing view, the main reasons that this Agreement failed to fly were its modified language and litigation arrangements.[22] Under its language arrangements, patentees would have been required to translate specifications as a whole rather than merely the patent claims into an official language of each Member State,[23] which would have been extremely expensive, particularly as Community membership increased. So too the Agreement's litigation arrangements were complex and likely to be costly. Under them, jurisdiction was to be vested in national courts designated as Community patent courts, with appeals to a new Community patent appeal court common to the Contracting States (COPAC).[24] In addition, preliminary referrals to the ECJ were to be allowed from the COPAC 'whenever there is a risk of an interpretation of this Agreement being inconsistent with [the EEC] Treaty',[25] and from certain national courts on matters of jurisdiction,[26] with the delays that such references entail; and so too infringement actions were to be subject to stays pending the outcome of related validity proceedings.[27] Finally, the increase in Community membership meant that 12 ratifications were now required for the system to take effect,[28] with some facing the same national constitutional obstacles as previously.[29]

When the European Commission took up the challenge of creating a unitary European patent again in the 1990s, it was in the context of a rapidly developing European intellectual property field. Aside from the growing body of EPO jurisprudence on the principles of patentability and patent scope contained in the EPC, there was by this time a developing body of Community intellectual property law, facilitated by the introduction of the Single European Act in 1987,

[20] See CPC, Art 82.

[21] Cf Pila (n 4).

[22] See Commission Green Paper 1997.

[23] See Luxembourg Agreement, Art 30.

[24] See Protocol on the Settlement of Litigation concerning the Infringement and Validity of Community Patents annexed to the Agreement.

[25] See Luxembourg Agreement, Art 2(2).

[26] See ibid, Art 3(2).

[27] Luxembourg Agreement, Art 73.

[28] Ibid, Art 6. A diplomatic conference convened in May 1992 to modify the conditions of the Agreement's entry into force did not produce any results: O Montalto, 'Patent and Trademark Developments in the European Community' (1993) 4 *Fordham Intellectual Property, Media and Entertainment Law Journal* 299, 300.

[29] Cf Montalto, ibid.

and including a plant variety Regulation,[30] two supplementary patent protection certificate (SPC) Regulations,[31] and a biotech patenting Directive.[32] In addition to these harmonization measures, the European Court had been busy explaining the implications of the free movement and competition provisions of the EEC Treaty for national compulsory licensing and acts involving the infringement of national patent grants.[33] For example, in 1992 it issued two decisions rejecting the validity of compulsory licences for failure to work at all, or sufficiently, a patent for an invention the local demand for which was satisfied by imports from other parts of the Community.[34] The effect was to render invalid Articles 89 and 83 of the CPC and Luxembourg Agreement respectively, by which Member States were permitted to reserve the right to require full local exploitation of a Community patent, and to grant compulsory licences in respect of a patentee who had failed to comply.[35] When combined with other ECJ decisions during this period,[36] the cases confirmed the Court's preparedness to ensure that the exercise of patent and other intellectual property rights served Community goals.[37]

In addition to this change in the legal landscape into which a unitary patent system would be introduced, there was a new concern on the part of the Commission in the 1990s, following the failures of the CPC and Luxembourg Agreements, to understand and accommodate the wishes of the public, including users of the patent system particularly. Hence its 1997 Green Paper,[38] the results of which were described in its follow-up document[39] as follows:

> The general message emerging from all of these discussions is the need to put greater emphasis on the practical aspects of the patent system, which should take full account of users' needs. Patents are very important instruments for promoting innovation, creativity and employment. They must form an integral part of the economic reality of enterprises, inventors and SMEs, providing them with adequate protection at a reasonable cost and

[30] Regulation (EC) No 2100/94 of 27 July 1994 on Community plant variety rights, OJ L227/1 (1 September 1994).

[31] Regulation (EEC) No 1768/92 of 18 June 1992 concerning the creation of a supplementary protection certificate for medicinal products, OJ L182/1 (2 July 1992); Regulation (EC) No 1610/96 of the European Parliament and of the Council of 23 July 1996 concerning the creation of a supplementary protection certificate for plant protection products, OJ L198/30 (8 August 1996).

[32] Directive 98/44/EC of the European Parliament and of the Council of 6 July 1998 on the legal protection of biotechnological inventions, OJ L213 (30 July 1998) (Biotech Directive).

[33] See, eg C-191/90 *Generics and Harris v Smith Kline and French* [1992] ECR I-5335; C-316/95 *Generics BV v Smith Kline & French Laboratories Ltd* [1997] ECR I-3929.

[34] See C-235/89 *Commission v Italian Republic* [1992] ECR I-3; C-30/90 *Commission v United Kingdom* [1992] ECR I-4.

[35] According to the Commission Green Paper 1997, the compulsory licensing provisions of the Luxembourg Agreement were in any case displaced by those of the TRIPS Agreement.

[36] See, eg Joined Cases C-241/91 P & C-242/91 P *RTE and ITV v Commission* [1995] ECR I-485.

[37] See the discussions by Stefan Enchelmaier and Steven Anderman in chs 7 and 8 of this volume; also F Fine, 'European Community Compulsory Licensing Policy: Heresy versus Common Sense' (2004) 24 *Northwestern Journal of International Law & Business* 619.

[38] See above n 18.

[39] 'Promoting Innovation through Patents: The Follow-Up to the Green Paper on the Community Patent and the Patent System in Europe' COM(99) 42 (5 February 1999) (Follow-Up to the Commission Green Paper 1997).

with optimum legal certainty. Above all, patents should not hinder innovation. ... Most comments emphasise the need to reverse priorities.[40]

Central to the Commission's 'reversal of priorities' regarding the unitary patent agenda was a new emphasis on cost and efficiency, including through the closer integration of the proposed patent system and the EPC. In the light of this particularly, one is able better to understand the CPR 2000. For one, its legal basis was an EC Regulation rather than an international agreement; the European Parliament having concluded that harmonization of 'the concrete provisions of national patent legislation' was 'no longer sufficient, and that it is necessary to draw up a Community Regulation with its legal basis in Article 235 of the EC Treaty' instead.[41] In addition, and partly as a consequence of this, the new Community patent was to be an autonomous *EC* right, governed in its essential aspects by the Regulation itself.[42] Further, the CPR 2000 sought to abolish domestic compulsory licensing altogether, and to replace it with Community-wide compulsory licences granted by the Commission.[43] It also proposed a simplified and cheaper language regime, whereby claims would be translated into the three official languages of the EPO (French, German and English) following the EPO's grant of the patent in one of the same.[44] And finally, it sought to displace the jurisdiction of national courts in respect of Community patents completely, by creating a Community intellectual property court with chambers of first instance and appeal, and vesting it and the EC Court of First Instance (CFI) with exclusive jurisdiction in respect of Community patents and Commission-granted patent licences respectively, with preliminary referrals to the ECJ from the CFI.[45] The net effect of these provisions was to increase the efficiency of the proposed unitary patent system, and to strengthen its community character as well, including by involving the CFI. This was even truer under a 2003 refinement of the proposal, which envisaged appeals from the Community court to the CFI.[46] On the other hand, the CPR maintained the international focus of its predecessors, supporting a closer cooperation between the proposed system and the EPC[47] by providing for Community accession to the Convention, and conceiving Community patents as European bundle patents designating the Community. It also followed the EPC model by giving a specialist tribunal first instance jurisdiction at least for interpreting and applying European patent law.

[40] Ibid, [1.1].

[41] See ibid, [1.2].

[42] See CPR 2000, Art 2(2).

[43] See ibid, Arts 21 and 22.

[44] See ibid, Art 11(2). Defendants were also to be shielded from liability for infringing a Community patent that had not been translated into the defendant's own language: see ibid, Art 44(3).

[45] See generally ibid, [2.4.5].

[46] See Proposal for a Council Decision establishing the Community Patent Court and concerning appeals before the Court of First Instance, COM(2003) 324 final (23 December 2003), Art 26.

[47] See ibid, [2.3]: 'The main thrust of this proposal is the creation of a "symbiosis" between two systems: that of the Regulation on the Community patent, a European Community instrument, and that of the Munich Convention, a classic international instrument'.

Between the first and last of the CPR proposals, in 2000 and 2009 respectively, further changes in the EU legal order had taken place. Above all, the Lisbon Treaty had come into force, conferring express competence on the EU to create intellectual property rights by TFEU, Article 118,[48] and elevating the Charter of Fundamental Rights[49] (including its requirement that 'intellectual property … be protected', consistent with the European Convention on Human Rights (ECHR)[50]) to the status of the EU Treaties.[51] In addition, the ECJ had rejected a challenge by the Netherlands to the constitutional validity of the Biotech Directive,[52] whose provisions had then been implemented by all Member States. On the other hand, however, a proposal for a further EU Directive on the patenting of computer-implemented inventions[53] had been rejected by the European Parliament after a controversial and drawn out legislative passage in which the EU was accused, among other things, of giving its imprimatur to 'casuistical' EPO case law that all but abolished the EPC's exclusion of computer programs from patentability.[54] And finally, the CJEU had published two decisions precluding reliance on the Brussels I Regulation to enforce simultaneously European bundle patents in multiple European jurisdictions in the majority of patent cases.[55]

Once again, this context helps to explain the last of the CPR proposals, concluded in 2009, including its somewhat ambivalent connection to the EU legal order. For example, the CPR's litigation agreement was now to be concluded not only by EU States, but also by non-EU members of the EPC.[56] According to the CJEU in an opinion on the constitutional validity of the agreement in 2011, its provisions tipped the balance too far in favour of internationalism at the expense of the Union, and in doing so breached the EU Treaties.[57] In the Court's opinion,

[48] According to the first paragraph of that Article: 'In the context of the establishment and functioning of the internal market, the European Parliament and the Council, acting in accordance with the ordinary legislative procedure, shall establish measures for the creation of European intellectual property rights to provide uniform protection of intellectual property rights throughout the Union and for the setting up of centralised Union-wide authorisation, coordination and supervision arrangements'.

[49] Charter of Fundamental Rights of the European Union, OJ C364/1 (18 December 2000).

[50] See Art 1 of Protocol 1; *Anheuser-Busch Inc v Portugal* [2007] 44 EHRR 42 (Grand Chamber) (interpreting the ECHR right to the peaceful enjoyment of one's possessions to include a right to the peaceful enjoyment of one's patents).

[51] See TEU, Art 6(1).

[52] See C-377/98 *Kingdom of Netherlands v Parliament and Council* [2001] ECR I-07079.

[53] See Proposal for a Directive of the European Parliament and of the Council on the patentability of computer-implemented inventions, COM(2002) 92 final (20 February 2002).

[54] See Opinion of the Economic and Social Committee on the Proposal for a Directive of the European Parliament and of the Council on the patentability of computer-implemented inventions, COM(2002) 92 final (19 September 2002) [3.1].

[55] See Case C-4/03 *Gesellschaft für Antriebstechnik mbH & Co KG v Lamellen und Kupplungsbau Beteiligungs KG* [2006] ECR I-6509; Case C-539/03 *Roche Nederland BV v Frederick Primus* [2006] ECR I-6535.

[56] See Working document on a revised Presidency text on a draft Agreement on the European and EU Patents Court and Draft Statute of 23 March 2009 (doc 7928/09), Preamble ('the present Agreement shall be open to accession by any Contracting State to the European Patent Convention').

[57] See Opinion 1/09 (8 March 2011).

the expansive jurisdiction of the proposed European and Community Patents Court meant that it would inevitably be called upon to read and interpret Treaty provisions concerning the internal market and competition law, as well as fundamental rights and general EU legal principles.[58] Given the exclusive nature of that jurisdiction, the effect of the agreement would have been to divest national courts of their powers in relation to the interpretation and application of EU law, and the power of the CJEU itself to respond to questions put to it under the preliminary referral mechanism of TFEU, Article 267.[59] In this way, the CJEU held, the agreement 'would alter the essential character of the powers which the Treaties confer on the institutions of the European Union and on the Member States and which are indispensable to the preservation of the very nature of European Union law'.[60] Hence the need for the EU to return once again to the unitary patent drawing board to produce yet another version of the CPC; the result this time being the UPP.

B. The UPP in the Light of Prior Unitary EU Patent Initiatives

The UPP clearly has much in common with the earlier unitary patent proposals, including the CPR proposals particularly. Above all, it seeks to create a new species of European patent providing uniform protection and having equal effect throughout EU Member States.[61] In addition, it builds on the existing system of the EPC, preserving its substantive law of patentability and patent scope,[62] and the role of the EPO as the granter of all European patents and the keeper of all European patent registers.[63] Third, it seeks to supplement, rather than displace, the European bundle patent for participating EU Member States in order to maximize patent owners' choice, and adopts a comparatively simple and user-friendly language regime by requiring that only patent claims be translated into the three official languages of the EPO.[64]

Beyond these basic similarities, however, the UPP differs from its predecessors in varied and significant ways. For example, while the unitary patent will have its legal basis in an EU Regulation, it will not be an autonomous right in the sense of deriving its content from its founding (EU) instrument. Instead, its content will be derived from the national laws of participating Member States, incorporating the provisions of the EPC and UPC Agreement,[65] making it little different *qua*

[58] See ibid, [78].
[59] See ibid, [79], [80] and [89].
[60] See ibid, [89].
[61] See Regulation 1257/2012, Art 3(2).
[62] See ibid, Recital 5, Art 2.
[63] See ibid, Art 9.
[64] See Regulation 1260/2012.
[65] See Regulation 1257/2012, Art 5(3).

right from a national or European bundle patent.[66] Nor, more generally, does the UPP support the autonomy and application of EU law to the extent of its predecessors. For example, under the unitary patent system the effect of each grant will be confined to the 13 or more participating EU Member States that have ratified the UPC Agreement and recognized the exclusive jurisdiction of the Court at the date of the patent's registration, with the Court's jurisdiction confined accordingly.[67] As a result, neither the unitary patent nor its supporting judicial system will necessarily extend throughout the EU, as each of the Community patents and patent systems would have done. Further, while the UPC is described as having exclusive jurisdiction in respect of all European (unitary *and* bundle) patents, as well as SPCs, for the first seven years of its existence at least litigants will be able to opt-out of its jurisdiction in respect of bundle patents and SPCs by initiating proceedings before national courts, ensuring the continued development of parallel national jurisprudence with respect to 'European' patent principles.[68] And finally, in contrast to several of the earlier UP proposals, the UPP limits the substantive jurisdiction of the CJEU and ensures that a specialist, supranational tribunal will remain the primary first and last instance court across the breadth of the European patent field.[69]

These limits on the CJEU's jurisdiction in favour of the UPC and even national courts raise the continued impact of non-EU sources of law more generally. Key in this context is that the UPP does not increase the scope of substantive EU law in the patent field, which will continue to be confined, in effect, to the Biotech Directive.[70] Given this, it is not surprising that the UPC Agreement requires the Unified Patent Court to base its decisions on a variety of non-EU legal sources as well as EU law, including the UPC Agreement, the EPC, 'other international agreements applicable to patents and binding on all the Contracting Member States',

[66] In effect the unitary patent will be a bundle patent exempt from the usual validation and renewal procedures imposed by the designated states.

[67] See Regulation 1257/2012, Arts 3(1) and 18(2).

[68] UPC Agreement, Art 83. On this opt-out mechanism see the discussions by Paul Torremans and Alan Johnson in chs 10 and 11 of this volume.

[69] As a Member State Court for EU legal purposes, the UPC will be subject to the preliminary referral procedure of TFEU, Art 267 with respect to questions of EU law which, under the UPP, will be confined (in relation to substantive law) to questions arising from the Biotech Directive. Under UPC Agreement, Art 32, and subject to the opt-out provision of Art 83, the UPC will otherwise have exclusive competence in respect of infringement and validity/revocation proceedings involving European (bundle and unitary) patents and SPCs, as well as actions relating to prior user rights, actions for compensation for licences of right, and actions concerning decisions of the EPO with respect to unitary patents. By express provision of Art 32(2), national courts remain competent for all other actions.

[70] On the TRIPS Agreement as a further source of substantive EU patent law see Case C-414/11 *Daiichi Sankyo and Sanofi-Aventis Deutschland* [2013] ECR I-0000, and the discussion by Angelos Dimopoulos and Tuomas Mylly in chs 5 and 6 of this volume. On the omission of substantive law in the UP Regulations, see C Wadlow, 'Hamlet without the Prince: Can the Unitary Patent Regulation Strut its Stuff without Articles 6–8?' (2013) 8 *Journal of Intellectual Law & Practice* 207.

and participating states' national laws,[71] since it is in such other sources that the law governing unitary patents must be found.

This leads to another way in which the UPP could be said to offer less support for the autonomy and development of EU (patent) law, which is its unconcern with the contractual rights of third parties, including compulsory licences. By express provision of Regulation 1257/2012, such rights will arise under and be governed by national laws, and confined in their scope to the territory of the granting state.[72] As seen above, this is notwithstanding the CPC and Luxembourg Agreement's restriction of the right of national authorities to grant compulsory licences in respect of Community patents to a 'short transitional period' for competition-related reasons,[73] and the CPRs' prohibition of national compulsory licensing altogether in preference for Community-wide, Commission-granted licences regulated by the CFI, once again in the service of competition policy.[74] It is also without regard to the effect of CJEU case law concerning the compatibility of national compulsory licensing with the EU Treaties.[75]

The explicit linkage under the prior unitary patent proposals of compulsory licensing with competition rules and values—as well as with social rights such as public health—underlines the effect of leaving such licensing to national authorities. As others have noted, however, that effect will be to create an imbalance between the rights of third parties and patentees and, by requiring that the former be dealt with domestically by Member States, to support a view of them and their aims as somehow peripheral to the (European) patent regime.[76]

In sum therefore, the UPP differs from its predecessors in ways that make it less *communitaire* overall, in the sense of being less supportive of EU legal autonomy and of the integration of general EU law and policy into the European patent system. Indeed, such is the minimalism of UP Regulation 1257/2012 in particular that one could say, as Italy and Spain have said, that it does not create a new species of EU patent right at all, as envisaged by TFEU, Article 118, and that it is therefore not authorized by the EU Treaties.[77] For these reasons, it is clear that the UPP is not simply a case of *plus ça change* but rather a substantively different proposal. The question that then remains is how, if at all, it can be justified.

[71] See UPC Agreement, Art 24. By Art 20, the UPC will be required to recognize and respect the primacy of EU law.

[72] See Regulation 1257/2012, Recital 10.

[73] See Resolution on Common Rules on the Granting of Compulsory Licences in Respect of Community Patents.

[74] See CPR 2000 and CPR 2009, Art 22(2); CPR 2000, [2.4.5.2].

[75] On this case law see the discussion by Steven Anderman in ch 8 of this volume.

[76] See, eg Hilty et al (n 5). Compare the view of the CJEU in Opinion 1/09, that the Court proposed to support the CPR 2009 would, given its expansive jurisdiction, be called upon to read and interpret Treaty provisions concerning the internal market and competition law, and even fundamental rights and general principles of EU law; see n 58.

[77] See Joined Cases C-274/11 & C-295/11 *Kingdom of Spain v Council of the European Union* (16 April 2013).

III. The UPP in the Light of its Legal and Political Context

As discussed above, the UPP is very much a product of its context, including its historical context, and it is therefore in the light of that context that it must be understood and assessed. Important in that regard is the existing European patent system created by the EPC, alongside which the original proposal for a Community patent and patent system was drafted. Aside from explaining the UPP's dependence on non-EU law and institutions (in the form of the EPC and EPO), this helps to explain the UPP's international focus, as well as that of its predecessors. Another important aspect however is the Lisbon Treaty, including its elevation of the Charter to the status of the Treaties and its introduction of TFEU, Article 118, both of which have had ambivalent results for the UPP. For example, the fundamental rights and freedoms recognized in the Charter—including Article 17(2) requiring that 'intellectual property … be protected' and Articles 1 and 3 requiring that human dignity and the integrity of the person be respected—support, and have been invoked by the EU to support, both the strengthening and limitation of patent protection.[78] So too while TFEU, Article 118 for the first time confers express competence on the EU to establish new intellectual property rights, as well as procedural and language requirements to support them,[79] the apparent exclusivity of that competence puts into doubt the constitutional validity of the UPP. The reason is that such validity depends on the legitimacy of the Council's decision under TEU, Article 20 to authorize the use of enhanced cooperation to create the package following the refusal by Spain and Italy to agree to the proposed tri-language regime, and Article 20 only permits the approval of enhanced cooperation in 'the framework of the Union's *non-exclusive* competences' (emphasis added).[80] Third, there is the use of enhanced cooperation itself to establish the UPP, which explains the UPP's potentially limited territorial reach, as well as its abandonment of the former (CPR) proposal that the EU accede to the EPC to enable the grant of European bundle patents designating the EU as a Contracting State, and some of the political and legal controversy which the UPP has attracted. According to Spain and Italy, for example, their continued willingness to collaborate in the creation of a unitary patent system for Europe

[78] See, eg n 100; Biotech Directive.

[79] The EU had previously relied on its implied competence to create new intellectual property rights under EC Treaty, Art 308 (ex EEC Treaty, Art 235) to create Community trade mark and designs systems. See Case C-350/92 *Spain v Council* [1995] ECR I-1985, [23]; Regulation EC/40/94 of 20 December 1993 on the Community trade mark, OJ L11/1 (14 January 1994); Regulation EC/6/2002 of 12 December 2001 on Community designs, OJ L3/1 (5 January 2002). On the exclusivity of that competence see I Schwartz, 'Article 235 and Law-Making Powers in the European Community' (1978) 27 *ICLQ* 614, arguing that the EU's competence under EEC Treaty, Art 235 (and by extrapolation under EC Treaty, Art 308) were exclusive once the conditions for their exercise were satisfied.

[80] See n 77.

demonstrates that enhanced cooperation was not 'a last resort', as also required by TEU, Article 20.[81]

Another related change of importance to the UPP's context is the political challenge recently to the legitimacy and viability of the EU in general,[82] and the widespread and keenly felt opposition to its role in the intellectual property field. According to Lord Justice Kitchin, for example, supporting the 11th-hour call in 2011 to limit the CJEU's role under the then draft UPP, 'the CJEU has no real patent expertise and its track record in intellectual property cases does not inspire confidence';[83] a statement supported with reference to its decisions concerning the SPC Regulations and the impact of human dignity on patentability in *Brüstle v Greenpeace*.[84] This call was accepted by removing from draft UPP Regulation 1257/2012 its definition of patent rights and infringement, explaining the absence of substantive law in either of the two UPP Regulations.[85]

As Lord Justice Kitchin's reference to *Brüstle* suggests, it is possible to attribute these challenges in part at least to the change in focus and raison d'etre of the EU over the past 50 years.[86] Initially occupied with the project of supporting economic cooperation among Member States, the EU has become increasingly concerned with protecting human rights and strengthening Europe's position internationally.[87] Indeed, it is interesting to see 'respect for fundamental social rights' immediately above the establishment of an EU unitary patent in the 10 actions from the Single Market Act 2011 considered most important by the public.[88] One of the difficulties in respect of the UPP, however, is the tension that exists between these things. On one hand, the establishment of a unitary patent system is an obvious way for the EU to strengthen its role internationally, while also increasing its political legitimacy locally, and to support the protection of intellectual property in accordance with Article 17(2) of the EU Charter. On the other hand, however, the EU's international and local legitimacy depend on its commitment to *all* fundamental rights, and not only those that support the interests of patentees, and yet attempts to make patent law in particular accountable to such rights are often met with scepticism from patent specialists, as responses to *Brüstle* demonstrate. The solution offered by the UPP is an EU patent and patent system in which the risk of this will be limited by minimizing the role of the CJEU.

[81] Ibid.

[82] See JHH Weiler, 'The Political and Legal Culture of European Integration: An Exploratory Essay' (2011) 9 *International Journal of Constitutional Law* 678. See also Pila (n 4).

[83] See D Kitchin, 'Congress dinner—October 2012: The Rt Hon Lord Justice Kitchin' <http://www.cipa.org.uk/pages/Congres-Dinner-2012-Lord-Justice-Kitchin>.

[84] Case C-34/10 *Brüstle v Greenpeace* [2011] ECR I-09821.

[85] For a discussion, see Wadlow (n 70).

[86] See G de Búrca, 'Europe's Raison d'être' (2013) *Public Law & Legal Theory Research Paper Series* No 13/09 <http://ssrn.com/abstract=2224310>.

[87] Ibid.

[88] See European Commission, 'Single Market Act: Public Consultation—First Overview of Responses' <http://ec.europa.eu/internal_market/smact/consultations/2011/debate/docs/overview-summary_en.pdf>.

The possibility that the European patent system will consequently be developed 'in isolation' from the economic and social reality of which it is part—as warned against by the Commission in the 1990s[89]—seems not to have been considered, reinforcing a wider perception of the UPP as insular and out of date. One reason for that wider perception is the UPP's reliance on substantive law from the 1950s and 1960s that was drafted for inclusion in the Strasbourg and European Patent Conventions, and that, 40 years later, is beginning to show signs of age. To give an example of current relevance, its consent-based definitions of patent rights and exhaustion have been criticized for being passé and prejudicial to the rights and interests of third parties.[90]

In sum, my suggestion is that generalist courts such as the CJEU are more likely and better equipped to take account of the EU Treaties and requirements of general EU law when interpreting patent legislation than their specialist counterparts. This could be said to be surprising given the deep and long-established connections between patent law and fundamental social and economic rights and freedoms particularly. For example, the patent system has its roots in competition policy, having originated in England at least from a practice of encouraging the introduction of new trades into the realm by offering foreign workers exemption from the strict guild rules of the fourteenth century.[91] In addition, even modern patent grants—which confer monopolies rather than exemptions from them—were first conceived as limited exceptions to a constitutional prohibition against monopoly grants, and have traditionally been defined narrowly to protect third-party rights and freedoms, including by excluding from patentability methods that would impede the public's ability 'to use materials in everyday use to achieve an everyday object',[92] as well as products essential for human health, such as foods, medicines and surgical or curative devices.[93] Thus, while it may be true that patent law and decision makers have not always deployed the language of 'competition' or 'fundamental rights and freedoms' explicitly, it is also true that the patent jurisprudence of EU Member States has been informed by the values of each over many centuries. In addition, while in some jurisdictions those values have served primarily to limit the availability and scope of patent protection, in others they have served to strengthen such protection by affirming a conception of patent grants as having their basis in morality and constitutional/natural law, or as encouraging the invention and disclosure of new and other socially beneficial technologies in the public interest. Whatever one's view, the essential aim of

[89] See, eg M Brandi-Dohrn, 'Some Critical Observations on Competence and Procedure of the Unified Patent Court' (2012) 43 *International Review of Intellectual Property and Competition Law* 372, 377, 380–81.

[90] See Follow-Up to the Commission Green Paper 1997, [2.1].

[91] J Pila, *The Requirement for an Invention in Patent Law* (Oxford, Oxford University Press, 2010) ch 1. See F Machlup, *An Economic Review of the Patent System: Study of the Subcommittee on Patents, Trademarks, and Copyrights of the Committee on the Judiciary* (Washington, US Govt Printing Office, 1958) 2.

[92] *Rogers v Commission of Patents* (1910) 10 CLR 701, 709 (Griffiths CJ).

[93] Pila (n 91) ch 3.

patent legislation in all jurisdictions is, and has always been, to define the scope of monopoly grants in a manner that appropriately reconciles different social and economic interests and values; and central in that regard is ensuring that such grants do not interfere with third-party rights and freedoms disproportionately.

This view of patent systems as seeking and having always sought (in principle at least) to regulate the use of inventions with a view to recognizing and protecting social and economic freedoms and rights is even more apparent at the EU level. For example, under the EEC Treaty—mirroring the position under the Statute of Monopolies 1623 (Eng)—national patent monopolies were recognized and protected as limited exceptions to the general prohibition against impediments to free movement,[94] and regulated by the ECJ as such. A landmark decision in that regard was *Merck v Stephar*,[95] where the Court redefined the essential nature of a patent grant to accommodate EU competition policy. According to its definition, 'the substance of a patent right lies essentially in according the inventor an exclusive right of first placing the product on the market', after which the patent rights in respect of that product were held to be exhausted.[96] The premise of its decision was a view (which the Court made explicit) that while patent rights are legitimate as rewards for an inventor's creative efforts, the protection they confer must nonetheless accommodate EU single market policies and correlative third-party rights and freedoms.[97] So too in the EU Biotech Directive, the general principles of patentability contained in the EPC were adapted to ensure respect for 'fundamental rights, as guaranteed by the [ECHR] and as they result from the constitutional traditions common to the Member States, as general principles of Community law'.[98]

In sum, EU lawmakers have always recognized and emphasized the connection between patent systems and the protection of social and economic rights and freedoms. Nonetheless, it is surely right that these connections are underlined by current realities, including those created by new technologies and the growing focus on fundamental rights in domestic and international regimes. One reason for the impact of new technologies is the challenge they pose to conceptions of life and nature, and the moral and legal issues that arise when patents are sought for living and natural phenomena, such as isolated human genes and recombinant animals. Another is the increasing belief that, in addition to rewarding inventors'

[94] See EEC Treaty, Art 36.

[95] Case 187/80 *Merck & Co Inc v Stephar BV* [1981] ECR 2063.

[96] Ibid, [9].

[97] See ibid, [10].

[98] See Biotech Directive, Recital 43; see also Case C-377/98 *Kingdom of Netherlands v Parliament and Council* [2001] ECR I-07079, [71]. Cf Regulation 1257/2012, Recital 1 (linking the unitary patent and patent system to 'the attainment of the objectives of the Union set out in Article 3(3) of the Treaty on European Union', including 'the sustainable development of Europe based on [inter alia] a highly competitive social market economy'); Recital 4 (offering as a further aim and justification of the UPP that unitary patent protection will 'improve the level of patent protection by making it possible to obtain uniform patent protection in the participating Member States and eliminate costs and complexity for undertakings throughout the Union').

creative efforts, and encouraging research and development in areas of pressing social need (such as health and the environment), patents and other intellectual property rights have an important role to play in promoting competition between states and businesses, and ensuring equilibrium among competing social rights and interests.[99] In this way, patents emerge as champions of the 'social single market' and fundamental rights and freedoms generally.[100]

The relevance of this for the UPP may be summarized as follows. First, it underlines the complex relationship between inventors' rights on the one hand and economic and social rights and freedoms on the other, and the difficulty and importance of questions about the purpose of patent systems and the implications of conceptions of that purpose for substantive law. Second, and relatedly, it underlines the importance of ensuring that the field of patent law is not defined restrictively, and that its development is not insulated from other areas of law and policy, including the law of fundamental social and economic freedoms and rights. This is equally true in the EU, where such freedoms and rights are given constitutional protection under the EU Treaties and EU Charter, making their implementation across all European legal fields in accordance with EU law essential. And it is in this context particularly that the attempt to limit the role of the generalist EU Courts in patent law- and decision-making is problematic, as the effect will almost certainly be—as it was apparently designed to be—to minimize the influence of general law and policy on the European patent system.

IV. The UPP in the Light of the EU's Prior Involvement in Patent Law

As noted above, the drafting of the UPP was substantively influenced by perceptions of the impact of EU law on the European patent system to date as having been sufficiently negative to require that the CJEU be kept out of the future European unitary patent system. Given this, it seems important to consider that impact and to ask whether it has in fact been negative, as alleged. It is submitted that it has not been.[101]

99 See F Gurry, 'Re-Thinking the Role of Intellectual Property' (transcript of speech delivered at the University of Melbourne, August 2013) <http://www.law.unimelb.edu.au/files/dmfile/dg_speech_melbourne_20131.pdf>.

100 See, eg Communication from the Commission to the European Parliament, the Council, the Economic and Social Committee and the Committee of the Regions, 'Single Market Act: Twelve levers to boost growth and strengthen confidence' SEC(2011) 467 final, [2.3].

101 On the impact of EU law on the European patent system see further J Pila, 'Some Reflections on Method and Policy in the Crowded House of European Patent Law and their Implications for India' (2012) 12 *National Law School of India Review* 54; J Pila, 'A Constitutionalized Doctrine of Precedent and the *Marleasing* Principle as Bases for a European Legal Methodology' in A Ohly and J Pila (eds),

To date, EU law has impacted upon the European patent system primarily through, and as a result of, the Biotech Directive; this being the only EU instrument in the field of substantive patent law.[102] To consider the impact of EU law it is therefore necessary to consider the effect of the Directive.

The immediate effect of the Biotech Directive was to trigger an amendment of the EPC. That amendment involved the incorporation of the Directive's provisions into the EPC's Implementing Regulations, and the insertion of a requirement that they be interpreted consistent with their interpretation under the Directive.[103] Several things may be said to have resulted from this. Most obviously, the provisions contained in the EU instrument are now also provisions of the EPC, with the result that both the EPO and the 10 non-EU EPC Contracting States must comply with them. Given that the other 28 EPC Contracting States are also EU Member States, and that their obligations with respect to EU law will almost certainly be stronger than their obligations with respect to other international agreements, including the EPC, the EPO's amendment of the EPC's Implementing Regulations to incorporate the Biotech Directive could be seen as an inevitable act of self-preservation. The reason is that any conflict between the EPC and EU law would result in those 28 EU Member States having to abandon the EPC in order to fulfill their obligations with respect to EU law. On the other hand, the fact that the Biotech Directive was incorporated by amendment of the Implementing Regulations rather than the EPC's main text raises democratic issues regarding the imposition of EU law beyond EU territory without submitting to the legislative process of a full diplomatic conference. It also reveals important aspects of the relationship between the EPO and EU institutions. On the one hand, and as the EPO has emphasized, the EPC and EU legal orders are separate and distinct: notwithstanding the CPR 2000 proposal, the EU is not a party to the EPC, and nor is the EPO a member of the European Union. That is why the EPO's Enlarged Board of Appeal in *Use of embryos/WARF*[104] refused to refer a matter of interpretation concerning a provision of the Directive (as incorporated into the EPC) to the EU's Court of Justice.[105] On the other hand, and as noted above, this formal position is belied by the need for the EPO in practice to ensure that no conflict between EPC and EU law arises, lest the EPC's authority be diminished by Contracting States' non-compliance with it. Seen again in this self-preserving light, the EPO's

The Europeanization of Intellectual Property Law: Towards a European Legal Methodology (Oxford, Oxford University Press, 2013) ch 13.

102 Cf the Plant Variety and SPC Regulations (n 31).

103 See EPC Implementing Regulations, Ch V (Biotechnological inventions); r 26(1) (requiring that the Biotech Directive be used as a supplementary means of interpretation when applying and interpreting the provisions of Ch V).

104 See G2/06 *Use of embryos/WARF* [2009] OJ EPO 306.

105 See ibid, [11]. According to the Enlarged Board, the EPO 'has no power to ask the ECJ for a preliminary ruling under the existing provisions of the EPC'.

approach of simultaneously asserting its independence of the EU legal order while ensuring consistency between EPC and EU law makes perfect sense.[106]

To consider further the implications of the incorporation of the Biotech Directive into the EPC, it is necessary to have regard to the content of the Directive's provisions themselves. To a large extent, the Directive merely restates the principles of European patent law contained in the EPC. For example, it provides for the availability of patents for inventions that are new, inventive, susceptible of industrial application, sufficiently described and supported, and not excluded from patentability by any of the EPC, Article 53 public policy exclusions.[107] In so doing it reinforces EU Member States' obligations to comply with these principles using the stronger arm of EU law. More significant are the two other types of provisions that the Biotech Directive contains. The first of these give legislative expression to pre-existing principles of EPO case law, including some of considerable importance and controversy, such as that establishing the inherent patentability of isolated human genes.[108] On the one hand, giving EU statutory form to EPO principles increases legal certainty to the benefit of all EPC Contracting States and their citizens, thereby fulfilling one of the central aims of the Biotech Directive and EU harmonizing measures generally. This is particularly so given that the national courts of 28 of those states are able to refer questions regarding the meaning of the relevant principles to the Court of Justice under TFEU, Article 267, enabling further clarification of patent law and greater involvement by national courts in its development. Given the absence of any preliminary referral mechanism under the EPC (notwithstanding attempts by Lord Justice Jacob in *Aerotel v Telco Holdings Ltd*[109] to create one), this is a development of especial significance. On the other hand, the fact that superior courts in other jurisdictions are currently reconsidering or have recently reconsidered and rejected the inherent patentability of isolated DNA[110] underlines the dangers of statutorily entrenching principles as contentious (and in as fast-a-moving area) as these—particularly given the explicit concern of European patent lawmakers to ensure the law's capacity to reflect and adapt to standards set by other leading patent jurisdictions.

The second type of provision contained in the Biotech Directive clarifies the meaning of the general EPC patentability requirements for the biotechnological field. Two examples will suffice. The first is the statement in Article 9 that 'The protection conferred by a patent on a product containing or consisting of genetic information shall extend to all material … in which the product is incorporated and in which the genetic information is contained and performs its function'.

106 In addition, it creates a dynamic between the EPO and CJEU that mirrors the dynamic between the CJEU and other European and national courts; see the discussion below.

107 See, eg Biotech Directive, Arts 3(1), 4(1), 5(1) and 6(1).

108 See Biotech Directive, Art 5(2).

109 *Aerotel v Telco Holdings Ltd* [2007] RPC 7 (CA).

110 See, eg *Association for Molecular Pathology v Myriad Genetic, Inc*, 133 S Ct 2107 (2013); *D'Arcy v Myriad Genetics Inc* [2014] FCAFC 115 (appeal to the HCA pending).

And the second is the statement in Article 6(2)(c) that the Biotech Directive, Article 53(a) EPC/Article 6(1) patentability exclusion for inventions the commercial exploitation of which would be contrary to *ordre public* or morality must be interpreted to include certain specific types of subject matter, including uses of human embryos for industrial or commercial purposes. Revealed in these two clarificatory provisions are further impacts of EU law on the European patent system. One is to restrict the scope of patent protection beyond that which existed previously: (a) by excluding more subject matter from patentability than was previously excluded under EPC, Article 53(a);[111] and (b) by limiting the protection conferred by a patent with reference to the purpose of the initial grant reflected in its patentability criteria. Of especial interest regarding (b) is its consistency with other areas of EU intellectual property, including copyright, the scope of which is similarly defined with reference to the criteria for its initial subsistence.[112] Thus, just as the protection conferred by a patent for genetic material extends only to the material when performing its specifically disclosed function, so too the protection conferred by copyright for a subject matter extends only to those aspects of the subject matter which are original. The similarity is important in underlining the effect of EU law in ensuring consistency between the different fields of intellectual property, and thereby increasing its coherence more generally.

Of even more importance for current purposes, the impact of EU law in exposing the European patent system to influences from other legal areas is further revealed in the jurisprudence regarding the Article 6(2)(c) exclusion from patentability. According to the Enlarged Board of Appeal in *Warf*, pre-empting the decision of the Court of Justice in *Brüstle*, the explicit basis of that exclusion in the legislative concern to protect the dignity and the integrity of the person required that it be interpreted expansively.[113] Once again, the decision marked a divergence from the restrictive approach to patentability supported by the EPO previously,[114] prompted this time by the European law of fundamental rights. According to the EPO's earlier approach, the exclusion from patentability of subject matter on morality or *ordre public* grounds—of which Article 6(2)(c) was an example—was 'to be invoked only in rare and extreme cases, for example that of a letter bomb', consistent with the nature of the exclusion as 'a measure to ensure that patents would not be granted for inventions which would universally be regarded as outrageous'.[115] By expressly requiring that patent law accommodate human dignity and the integrity of the person,[116] however, the Biotech Directive led the EPO

[111] See, eg *Howard Florey/Relaxin* [1995] EPOR 541; *Plant Genetic Systems* [1995] EPOR 357.

[112] See Case C-5/08 *Infopaq International A/S v Danske Dagblades Forening* [2009] ECDR 16; J Pila, 'Patent Eligibility and Scope Revisited in the Light of *Schütz v Werit*, European Law and Copyright Jurisprudence' in RC Dreyfuss and JC Ginsburg (eds), *Intellectual Property at the Edge: The Contested Contours of IP* (Cambridge, Cambridge University Press, 2014) ch 18.

[113] *Brüstle* (n 84) [34].

[114] See n 111.

[115] *Howard Florey* (n 111) [6.2.1].

[116] See Charter, Arts 1 and 3.

in *Warf* to reject this approach for the purposes of Article 6(2)(c) at least, and to 'discover' its jurisprudence in substantive human rights.[117] In so doing it repeated the chain of events 50 years ago, when the German Constitutional Court challenged the compatibility of EU law with (German) fundamental rights, prompting the CJEU to make the same fundamental rights 'discovery'. Indeed, it is difficult to ignore the similarity between the EPO's reasoning in *Warf* and the ECJ's reasoning in *Stauder v City of Ulm*[118] and *Internationale Handelsgesellschaft*[119] from the late 1960s and early 1970s. Similar to the CJEU in those two cases, the EPO in *Warf* responded to the Biotech Directive by asserting its preparedness to recognize and enforce fundamental rights in the context of patent law, and conceiving those rights simultaneously as autonomous aspects of the EPC and as derived from EU law;[120] just as the ECJ in *Stauder* and *Internationale Handelsgesellschaft* had responded to the German challenge by asserting its preparedness to recognize and enforce fundamental rights in the context of EU law, and conceiving those rights as autonomous EU legal rights derived from the constitutional traditions of Member States. The decision was a prelude to the Enlarged Board's adoption in 2010 of the ECJ's constitutional model of the (then) European Economic Community more than 50 years ago in *Costa v Enel*[121] as comprising an autonomous legal community. According to the Court in *Costa*:

> By creating a community of unlimited duration, having its own institutions, it own personality, its own legal capacity and capacity of representation on the international plane and, more particularly, real powers stemming from a limitation of sovereignty or a

[117] Previously the EPO Boards of Appeal had accepted their jurisdiction in respect of fundamental *procedural* rights under EPC, Art 125. According to that Article: 'In the absence of procedural provisions in this Convention, the European Patent Office shall take into account the principles of procedural law generally recognized in the Contract States'. In T377/95 *Herpes simplex virus/ UNIVERSITY PATENTS INC* [1999] OJ EPO 11, for example, the Technical Board of Appeal accepted the ECHR as a relevant source of 'guidance' for the Boards as to such 'principles of procedural law' because 'all member states to the EPC adhere to the ECHR' (at [36]; see also G3/98 *Six-month period/ UNIVERSITY PATENTS* [2001] OJ EPO 62, [2.5.3]). By anchoring the Boards' jurisdiction to EPC, Art 125, this represented a more cautious view than that earlier expressed by the Disciplinary Board of Appeal in D11/91 *Disciplinary penalty* [1995] OJ EPO 721, where it affirmed that while the ECHR could not 'be applied directly to the EPO because the EPO is not a signatory state[,] to the extent that the [ECHR] contains rules which express general principles of law, these rules must be considered as forming part of the legal system of the EPO and must therefore be observed by all its departments'. Note that even *Disciplinary penalty* concerned a matter of procedural law, and in particular the guarantee contained in ECHR, Art 13 concerning 'each individual's right to be heard by a duly constituted tribunal'. According to the Board in *Disciplinary penalty*, 'This is an expression of a general principle of law common to the member states of the European Patent Organisation, which is thus binding on the Organisation'.

[118] Case 29/69 *Stauder v City of Ulm* [1969] ECR 419.

[119] Case 11/70 *Internationale Handelsgesellschaft* [1970] ECR 1125.

[120] This can be seen on the legislative plane in the EPO's introduction of the Biotech Directive and the r 26(1) interpretive provision into the EPC, and on the judicial plane in the Enlarged Board's simultaneous refusal in *Warf* to refer the interpretation of r 28(c) EPC to the CJEU and reliance on the intent of the EU legislators when interpreting that rule.

[121] Case 6/64 *Costa v ENEL* [1964] ECR 585, [3].

> transfer of powers from the [member] states to the community, the member states have limited their sovereign rights, albeit within limited fields, and have thus created a body of law which binds their nationals and themselves.

So too in G3/08 *PRESIDENT'S REFERENCE/Computer program exclusion*, the Enlarged Board of Appeal, in a striking example of EU law spill-over, similarly described the European Patent Organisation as comprising an autonomous legal community. In its decision:

> The European Patent Organisation is an international, intergovernmental organisation, modeled on a modern state order and based on the separation of powers principle, which the sovereign contracting states have entrusted with the exercise of some of their national powers in the field of patents.[122]

By thus modelling the legal order of the EPC on the legal order of the EU, down to the place within that order of fundamental rights, the Board has helped to create a dynamic between the EPO and the CJEU that mirrors the 'cold war' dynamic that has existed over half a century between the CJEU and the German Constitutional Court.[123] In addition, since the elevation of the EU Charter to the status of the EU Treaties in 2009, and the EU's commitment to accede to the European Convention on Human Rights, the 'anxiety of influence'[124] that is a defining feature of that dynamic has similarly come to characterize the CJEU's relationship with the European Court of Human Rights. To quote from one commentator writing recently: 'Each court wants to retain autonomy and control, while avoiding conflict … Each recognizes the significance of human rights in European integration but also recognizes the need to tread carefully in the present complex jurisdictional arena'.[125] Just so now also for the EPO and CJEU.

This comparison between the impact of the Biotech Directive on the European patent system on one hand and of German constitutional law and the ECHR on the EU legal system on the other underlines the extent and significance of EU law's impact in having challenged the traditional insularity of the European (EPC) patent regime (focused on the technical aspects of patentability) by requiring it to recognize and take account of social and economic rights, along with the jurisprudence of the tribunals responsible for protecting them. Aside from the CJEU itself, those tribunals include the European Court of Human Rights and EU Member State courts under TFEU, Article 267.

Try as the EPO might to pre-empt and emulate the Court of Justice's approach to the intersection of patent law and fundamental rights, it is unlikely ever to succeed completely. Some indication of this can be found in the *Warf* and *Brüstle* cases. Whereas the EPO in *Warf* had confined its decision to the facts of the case

[122] [2011] OJ EPO 10, [7.2.1].

[123] On the cold war dynamic, see JHH Weiler and UR Haltern, 'The Autonomy of the Community Legal Order—Through the Looking Glass' (1996) 37 *Harvard International Law Journal* 411.

[124] With apologies to Harold Bloom.

[125] S Douglas-Scott, 'A Tale of Two Courts: Luxembourg, Strasbourg and the Growing European Human Rights *Acquis*' (2006) 43 *CML Rev* 629.

and refrained from defining 'human embryo'[126]—whether or not out of deference to EPC Contracting States and the margin of appreciation shown by the European Court of Human Rights with respect to human dignity[127]—the Court of Justice in *Brüstle* had neither the luxury of confining the legal effect of its decision (given its basis in TFEU, Article 267) nor the restraint to leave 'human embryo' undefined. The result was a difference in the substantive legal outcome of each case: whereas the Enlarged Board had declared 'human embryo' to be a matter for definition on the facts of each case,[128] the CJEU invoked the requirements of human dignity to support its definition of that term to mean 'any human ovum ... as soon as fertilized'; a definition with far-reaching consequences beyond patent law.[129]

In sum, the impact of the EU Biotech Directive on the European patent system may be said to have been as follows. First, it has given the CJEU jurisdiction in respect of substantive patent law, thereby enabling it and all EU Member States to play a more active role in the law's development. Second, and relatedly, it has effectively required the EPO to anticipate or abide by decisions of the Court of Justice so as to avoid any conflict between the EPC and EU law, which conflict would be disastrous for the EPC's legitimacy and authority. Third, it has put certain previously un-codified principles of European patent law on a statutory footing, precluding their revision by any European tribunal, even as they are revised in other leading patent jurisdictions (as for the patentability of isolated human genes). And fourth, and perhaps most strikingly, it has opened the existing system of the EPC up to a wider range of values and influences than those to which it has historically been receptive, requiring (among other things) the EPO to 'discover' its fundamental rights jurisprudence, and making it additionally accountable—informally speaking at least—to the CJEU, as well as the European Court of Human Rights and national courts.

There is no doubt that these developments create a degree of legal uncertainty, and are in this sense regrettable from both a single market and a rule of (patent) law perspective. On the other hand, putting aspects of European patent law on an EU legal footing promotes harmonization within and outside the EU, strengthens the functioning of the single market, and increases legal certainty with respect to those harmonized aspects at least. So too while the imposition of EU law on non-EU EPC Contracting States raises democratic issues, increasing the accountability of the EPC to fundamental rights and other external legal and policy influences, and requiring the EPO to engage with the jurisprudence of the CJEU, the European Court of Human Rights, and (via their references to the CJEU) the national courts of at least 28 of its Contracting States, must be regarded as beneficial overall. Indeed, there can be no justification for insulating patent or any

[126] *Warf* (n 104) [20].

[127] See A Plomer, 'After *Brüstle*: EU Accession to the ECHR and the Future of European Patent Law' (2012) 2 *Queen Mary Journal of Intellectual Property* 110.

[128] *Warf* (n 104) [20].

[129] *Brüstle* (n 84) [35].

other area of law from fundamental rights scrutiny, or from complying with other areas of general law. By introducing fundamental rights and other values into the European patent system, the EU has challenged the self-sufficiency and insularity of the EPC and EPO tribunals, and served as an important reminder of the deep connections that exist and have always existed between patent law and other substantive legal fields. As suggested above, in our current era particularly, in which biotechnological research is challenging the distinction between nature and artefact on which patent law depends, patents in all areas are increasingly relied on to solve social and economic problems, and the recognition and protection of fundamental rights are of increasing national and international concern, explicit and active support for these connections is especially important and timely—and, it is submitted, best ensured by the oversight of a generalist superior court, including, in Europe, of the CJEU.

V. Conclusion

Whether assessed from a harmonization or patent law perspective, much depends on the future of the UPP, which remains a matter of considerable uncertainty. Three things in particular will be key to its success: how many EU Member States decide to participate; how the UPC makes sense of the 'sources' provision of Article 24 of the UPC Agreement, and what substantive body of patent jurisprudence it develops in accordance with the same; and how EU Member States and the CJEU interpret the effect of the UPP on the scope of EU competence in respect of substantive patent law. The experience of the EPO and CJEU to date underlines the latter as an issue of especial importance. As seen above, a central aim in drafting the UPP has been to confine the CJEU's competence to what it is currently. The effect of this—consistent perhaps with its aim—will likely be to limit the future impact of general EU legal principles on the European patent system, as well as the influence of tribunals exercising jurisdiction in respect of them (formally or informally). Once again, in a context in which specialist patent courts in other jurisdictions, such as the United States, are being reined in by generalist appellate tribunals,[130] European developments in this regard seem out of step and retrograde.

It must be acknowledged, however, that there is some uncertainty as to whether this will in fact be the UPP's result. The reason is that if the history of EU law tells us anything, it is that the CJEU is not naturally disposed to narrow interpretations of its own jurisdiction,[131] and that national courts have been only too pleased to

[130] See the discussion by Rochelle Dreyfuss in ch 10 of this volume.

[131] See, eg Case C-380/03 *Tobacco Advertising II: Germany v Parliament and Council* [2006] ECR I-11573 (12 December 2006); Case C-58/08 *Vodafone* [2010] ECR I-04999 (8 June 2010); Case T-526/10 *Inuit* (25 April 2013); Case C-270/12 *UK v Council and Parliament* (7 March 2014). In respect

support the CJEU to that end.[132] Given this especially, it is difficult to imagine a restrained interpretation of EU competence vis-à-vis the law of unitary patents should the system take effect. On the contrary, it seems at least as likely that the Court will seize on the patent's legal basis in Regulation 1257/2012 as sufficient to bring its validity and content within the scope of EU law, notwithstanding that both the criteria of patentability and the rights conferred by the patent are defined in non-EU instruments.[133] Following recent case law, the Court may even derive assistance to that end from the requirement in Article 17(2) of the Charter that intellectual property 'be protected', of which the UPP—with its explicit focus on 'improv[ing] the level of patent protection'—could be seen as an expression.[134] And if the CJEU does declare itself to have interpretive jurisdiction in respect of the substantive law governing unitary patent grants, and the history of the EU's involvement in the patent field to date is any indication of the result, the UPP will likely develop into a system that recognizes and protects the deep connections between substantive patent law and fundamental social and economic rights and freedoms. That is an outcome worth striving for.

of the patent field specifically, see further Case C-377/98 *Kingdom of Netherlands v Parliament and Council* [2001] ECR I-07079 (9 October 2001).

132 For a recent example of the national courts' enthusiasm for referring questions to the CJEU, even when not required to, see *Public Relations Consultants Association Ltd v Newspaper Licensing Agency Ltd* [2013] UKSC 18.

133 See further the discussions by Angelos Dimopoulos and Tuomas Mylly in chs 5 and 6 of this volume.

134 On EU legislation as an expression of fundamental rights and freedoms see, eg Case C-555/07 *Seda Kücükdeveci* [2010] ECR I-365. On the UPP as a measure aimed at ensuring patent protection see Regulation 1257/12, Recital 4 (n 98). See further discussion by Tuomas Mylly in ch 6 of this volume.

3

An Historical Perspective II: The Unified Patent Court

CHRISTOPHER WADLOW*

I. The Background to the Unified Patent Court

A. The Texts and the Issues

The Unitary Patent and the Unified Patent Court are the culmination of a process which began at the Council of Europe as long ago as 1950.[1] Since then, numerous proposals have been made for European patents, and corresponding patent litigation systems, some of which have enjoyed resounding success, while others have fallen into well-deserved obscurity. In this paper I examine and compare five systems which have been proposed for pan-European patent litigation.[2] These are: (1) the Community Patent Convention (1975);[3] (2) the Agreement relating to Community Patents (1989);[4] (3) the proposed Community Patent Regulation (*c* 2000–04) and its associated instruments;[5] (4) the proposed European Patent Litigation Agreement (*c* 2004);[6] and (5) the Unified Patent Court Agreement.[7]

Each of these will be described by reference to three principal issues, namely: (1) centralisation of the specialised patent court system vs decentralisation and local accessibility; (2) consolidation of the issues of infringement and validity vs bifurcation; and (3) independence of the patent court from existing institutions

* Emeritus Professor of Law, University of East Anglia.

[1] CM Wadlow, 'Strasbourg, the Forgotten Patent Convention, and the Origins of the European Patents Jurisdiction' (2010) 41 *International Review of Intellectual Property and Competition Law* 123.

[2] I omit the very earliest proposals, never officially published, namely those by Reimer and de Haan for the Council of Europe (*c* 1950–55); and those by Haertel for the EEC (1960).

[3] Convention for the European Patent for the Common Market (15 December 1975) (Community Patent Convention) (CPC).

[4] Agreement relating to Community Patents (15 December 1989). This comprises an amended version of the 1975 Convention and three Protocols relating to the litigation of Community patents.

[5] Proposal for a Council Decision establishing the Community Patent Court and concerning appeals before the Court of First Instance, COM(2003) 324 final (23 December 2003).

[6] Draft Agreement on the Establishment of a European Patent Litigation System and Draft Statute of the European Patent Court (EPO, Working Party on Litigation, 16 February 2004).

[7] Agreement on a Unified Patent Court, OJ C175/1 (20 June 2013) (UPC Agreement).

vs integration into pre-existing court or patent system(s), whether national or supranational.

B. The Community Patent Convention (1975)

Under the original version of the Community Patent Convention (1975),[8] the European Patent Office would have had exclusive jurisdiction over applications for the revocation of Community patents,[9] with national court hierarchies having exclusive jurisdiction over infringement.[10] The European Court of Justice would have had final instance jurisdiction (for issues of validity) by way of appeal from the EPO,[11] and would have entertained preliminary references (on issues arising from interpretation of the two Conventions,[12] as well as general Community law) from national courts.[13] Bifurcation would have been complete, and mandatory.

The Community Patent Convention failed to be ratified by all intending Contracting States, and never came into effect, though its provisions as to substantive patent law (as opposed to institutions and procedures) were widely adopted into national law.

C. The Agreement Relating to Community Patents (1989)

The 1975 Community Patent Convention was superseded by the Agreement relating to Community Patents (1989).[14] Under the Protocols to the 1989 Agreement,[15] designated courts of Member States were to have first instance jurisdiction over both infringement and validity.[16] A new centralised Community institution under the name of the Common Appeal Court (more conveniently COPAC) would be created to hear 'references' from national appellate courts.[17] The role of the national second instance courts was purely nominal, and to all

[8] See above n 3.

[9] CPC, Art 56. The national court was obliged to treat the Community patent as valid: CPC, Art 76.

[10] CPC, Art 69.

[11] CPC, Art 63. There was an intermediate appeal (Art 62) from the revocation divisions established by the Convention to the EPO's internal Boards of Appeal.

[12] The Community Patent Convention itself, and those provisions of the European Patent Convention incorporated into it.

[13] CPC, Art 73.

[14] See above n 4; CM Wadlow, 'The Community Patent Appeal Court' (1986) 11 *EL Rev* 295.

[15] Principally the Protocol on the Settlement of Litigation concerning the Infringement and Validity of Community Patents (Protocol on Litigation) and the Protocol on the Statute of the Common Appeal Court.

[16] Protocol on Litigation, Arts 1 and 15. These courts were somewhat misleadingly designated 'Community patent courts', though they were not Community institutions. The number of courts in a given state was supposed to be 'as limited a number as possible', but proposals current at the time envisaged low double figures for the number of Community patent courts in some of the larger Member States.

[17] Protocol on Litigation, Art 2.

intents and purposes COPAC would have acted as a true second-tier appeal court with jurisdiction over all issues of infringement and validity, and matters of both fact and law.[18]

National appeal courts (and final instance courts, if relevant) retained jurisdiction over issues governed by national law, as well as any issues of Community law outside the exclusive jurisdiction of COPAC. There were provisions for preliminary references both from national courts and COPAC to the ECJ,[19] and from national courts to COPAC on any issues of interpretation relating to the Agreement, but not within the exclusive jurisdiction of the latter.[20] There was no bifurcation at any stage of the proceedings, and no special role for the EPO except for entertaining free-standing revocation actions,[21] with an appeal to COPAC.[22]

D. The Community Patent Regulation Period (*c* 2000–04)

The 1975 and 1989 proposals had both envisaged the Community Patent (and its associated institutions) being established by treaty between the Member States, rather than by Community secondary legislation, but in both cases the proposed Convention or Agreement failed to receive the necessary degree of ratification. However by 2000 the competence of the Community was considered to be sufficiently extensive for the Commission to propose a series of draft Regulations and Decisions on a Community Patent,[23] though these too never came to fruition.

Under the system associated with the proposed Community Patent Regulation, first instance jurisdiction over both infringement and validity would have been assigned to a new 'judicial panel' to be known as the Community Patent Court.[24] This would have been attached to the Court of First Instance and situated in Luxembourg, but with the power to conduct proceedings in other Member States.[25] The panel was to consist of a total of seven judges 'having an established high level of legal expertise in patent law', normally sitting in chambers of three judges,[26] and assisted by technical experts acting as 'assistant rapporteurs'.[27] The jurisdiction of the new court would have extended only to Community patents (and Community Supplementary Protection Certificates), and not to national

[18] Protocol on Litigation, Arts 21–24.

[19] Agreement relating to Community Patents, Arts 1 and 2. References by COPAC to the European Court of Justice were confined to situations where the interpretation of the Agreement might conflict with general Community law.

[20] Protocol on Litigation, Art 30.

[21] Agreement relating to Community Patents, Art 55.

[22] Protocol on Litigation, Art 28.

[23] Initially the Proposal for a Council Regulation on the Community Patent, COM(2000) 412 final (28 November 2000).

[24] Proposal for a Council Decision establishing the Community Patent Court and concerning appeals before the Court of First Instance, COM(2003) 828 final (23 December 2003), Art 1.

[25] Ibid, Art 4; proposed Annex II to the Protocol of the Statute of the Court of Justice, Art 24.

[26] Proposed Annex II to the Protocol of the Statute of the Court of Justice, Arts 2 and 8.

[27] Ibid, Art 7.

patents or ordinary European patents.[28] Appeals from the Community Patent Court would lie to the Court of First Instance.[29]

The practical importance of this proposed system would have depended entirely on the degree of uptake of Community patents, subject to a further delay between the first such patents being granted, and their being litigated. The seven specialist patent judges of the Community Patent Court might well have sat out their initial six-year terms without adjudicating a single case.[30] At least the three appellate judges of the Court of First Instance would have been able to fill in their time on Community Trade Marks and Designs.

E. The European Patent Litigation Agreement (*c* 2007)

Even if the Community Patent Regulation had been adopted, there would have been no place in its provisions for the many hundreds of thousands of pre-existing European patents, nor for the European patents (not designating the whole Community) which would presumably have continued to be granted long afterwards. Scepticism as to the demand for the Community patent and the more pressing need to provide for an efficient, pan-European jurisdiction to accommodate existing and prospective European patents led to proposals for a European Patent Litigation Agreement,[31] associated with the existing European Patent System (based on the European Patent Convention of 1973),[32] rather than as part of the Community legal order.

The European Patent Litigation Agreement would have established a 'European Patent Judiciary',[33] whose organs were the European Patent Court and the Administrative Committee, with the Court comprising a single Court of First Instance, a Court of Appeal, and a Registry.[34] The system would have had jurisdiction over the infringement and validity of European patents (present and future) effective in any of its Contracting States, and any Community patents yet to be granted. Though nominally a single institution, the first instance court would

[28] Ibid, Art 1.

[29] Ibid, Art 26. A specialist patent chamber of the Court of First Instance, comprising three suitably experienced judges, was to be established. Ibid, Art 61a.

[30] Cf the assumptions of COM(2003) 828 final: 'The expected caseload in the initial phase is estimated for the first three consecutive years at around 50, 100 and 150 newly lodged cases which would mean a case load of 25, 50 and 75 new cases per year per chamber. This assumption is based on an expected number of 100 000 patents granted by the European Patent office per year of which around 50 000 would designate the Community and an annual litigation rate of 1 in 1 000 patents in force'. The naivety is stunning.

[31] See above n 6.

[32] Convention on the Grant of European Patents (8 October 1973).

[33] Draft Agreement on the Establishment of a European Patent Litigation System, Art 3(1).

[34] Ibid, Art 3(2).

have comprised both central and regional (or local) divisions.[35] Appeals from any of the divisions of the first instance court would have been to the central second instance court.[36] Both levels of court would have comprised both legally and technically qualified judges,[37] with panels consisting of at least two legally qualified judges (of different nationalities) and one technically qualified judge.[38] Bifurcation was not contemplated.

The European Patent Litigation Agreement was intended to co-exist with the Community legal order, though not as a part of it. There would have been provisions for preliminary references to the Court of Justice of the European Communities on matters of Community law,[39] which did not include the substantive law of the European Patent Convention or the European Patent Litigation Agreement itself. However, insoluble problems arose between the intended jurisdictional provisions of the Agreement, and those of the Community Jurisdiction Regulation,[40] as interpreted by the Court of Justice in its decisions in *GAT v LuK* and *Roche v Primus*.[41]

F. The Unitary Patent and Unified Patent Court

Finally there is the proposed Unified Patent Court Agreement, which is discussed extensively in the rest of this volume. To facilitate comparison with the various earlier proposals, the Unified Patent Court Agreement is rather similar to the European Patent Litigation Agreement, except that the central first instance division is further divided between Paris, Munich and London according to technical subject matter. Unlike the European Patent Litigation Agreement, there is discretionary provision for bifurcation of the issues of infringement and validity,[42] and the role of the Court of Justice is (as far as possible) even further marginalised.

[35] Ibid, Art 10; Draft Statute of the European Patent Court, Art 19.

[36] Draft Agreement on the Establishment of a European Patent Litigation System, Art 11; Draft Statute of the European Patent Court, Arts 44, 76–81.

[37] Draft Statute of the European Patent Court, Art 3.

[38] Ibid, Arts 26(1) and 27.

[39] Draft Agreement on the Establishment of a European Patent Litigation System, Art 40.

[40] Regulation 44/2001 on jurisdiction and the recognition and enforcement of judgments in civil and commercial matters, OJ L12/1 (16 January 2001).

[41] Case C-4/03 *Gesellschaft für Antriebstechnik mbH & Co KG (GAT) v Lamellen und Kupplungsbau Beteiligungs KG (LuK)* [2006] ECR I-6509; Case C-539/03 *Roche Nederland BV v Primus* [2006] ECR I-6535.

[42] Agreement on a Unified Patent Court, Art 33(3)(b).

II. A Thematic Comparison

A. Centralisation versus Local Accessibility

A unified system for patent litigation implies a degree of centralisation of institutions, though only one of the systems under consideration here (the Community Patent Regulation) committed itself to 100 per cent centralisation.[43] Of the others, the 1975 Community Patent Convention combined maximum centralisation for the issue of validity, to be decided by the European Patent Office with a final appeal to the European Court of Justice, with maximum decentralisation of infringement issues, which were adjudicated by existing national courts of first, second and final instance, with a more limited preliminary reference procedure to the Court of Justice.[44]

In 1975, the bright line between centralised and decentralised jurisdiction had been defined functionally, in a similar manner to the bifurcated German national system. With the 1989 Agreement relating to Community Patents a different split was adopted, with local court systems having jurisdiction over both infringement and validity at first instance, and the centralised Community Patent Appeal Court having jurisdiction over both sets of issues on appeal.[45] In this system the bright line between centralisation and localism was defined according to the level of the proceedings, rather as in the American federal patent litigation system following the creation of the Court of Appeals for the Federal Circuit.[46]

The European Patent Litigation Agreement maintained this distinction between first instance and appellate courts, but with a greater degree of centralisation, less localism, and next to no reliance on national court systems.[47] Though formally a single institution, the Court of First Instance was composed of a central division and an (unspecified) number of regional divisions. Depending on the volume of patent cases, a regional division could exist for a grouping of several Contracting States, a single Contracting State, or a region within a Contracting State.[48] The system of the Unified Patent Court Agreement is essentially the same as that of the European Patent Litigation Agreement, but elaborated in more detail.[49]

[43] See above nn 5 and 24.

[44] See above nn 3 and 8.

[45] See above nn 4 and 14.

[46] See the discussion by Rochelle Dreyfuss in ch 9 of this volume.

[47] See above nn 6 and 31.

[48] Draft Agreement on the Establishment of a European Patent Litigation System, Arts 7(2) and 10; Draft Statute of the European Patent Court, Arts 19–20.

[49] Agreement on a Unified Patent Court, Art 7(3)–(5); Statute of the Unified Patent Court, Art 18.

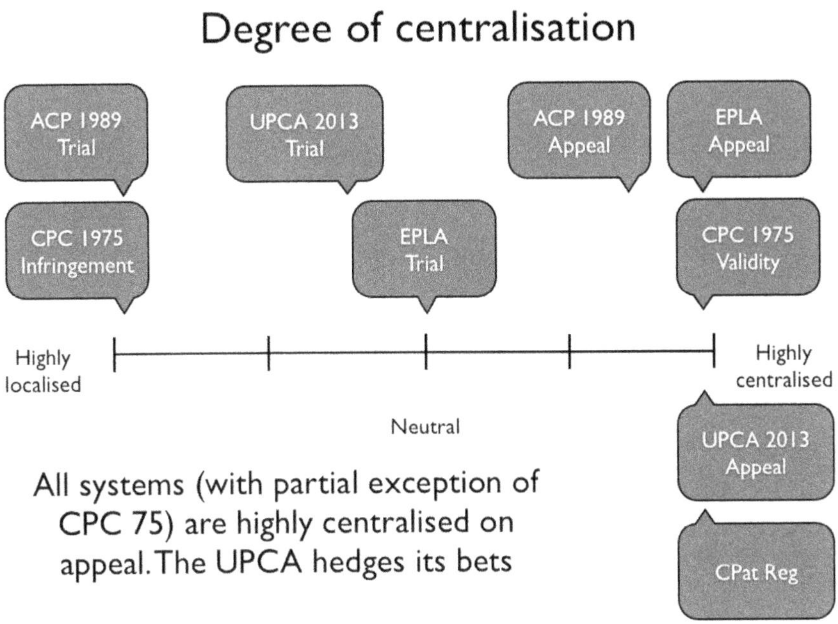

Figure 1: Degree of centralisation

B. Consolidation versus Bifurcation of Infringement/Validity Issues

Centralisation is (inversely) linked to bifurcation of the issues of infringement and validity. Bifurcation (which is normal only in Germany) is supposed to reassure patent proprietors, especially when there is a multiplicity of inexperienced local trial courts. However, bifurcation increases the risk of inconsistent interpretations of the patent in suit. It also creates procedural complications, opportunities for delay and problems of coordination.

Only the Community Patent Convention 1975 was wholly committed to bifurcation, at all levels below the European Court of Justice.[50] The Unified Patent Court Agreement contemplates discretionary bifurcation,[51] but it remains to be seen to what extent this will be exercised in practice. All intermediate systems rejected bifurcation, though the associated risks of important patents being revoked on spurious grounds by inexperienced trial judges, and only reinstated much later on appeal, or not at all, may have undermined support for these proposals and contributed to their lack of success.

[50] See above n 3. Even so, it was by no means certain that the two sets of issues would both reach the European Court, and if they did, it would not necessarily be at the same time, or under the same circumstances.

[51] Agreement on a Unified Patent Court, Art 33(3)(b).

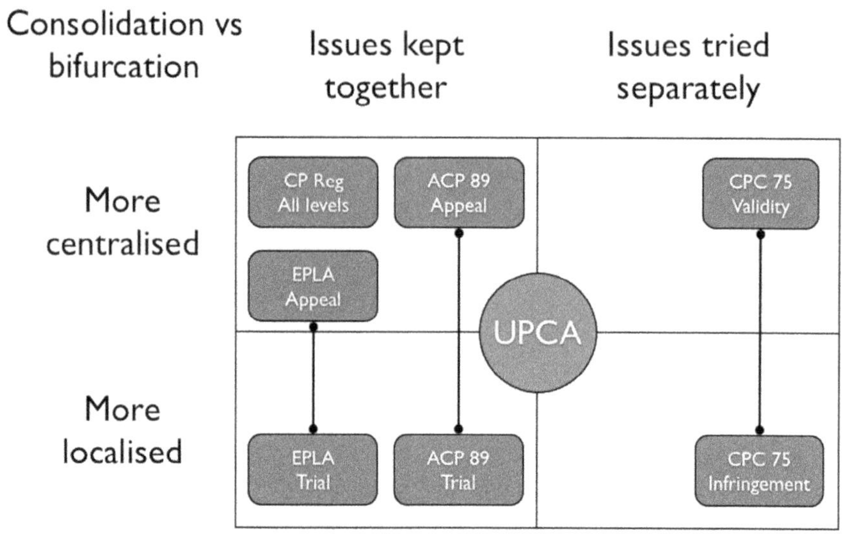

Figure 2: Consolidation vs bifurcation

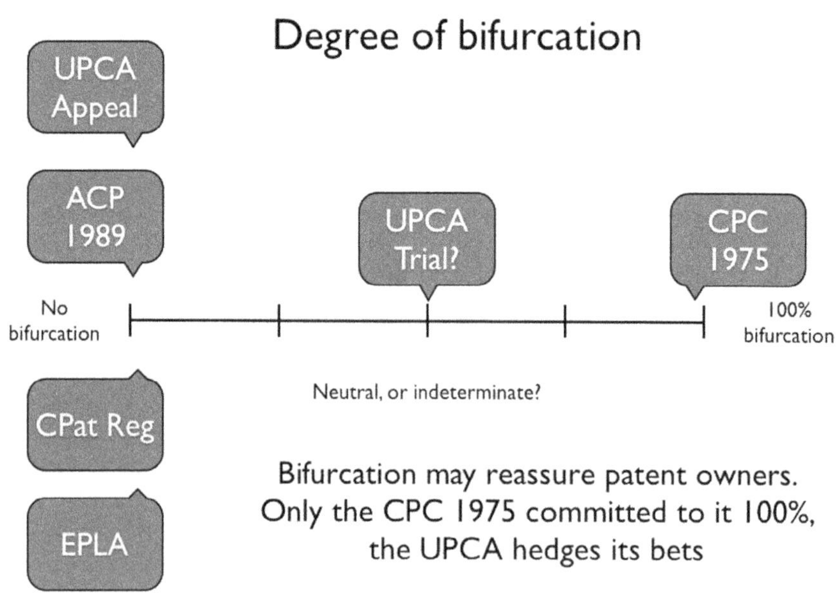

Figure 3: Degree of bifurcation

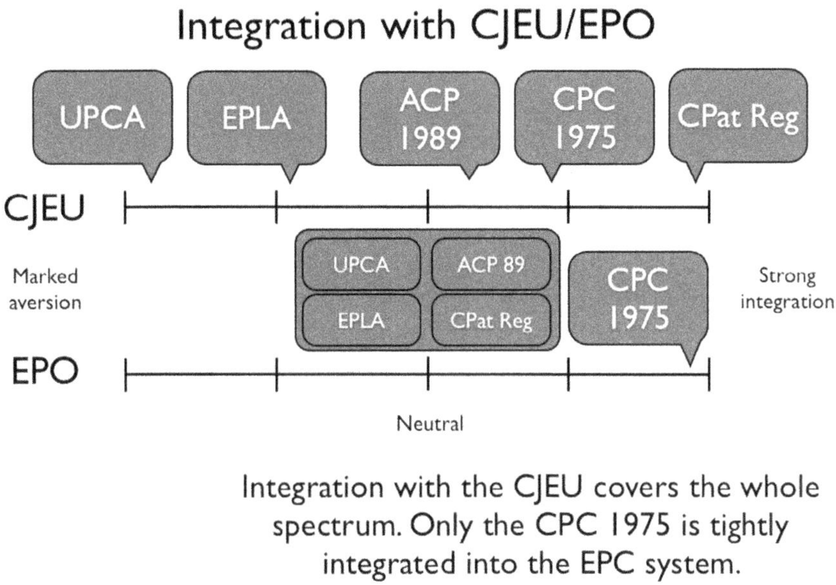

Figure 4: Integration with Court of Justice and European Patent Office

C. Integration versus Separation

Integration cannot be mapped onto a single scale, since integration can be measured in relation to national courts, other Community institutions, and the European Patent Office. The Unified Patent Court Agreement (and the European Patent Litigation Agreement before it) are marked by an intentional distancing of the system from all and any of these. Of the other systems considered, the Community Patent Convention (1975) and the Agreement on Community Patents (1989) featured strong (but partial) reliance on existing national court systems; the Community Patent Regulation was tightly integrated into the general Community judicial system; while only the Community Patent Convention (1975) conferred significant litigation-related jurisdiction on the European Patent Office.

III. The Pedigree of the Unified Patent Court Revisited

A. The Issues Summarised

The five systems briefly considered here demonstrate almost every possible combination of variations on the three principal variables: centralisation, bifurcation and integration. For maximum centralisation, nothing compares to that of the

Community Patent Regulation.[52] No system is completely decentralised, though the Community Patent Convention (1975) combined mandatory bifurcation with maximum centralisation of validity and maximum decentralisation of infringement,[53] and the Agreement relating to Community Patents also contemplated (though it certainly did not encourage) a level of decentralisation within individual Contracting States.[54] Not surprisingly, all later systems have opted for fully centralised jurisdiction at least at appellate level, with varying (and to some extent discretionary or optional) degrees of decentralisation at first instance. Only the 1975 Community Patent Convention was intended to be integrated with the European Patent Office, which led inevitably to bifurcation. The system proposed under the Community Patent Regulation was unique in the degree of integration it intended with the European Court of Justice. More recent proposals have sought to marginalise the role of that Court.

Table 1: Summary table for centralisation, bifurcation, integration

	Centralisation	Bifurcation	Integration
Community Patent Convention 1975	Highly centralised for validity (EPO); completely decentralised for infringement.	Mandatory bifurcation at all levels.	Highly integrated with European Patent System for validity; moderately integrated with European Court of Justice.
Agreement relating to Community Patents 1989	Highly decentralised at first instance; fully centralised on appeal.	Not contemplated.	Entirely separate from EPO; COPAC largely independent from European Court of Justice.
Community Patent Regulation 2000	Totally centralised.	Not contemplated.	Highly integrated into Court of First Instance.
European Patent Litigation Agreement 2004	Wholly centralised on appeal; mixed system at first instance.	Not contemplated.	Intentionally separate from European Court of Justice.
Unified Patent Court Agreement 2013	Wholly centralised on appeal; mixed system at first instance.	Discretionary.	Intentionally separate from European Court of Justice.

[52] See above nn 5 and 24.
[53] See above nn 3 and 8.
[54] See above nn 4 and 14.

IV. Conclusions

From an historical perspective, the system embodied in the Unified Patent Court Agreement is the close and direct descendant of the abortive European Patent Litigation Agreement. Compared to that Agreement, the major innovations of present relevance are the (purely political) division of the first instance central division between Paris, Munich and London according to technical subject matter,[55] and the option of bifurcation of the issues of validity and infringement.[56] The more distant antecedents of the Unified Patent Court Agreement (with the partial exception of the 1989 Agreement relating to Community Patents) are by now of purely academic and historic interest, at least so far as procedures and institutions are concerned. In particular, the 1975 Community Patent Convention and the draft Community Patent Regulation of the 1980s were in their different ways strikingly doctrinaire and unworkable. If the Unified Patent Court Agreement is lacking in pedigree, it does at least demonstrate the virtues of pragmatism and compromise, and perhaps some of the wisdom of experience.

[55] Agreement on a Unified Patent Court, Art 7(2) and Annex II.
[56] Ibid, Art 33(3)(b).

4

An Institutional Perspective I: The Role of the EPO in the Unitary (EU) Patent System

STEFAN LUGINBUEHL*

I. Introduction

A. General

After decades of unsuccessful negotiations to establish a common patent for the European Union (EU),[1] it was decided to establish a European patent with unitary effect (commonly referred to as the 'unitary patent') by way of enhanced cooperation[2] under Article 20 EU Treaty and Articles 326–34 TFEU.[3] Enhanced cooperation allows some EU Member States as a last resort to move forward immediately, with others able to opt-in at a later stage. Twenty-five EU Member States agreed to participate in the enhanced cooperation scheme on the creation of unitary patent protection. Only Croatia, Italy and Spain do not participate in the scheme for the time being. On 20 January 2013 the two Regulations implementing the unitary patent and

* Stefan Luginbuehl, PhD (Utrecht), lawyer, Directorate International Legal Affairs, European Patent Office, Munich. The views expressed are those of the author.

[1] For an historical overview of the Community patent, see also J Pila, 'The European Patent: An Old and Vexing Problem' (2013) 62 *ICLQ* 917; E Ellyne, 'European Unitary Patent: Are We there Yet?' (2014) 31 *Queen Mary Journal of Intellectual Property* 57; S Luginbuehl, *Uniform Interpretation of European Patent Law with a Special View on the Creation of a Common Patent Court* <http://igitur-archive.library.uu.nl/dissertations/2009-0901-200115/luginbuehl.pdf> 11 ff.

[2] See critique by M Lamping, 'Enhanced Cooperation—A Proper Approach to Market Integration in the Field of Unitary Patent Protection?' (2011) 42 *International Review of Intellectual Property and Competition Law* 879, 904 ff; H Ullrich, 'Harmonizing Patent Law: The Untamable Union Patent', Max Planck Institute for Intellectual Property and Competition Law Research Paper No 12-03 <http://www.rzecznikpatentowy.org.pl/nie_dla_pat_jed/SSRN-id2027920.pdf> 17 ff.

[3] Council Decision of 10 March 2011 authorising enhanced cooperation in the area of the creation of unitary patent protection, OJ L76/53 (22 March 2011).

its translation regime[4] (Unitary Patent Regulations) entered into force for these 25 states. In spring 2013 Spain filed two nullity actions against the Regulations[5] with the CJEU. Both actions are still pending. The CJEU is expected to hand down its judgment by the beginning of 2015.

Despite having already entered into force, the Unitary Patent Regulations will only become fully applicable when the third legal instrument of the 'EU patent package'—the Agreement on a Unified Patent Court[6] (UPC Agreement)—enters into force.[7] This approach underscores that the unitary patent and the future common patent court form one inseparable package,[8] and that consequently there can be no unitary patent until the UPC Agreement takes effect.

The UPC Agreement was signed by 25 EU Member States in Brussels on 19 February 2013. It is interesting to note that although Poland is participating in enhanced cooperation, it was not among the signatories. Italy, on the other hand, which is not participating in enhanced cooperation, signed the Agreement. Consequently, Poland will remain outside the unitary patent protection system for now, while Italy's participation is limited to the common European patent court. Croatia, which joined the EU on 1 July 2013, indicated that it is currently not interested in acceding to the UPC Agreement. The UPC Agreement will enter into force as soon as it is ratified by 13 states, including France, Germany and the United Kingdom as the three states in which most European patents had effect in 2012, the year preceding the signature of the Agreement.[9]

So far, Austria, France, Sweden, Belgium and Denmark have deposited their instruments of ratification of the UPC Agreement.[10] Malta has concluded its parliamentary ratification procedure, and it is expected that the UK will deposit its ratification instrument after the 2015 general election.

The recast of the already revised Brussels I Regulation[11] is another requirement for the entry into force of the UPC Agreement. The recast which has the goal to ensure that there are no conflicts between the Brussels I Regulation and the

[4] Regulation (EU) No 1257/2012 of the European Parliament and of the Council of 17 December 2012 implementing enhanced cooperation in the area of the creation of unitary patent protection, OJ L361/1 (31 December 2012) (Regulation 1257/2012); and Regulation (EU) No 1260/2012 of 17 December 2012 implementing enhanced cooperation in the area of the creation of unitary patent protection with regard to the applicable translation arrangements, OJ L361/89 (31 December 2012).

[5] Joined Cases C-146/13 & C-147/13 *Kingdom of Spain v Council of the European Union*. See also in this regard W Tilmann, 'Spain's Action against the EU Patent Package: Arguments and Counter-Arguments in Case C-146/13' (2014) 36 *European Intellectual Property Review* 4.

[6] Agreement on a Unified Patent Court, OJ C175/1 (20 June 2013) (UPC Agreement).

[7] Regulation 1257/2012, Art 18(2).

[8] See the critique by J Pagenberg, 'Unitary Patent and Unified Patent Court—What Lies Ahead?' (2013) 8 *Journal of Intellectual Property Law & Practice* 480.

[9] See UPC Agreement, Art 89.

[10] For the status of UPC Agreement ratification process, see <http://ec.europa.eu/internal_market/indprop/patent/ratification/index_en.htm>.

[11] Regulation (EU) No 1215/2012 of the European Parliament and of the EU Council of 12 December 2012 on jurisdiction and the recognition and enforcement of judgments in civil and commercial matters, OJ L351/1 (20 December 2012).

UPC Agreement was initiated in July 2013.[12] It was adopted in record time and entered into force on 30 May 2014[13] so that the revised version of the Brussels I Regulation, including the latest recast, will become fully applicable on 10 January 2015.[14]

The Unitary Patent Regulations[15] will apply to only those states participating in enhanced cooperation that ratified the UPC Agreement.[16] Consequently, as it is to be expected that not all the 25 EU Member States participating in enhanced cooperation will have ratified the UPC Agreement when it enters into force, the first unitary patents registered will not cover the entire territory of the participating states. For example, the unitary patent will not cover the territory of Poland until such time as Poland accedes to the UPC Agreement, even though it is participating in the enhanced cooperation scheme.

B. The Unitary Patent Concept

The unitary patent is a European patent to which, at the request of its proprietor, unitary effect is given as from grant of the European patent.[17] The registration of unitary effect thus requires a European patent granted under the Rules of the European Patent Convention (EPC).[18] This makes it a unique construct under EU law, namely an EU title grantable only on the basis of a right conferred under an international convention. The approach chosen means that the European Patent Office's existing search, examination and grant procedure remains entirely unaffected. Consequently, an applicant seeking unitary protection in the states participating in enhanced cooperation will first have to file a European or international application. The applicant does not have to decide whether he wants unitary effect for the patent until such time as the patent is granted. The unitary patent is an additional option to 'classic' European and national patents.[19] However, double protection in the form of a classic European patent plus a unitary patent in the countries taking

[12] Proposal for a Regulation of the European Parliament and of the Council amending Regulation (EU) No 1215/2012 on jurisdiction and the recognition and enforcement of judgments in civil and commercial matters, COM(2013) 554 final (26 July 2013), adopted on 15 May 2014 as Regulation EU No 542/2014 of the European Parliament and of the Council of 15 May 2014 amending Regulation (EU) No 1215/2012 as regards the rules to be applied with respect to the Unified Patent Court and the Benelux Court of Justice, OJ L 163/1 (29 May 2014).

[13] Regulation 542/2014.

[14] Regulation 1215/2012, Art 81 2nd sentence and Regulation 542/2014, Art 2 2nd sentence. See also concerning the revised jurisdiction rules for patent litigation, S Luginbühl and D Stauder, 'Die Anwendung der revidierten Zuständigkeitsregeln nach der Brüssel I-Verordnung auf Klagen in Patentsachen' [2014] *Gewerblicher Rechtsschutz und Urheberrecht Int.* 885 ff.

[15] See n 4.

[16] Regulation 1257/2012, Art 18(2).

[17] Ibid, Art 4(1); see also EPC, Art 64(1).

[18] Convention on the Grant of European Patents (5 October 1973) (EPC). The EPC has 38 Contracting States (all members of the EU, plus Albania, the former Yugoslav Republic of Macedonia, Iceland, Liechtenstein, Monaco, Norway, San Marino, Switzerland, and Turkey).

[19] Regulation 1257/2012, Recital 26.

part in enhanced cooperation will not be possible.[20] The question of whether double protection in the form of a unitary patent plus a national patent for the territory of the participating states is possible will have to be answered at national level.[21] It is expected that quite a number of participating states will accept such double protection, not least in order to strengthen the national route.

Unitary patents, unlike classic European patents, have unitary character throughout the territories of those states taking part in the enhanced cooperation scheme[22] and having ratified the UPC Agreement.[23] In all those countries, they offer unitary protection and have the same effects.[24] Consequently, they can be limited, transferred or revoked only in respect of all participating states, although they can be licensed on a limited territorial basis.[25] It will also be possible for the patent holder to grant licenses of rights for unitary patents.[26]

II. Institutional Perspectives on the Unitary Patent

A. Introduction

Broadly speaking, institutional perspectives on the unitary patent relate in particular to aspects of legal policy in the Unitary Patent Regulations. This includes institutional matters facing the EU and the EPO,[27] such as how to attribute

[20] Ibid, Recital 8 and Art 4(2).

[21] The question of whether it is possible to have simultaneous protection by a 'classic' European patent and a national patent on the territory of an EPC Contracting State is left to national law: see EPC, Art 139(3). Only a few EPC Contracting States such as Austria, Hungary, Poland and the Scandinavian states allow such a double protection: see National Law Relating to the EPC, X. Miscellaneous <http://www.epo.org/law-practice/legal-texts/national-law.html>.

[22] As regards the range of protection of a unitary patent, see R Romandini and A Klicznik, 'The Territoriality Principle and Transnational Use of Patented Inventions—the Wider Reach of a Unitary Patent and the Role of the CJEU?' (2013) 44 *International Review of Intellectual Property and Competition Law* 524.

[23] See Regulation 1257/2012, Arts 3(2) and 18(2); EPC, Art 142(1).

[24] Spain argues in its action against Regulation 1257/2012 that because of the deletion of some Articles on substantive patent law (on scope of protection and limitations of a unitary patent, former Articles 6–8 draft Regulation on unitary patent protection) the Regulation does not provide for uniform protection anymore and thus that there is no act of the EU, or, alternatively that the legal basis of Art 118(1) TFEU for the Regulation is missing; see in this regard also C Wadlow, '"Hamlet without the Prince": Can the Unitary Patent Regulation Strut its Stuff without Articles 6–8?' (2013) 8 *Journal of Intellectual Property Law & Practice* 207; H Ullrich, 'The Property Aspects of the European Patent with Unitary Effect—A National Perspective for a European Prospect?' in I Govaere and D Hanf (eds), *Scrutinizing Internal and External Dimensions of European Law*, Liber Amicorum Paul Demaret, Vol I, ser Cahiers du Collège d'Europe/College of European Studies—vol 17 (Bruxelles et al, 2013) 481; Ellyne (n 1) 64 ff; Pagenberg (n 8) 481.

[25] Regulation 1257/2012, Art 3(2).

[26] Ibid, Art 8.

[27] Concerning the basic institutional aspects of the European patent system, see S Luginbuehl, *European Patent Law—towards a Uniform Interpretation* (Cheltenham, Edward Elgar, 2011) 1.

unitary effect to a European patent[28] and thus establish legal effect on the basis of an EU Regulation which applies to a patent granted by the EPO—an organ of an international organisation[29] outside the direct influence and judicial control of the EU[30]—as well as on the basis of the EPC, an international treaty binding on 38 European states, 10 of them not members of the EU. Another basic institutional question is whether the Unitary Patent Regulations are in line with the principles of autonomy and uniformity in the application of EU law as the Regulations only become applicable once, and only in those EU Member States in which the UPC Agreement has entered into force. One may also wonder whether there is a problem with Article 291(2) TFEU, which deals with delegated acts, because the Select Committee of the European Patent Organisation, not the European Commission, is charged with determining the level of the renewal fees and the distribution key for these fees.[31] These and other such questions on fundamental institutional issues are raised by Spain in the above-mentioned actions against the adoption of the Unitary Patent Regulations[32] and will not be addressed any further here.

However, institutional perspectives on the unitary patent also include more technical aspects of the law, such as:

(a) the decision taken in the Regulations on unitary patent protection to use the existing legal framework provided by the EPC (Part IX of the EPC) to implement the unitary patent within the current European patent system, and
(b) the relationship between the EPO and its Boards of Appeal, on one side, and the future Unified Patent Court, on the other.

B. Technical Aspects of the Law

i. Part IX of the EPC as the Legal Basis for Implementing the Unitary Patent in the existing European Patent System

(a) General

Article 1(2) and Recitals 6 and 16 of Regulation 1257/2012 hold that the unitary patent will be implemented under Part IX of the EPC. In 2000, the European Commission still envisaged that the European Community would accede to the EPC.[33] This is no longer the case. A revision of the EPC, and thus another

[28] See Regulation 1257/2012, Recitals 5 and 7.
[29] See EPC, Art 4(2)(a).
[30] See also Ullrich (n 2) 41 ff; M Troncoso, 'International Intellectual Property Scholars Series: European Union Patents: A Mission Impossible? An Assessment of the Historical and Current Approaches' (2013) 17 *Marquette Intellectual Property Law Review* 231, 245 ff; T Jaeger, 'Hieronymus Bosch am Werk beim EU-Patent?' (2013) *Europäische Zeitschrift für Wirtschaftsrecht* 15, 16.
[31] See II.B.i.(d) The Establishment of the Select Committee.
[32] See I.A. General.
[33] Proposal for a Council Regulation on the Community patent of 1 October 2000, COM(2000) 412 final, No 2.3.3, 8.

diplomatic conference with possible delays due to the ratification procedure involved, is consequently not necessary anymore.

Part IX of the EPC was established as an interface between the EPC and the unitary patent for the territory of the European Community envisaged in the former Community Patent Convention 1975 (CPC). It includes the legal, technical and institutional framework for establishing a unitary patent within the existing EPC system.

Using the existing EPC framework has the advantage that the unitary patent can be introduced without having to revise the EPC as mentioned above, but it also means having to fit the Regulations on unitary patent protection, which are binding for 25 EU Member States, into a framework that is binding for 38 states, 13 of them not bound by the Regulations.

(b) The Regulations on Unitary Patent Protection as a 'Special Agreement' under Article 142 EPC

Article 142(1) EPC, the first provision in Part IX of the EPC, expressly empowers a group of Contracting States to provide by special agreement that European patents granted for them may have unitary character throughout their territories. Switzerland and Liechtenstein have already made use of this authorisation and agreed to a unitary patent established by international treaty.[34] There seems to be a general consensus[35] that, even though the Regulations are not a treaty but secondary EU law, the two Regulations on the unitary patent are to qualify as 'special agreements':[36] the basic consideration underlying Part IX of the EPC is the wish of a group of Contracting States to have the possibility to establish a European patent with unitary character in the post-grant stage. Bearing this in mind, together with the fact that the relevant EPC provisions come under the general heading 'special agreements', it is clear that the fathers of the EPC and the legislator intended to make provision for any agreement between EPC Contracting States, whether embodied in an international treaty or in some other legal instrument expressing such agreement.

(c) Additional Tasks for the European Patent Office

Recital 16 of Regulation 1257/2012 furthermore sets out that the group of Member States making use of the provisions of Part IX of the EPC may delegate tasks to the EPO and set up a Select Committee of the Administrative Council of

[34] Treaty between the Swiss Confederation and the Principality of Liechtenstein on Patent Protection (Patent Treaty) of 22 December 1978, OJ EPO 1980, 407 ff.

[35] See, however, IB Stjerna, 'Die Beratungen zum "Einheitspatent" und der zugehörigen Gerichtsbarkeit—Auf dem Weg ins Desaster' (2012) *Mitteilungen der deutschen Patentanwälte* 54, 57; Troncoso (n 30) 258.

[36] This is also made clear in Regulation 1257/2012, Art 1(2) and Recital 6.

the European Patent Organisation.[37] Article 9 of Regulation 1257/2012 provides further details. The first paragraph holds that, as a group of EPC Contracting States, the participating states will, within the meaning of Article 143(1) EPC, give the EPO additional tasks to be carried out 'in accordance with the internal rules of the EPO'. The additional tasks include, in particular:

- receiving and examining requests for unitary effect, registering unitary effect or rejecting requests if the legal requirements are not met;
- setting up and administering a central unitary patent register; and
- collecting and administering renewal fees for unitary patents.

(d) The Establishment of the Select Committee

Paragraph 2 of Article 9 Regulation 1257/2012 sets out that, in their capacity as EPC Contracting States, the participating states will ensure the governance and supervision of these additional tasks and will ensure the setting of the level of renewal fees and their distribution. Furthermore, it holds that to that end, they will set up a Select Committee of the Administrative Council of the European Patent Organisation within the meaning of Article 145 EPC.

Against this background, the participating Member States had the duty to first set up the required Select Committee in order to fulfil their other tasks, in particular the adoption of the Implementing Rules dealing with the details of the tasks entrusted to the EPO, that is the 'internal rules of the EPO' as provided for in paragraph 1 of Article 9 Regulation 1257/2012 and the setting of the level of renewal fees for the unitary patent and their distribution among the 25 participating states.

Several approaches were discussed on how to officially set up the Select Committee in practice and fulfil the legal obligation as set out in Regulation 1257/2012. One was to establish the Select Committee by a separate declaration made by the 25 participating states. That, however, was considered too complex, not least because it would once again raise complicated issues of international law. Another proposal involved supplementing the Implementing Rules with a specific rule laying down that a Select Committee is set up with the adoption of the Rules. In the end, a more pragmatic solution was chosen. Very simply, the Select Committee formally agreed in a decision at its inaugural meeting in March 2013 to set up the Select Committee of the Administrative Council. This decision is recorded in the minutes of the meeting.

[37] In its action against Regulation 1257/2012, Spain claims that there is a misapplication of the *Meroni* case law (Case C-10/56 *Meroni & Co, Industrie Metallurgiche, SAS v High Authority of the European Coal and Steel Community* (13 June 1958) [1957–58] ECR 133) in delegating to the EPO certain administrative tasks relating to the unitary patent, and that consequently there is an unlawful delegation of powers to an international organisation. Without going into further details, it can be argued that it is the EU Member States and not the EU that entrust these tasks to the EPO, and consequently that the *Meroni* case law is not applicable.

The Select Committee as provided for in Article 145 EPC is a sub-body of the Administrative Council of the European Patent Organisation. It is currently composed of the representatives of the 25 participating states and the European Commission, as well as the EPC Contracting States that do not participate in the enhanced cooperation scheme, along with user organisations as observers.

At the end of June 2013, the EPO tabled a first draft of the Implementing Rules for a general round of discussions by the Select Committee. This draft was revised several times. The draft Rules include detailed provisions relating to the request for unitary effect, the competence and duties of the Select Committee and the President of the EPO, licences of right and lapse of the unitary patent, as well as Rules concerning the future register for unitary patent protection, which will be part of the existing European Patent Register.

The other important task of the Select Committee, which is to determine the level of renewal fees and the distribution scale as mentioned above, will be of key importance to users, but also to the participating states, non-participating EPC Contracting States and the EPO. In contrast to the arrangement in place today with regard to traditional European patents, renewal fees for the unitary patent will have to be paid to the EPO.[38] The EPO will retain 50 per cent of the fees and distribute the remaining part to the participating states according to the distribution scale.[39] As regards the level of the fees—a highly controversial topic—Regulation 1257/2012 only sets out general criteria.[40] It seems clear that these fees will have to be low enough to be attractive to users but high enough to ensure the EPO's financial sustainability. The discussions on the financial issues are still ongoing in the Select Committee.

ii. The Relationship between the EPO, its Boards of Appeal and the Unified Patent Court

(a) The establishment of a Unitary Patent Protection Division

As a European patent, the unitary patent will be open to opposition under Article 99 ff EPC, possibly followed by an appeal. Consequently, a European patent to which unitary effect is attributed can be revoked by the Opposition Division or the Boards of Appeal of the EPO. Limitation and revocation procedures under Article 105a ff EPC will also be available.

The Boards of Appeal, however, will not have jurisdiction over appeals against EPO decisions on tasks relating to the administration of the unitary patent. That jurisdiction will lie with the UPC.[41] In view of these circumstances, the Select Committee made a proposal during discussions on the Implementing Rules to establish a special department within the EPO with responsibility for carrying

[38] Regulation 1257/2012, Art 9(1)(e).
[39] Ibid, Art 13(1).
[40] Ibid, Art 12.
[41] Ibid, Art 9(3); UPC Agreement, Arts 32(1)(i) and 47(7).

out the tasks relating to the unitary patent.[42] The possibility of creating special departments of this kind is provided for in Article 143(2) EPC. The proposed Unitary Patent Protection (UPP) division will make a clear separation between the tasks performed by the EPO for the 38 EPC Contracting States in relation to the examination and grant of European patents, on the one hand, and the additional tasks entrusted to the EPO by the 25 participating Member States, on the other. The existing departments referred to in Article 15 EPC (Receiving Section, Search Divisions, Examining Divisions, Opposition Divisions, Legal Division, Boards of Appeal and Enlarged Board of Appeal) which carry out the application, examination, opposition and appeals proceedings will thus have no responsibility with regard to the additional tasks entrusted to the EPO on the basis of Regulation 1257/2012.

The UPP division's establishment will ensure that the UPC has a clear counterpart at the EPO. This will be important if an action is filed with the UPC against a decision of the UPP division. The latest version of the draft Rules of Procedure of the Unified Patent Court contains for example a proposal for the introduction of interlocutory revision.[43] This kind of remedy, which is also provided for in Article 109 EPC for appeals against a decision of the EPO, will make it possible for the court to inform the UPP division about an action against one of its decisions and enable it to rectify the contested decision.

(b) The UPC and the EPO (and its Boards of Appeal): Two Independent Institutions at European Level?

Both the UPC[44] and the EPO will apply uniform substantive European patent law:[45] the validity grounds,[46] the scope of protection[47] and the right to a European patent,[48] all determined by the EPC, will apply to classic European patents as well as unitary patents.[49] The aim of substantial legal uniformity in Europe can only be achieved if the authorities apply it in a consistent manner.[50] As the EPO and the

[42] Draft Rules relating to Unitary Patent Protection—revised and consolidated version, SC/21/14 (6 June 2014), r 4.

[43] Preliminary set of provisions for the Rules of Procedure ('Rules') of the Unified Patent Court, 16th draft (31 January 2014) <http://www.unified-patent-court.org/images/documents/revised-draft-rules-of-procedure.pdf>, r 91.

[44] The UPC has jurisdiction concerning disputes relating to 'classic' European patents and unitary patents: see UPC Agreement, Art 32.

[45] Concerning the terminology, see Luginbuehl (n 27) 4 ff. See also J Brinkhof and A Ohly, 'Towards a Unified Patent Court in Europe' in A Ohly and J Pila (eds), *The Europeanization of Intellectual Property Law* (Oxford, Oxford University Press, 2013) 199, 204 s.

[46] EPC, Arts 138 and 139(2).

[47] Ibid, Art 69.

[48] Ibid, Art 60.

[49] See UPC Agreement, Art 24(1)(c); as regards the validity grounds, see UPC Agreement, Art 65(2).

[50] See in this regard also HHJ Birss, 'Unitary Rights and Judicial Respect in the EU—"Bringing Cool Back"' (2013) 3 *Queen Mary Journal of Intellectual Property* 195, 197 ff; J Brinkhof, 'Dutch Courage?' in B van den Broek et al (eds), *Hoyng-bundel: Liber Amicorum Willem Hoyng* (Amsterdam, Jaar van uitgave, 2013) 357, 376 s.

UPC are independent institutions from a formal legal institutional perspective, it will be of crucial importance that both of them take each other's case law into account in order to achieve as harmonized an approach as possible. This implies that the two institutions are not as independent as they seem to be. The EPO has already invested a lot of effort in establishing mutual respect and recognition between national patent judges and the members of the EPO Boards of Appeal. The European patent judges' symposium, which has been taking place every two years for over 30 years,[51] and the annual EPLAW judges' forum[52] in Venice have become important opportunities for judges to meet and exchange views and experiences.[53] More than ever before, judges and members of the EPO Boards of Appeal are taking note of each other's decisions,[54] which are made easily accessible on the internet by many states and the EPO.[55] Most judges in the major European patent litigation states[56] are aware that they belong to a common European patent judiciary area,[57] and that a comparative interpretation of the law is required to achieve harmonized case law.[58] This means that the other's legal understanding and case law have to be taken into practical consideration before a decision is made. The need for this kind of understanding between judges and members of the EPO Boards of Appeal is set to become even more important with the establishment of the UPC, when two judicial institutions highly specialised in patent

[51] For an overview see Luginbuehl (n 27) 129 ff; G Kolle and D Stauder, 'Die Symposia europäischer Patentrichter' Festschrift für Rüdiger Rogge zum 65. Geburtstag [2001] *Gewerblicher Rechtsschutz und Urheberrecht* 955. For more detail, see speeches, articles, discussions and reports from the 16 symposia to date in Special Edition of the OJ EPO 2013; Special Edition 1, OJ EPO 2011; Special Edition 1, OJ EPO 2009; Special Edition 2, OJ EPO 2007, Special Edition, OJ EPO 2005; Special Edition 2, OJ EPO 2003; Special Edition 2, OJ EPO 2001; Special Edition, OJ EPO 1999; (1997) 28 *International Review of Intellectual Property and Competition Law* 785; (1996) 27 *International Review of Intellectual Property and Competition Law* 151; (1993) 24 *International Review of Intellectual Property and Competition Law* 689; (1991) 22 *International Review of Intellectual Property and Competition Law* 843; (1989) 20 *International Review of Intellectual Property and Competition Law* 271; (1987) 18 *International Review of Intellectual Property and Competition Law* 579; (1985) 16 *International Review of Intellectual Property and Competition Law* 283; (1983) 14 *International Review of Intellectual Property and Competition Law* 707. See also Brinkhof and Ohly (n 45) 205.

[52] <http://www.eplaw.org/>.

[53] See also R Jacob, 'The Relationship between European and National Courts in Intellectual Property' in Ohly and Pila (n 45) 185, 188 s.

[54] See, eg *Human Genome Sciences Inc v Eli Lilly and Co* [2011] UKSC 51, [43] ff or *Grimme Maschinenfabrik GmbH & Co KG v Derek Scott* [2010] EWCA Civ 1110 (n 79 ff); decision of the German Federal Court of Justice dated 15 April 2010 (Xa ZB 10/09)—*Walzenformgebungsmaschine (Roll-forming machine)*, OJ EPO 2010, 622, 626; decision of the Swiss Federal Court of 4 March 2011(4A_437/2010), 1st civil division, OJ EPO 2011, 452, 455 ff; decision of the Enlarged Board of Appeal dated 5 December 1984, G 5/83, OJ EPO 1985, 64 (n 18).

[55] See also the collections of case law of the EPO Boards of Appeal, *Case Law of the Boards of Appeal of the European Patent Office*, 7th edn (2013), and from the EPC Contracting States, *European National Patent Decisions Report 2004* and *Case Law from the Contracting States to the EPC, 2004–11*, Special Edition 3, OJ EPO 2011.

[56] 90% of all litigation in Europe on European patents takes place before the courts of France, Germany, the Netherlands and the United Kingdom: see Luginbuehl (n 27) 21 ff.

[57] See Brinkhof and Ohly (n 45) 205.

[58] See, eg Birss (n 50) 198 ff; J Smits and W Bull, 'The Europeanization of Patent Law: Towards a Competitive Model' in Ohly and Pila (n 45) 39, 50.

matters will exist at European level. This would be even more pertinent if the CJEU started to regularly construe substantive patent law that would be binding on the UPC and the EU Member States,[59] but not so directly on the EPO and its Boards of Appeal. This is explained by the fact that the EPO and the Boards of Appeal are not directly part of the EU judicial framework. Thus, they can neither submit questions to the CJEU on the interpretation of EU law, which was incorporated into the EPC, nor are they bound to any ruling of the CJEU.[60] However, 28 of the EPC Contracting States are bound by the CJEU's interpretation of EU law. This fundamental institutional problem has already been brought to light by the CJEU's famous judgment in *Brüstle v Greenpeace*.[61] The CJEU held that uses of human embryos for industrial or commercial purposes shall be considered unpatentable. This judgment was not in line with EPO practice. The CJEU ruling was based on Article 6(2)(c) of the EU Biotech Directive,[62] which was incorporated into the Implementing Rules to the EPC.[63] As the CJEU's decision was a narrower reading of the provision than that adopted by the EPO, the question arose as to whether the EPO should change its practice. On the one hand, this could have given the impression that CJEU judgments were binding on the EPO and its Boards of Appeal, and consequently indirectly on the 10 EPC Contracting States that are not members of the EU. Institutionally speaking, this would have been very problematic as these states had transferred their sovereignty rights only to the European Patent Organisation, not to the EU. On the other hand, if the EPO did not change its practice it would have had to either accept the risk that European patents granted on such inventions could be expected to be revoked or partly revoked during national proceedings in EU Member States, or apply a different kind of practice and interpretation of the substantive patent law, depending on where the European patent was going to take effect. In the end, it was decided to amend the examination guidelines to allow the EPO to take the CJEU judgment into account when interpreting the relevant provisions in the EPC Implementing Rules.

[59] See UPC Agreement, Art 20 ff; W Tilmann, 'The Compromise on the Uniform Protection for EU Patents' (2013) 8 *Journal of Intellectual Property Law and Practice* 78, 81; Brinkhof and Ohly (n 45) 216.

[60] See decision of the Enlarged Board of Appeal of the EPO, G 2/06, OJ EPO 2009, 306, 317 ff; EPC, Art 23(3).

[61] Case C-34/10 *Brüstle v Greenpeace* (18 October 2011) [2012] 1 CMLR 41. See also D Eyre and G Schlich, 'Brüstle: The Death of Stem Cell Patents?' [2011] *CIPA Journal* 681; H Schacht, 'Commencement or Completion: What Constitutes a "Human Embryo" within the Meaning of the EU Biotechnology Directive?' (2014) 36 *European Intellectual Property Review* 66; PHD Batista, 'Zur Patentierung menschlicher embryonaler Stammzellen—kritische Würdigung der Entscheidung des EuGH im Fall Brüstle' [2013] *Gewerblicher Rechtsschutz und Urheberrecht: Internationaler Teil* 514.

[62] Directive 98/44/EC of the European Parliament and of the Council of 6 July 1998 on the legal protection of biotechnological inventions, OJ L 213/13 (30 July 1998).

[63] EPC, r 28(c).

III. Summary and Conclusion

The states participating in enhanced cooperation and the European Parliament decided, with the adoption of the Unitary Patent Regulations, to implement the unitary patent in the current European patent system within the framework of the European Patent Organisation. The decision to use Part IX of the EPC for this purpose provides for an efficient and practical implementation of the unitary patent within the specific structures of the Organisation, that is by the Select Committee. This approach ensures that legal solutions are found that facilitate the smooth transition from the pre-grant proceedings provided by the EPC to the post-grant registration procedure of the unitary patent. Whether it is compatible with EU law will have to be decided by the CJEU in its judgment on Spain's actions against the Regulations.

With regard to the relationship between the EPO, on the one side, and the future UPC, on the other, a dedicated division will be established within the EPO, comprising lawyers who will deliver decisions related to the unitary patent.

For the EPO Boards of Appeal and the UPC, it will be of crucial importance that the two institutions maintain a steady discourse on their case law and the interpretation of the existing uniform substantive patent law that they both apply. As the Regulations on unitary patent protection come into force and with the establishment of the UPC, it could be anticipated that the CJEU will provide more rulings on the interpretation of substantive patent law. Institutional problems between the EU and the EPO—as exemplified by the CJEU's judgment in *Brüstle v Greenpeace*—are likely to arise more frequently. As things stand today, the EU will be more persistent and may thus increase its influence, not least via the CJEU, on the European Patent Organisation, the EPO and its Boards of Appeal.[64] This situation may lead EPC Contracting States to accept the de facto automatic adoption by the EPO of CJEU case law, as it seems neither advisable, nor even possible, in centralised and uniform patent application and examination proceedings, to apply different substantive patent law depending on the territory where the European patent is going to take effect. This is certain to reopen the question of whether the EPO and its Boards of Appeal should not in the long term be integrated into the EU system, provoking difficult political and institutional decisions on the part of the EPC Contracting States that are not members of the EU.

[64] See also J Pila, 'A Constitutionalized Doctrine of Precedent and the *Marleasing* Principle as Bases for a European Legal Methodology' in Ohly and Pila (n 45) 227, 235 ff.

5

An Institutional Perspective II: The Role of the CJEU in the Unitary (EU) Patent System

ANGELOS DIMOPOULOS*

I. Introduction

In 2013 a new era for EU patent law started. The creation of the EU patent with unitary effect (EPUE)[1] and the establishment of the Unified Patent Court (UPC)[2] established a new legal framework on substantive patent protection and patent litigation in Europe. However, the creation of the new EU patent system did not follow the usual path of EU harmonization, as the political compromise reached resulted in a complex and multi-layered system of patent protection in the EU.[3] Recognizing the existence of the European Patent Convention (EPC), as an extra-EU international agreement on patent protection,[4] and building upon it, a new system of patent protection was created, by allowing in essence different types of

* Lecturer in Law, Queen Mary University of London.

[1] Regulation (EU) No 1257/2012 of the European Parliament and of the Council of 17 December 2012 implementing enhanced cooperation in the area of the creation of unitary patent protection, OJ L361/1 (31 December 2012) (UPPR); Regulation (EU) No 1260/2012 of 17 December 2012 implementing enhanced cooperation in the area of the creation of unitary patent protection with regard to the applicable translation arrangements, OJ L361/89 (31 December 2012). The Regulations will enter into force as of 1 January 2014, or from the date when the international agreement enters into force, whichever is the latest.

[2] Agreement on a Unified Patent Court, OJ C175/1 (20 June 2013) (UPC Agreement). The international agreement creating a unified patent court will enter into force on 1 January 2014 or after 13 Contracting States ratify it, provided that the UK, France and Germany are among them.

[3] For a description and critique of the processes that led to this initiative, see T Jaeger, 'All Back to Square One? An Assessment of the Latest Proposals for a Patent and Court for the Internal Market and Possible Alternatives' (2012) 43 *International Review of Intellectual Property and Competition Law* 286; M Lamping, 'Enhanced Cooperation—a Proper Approach to Market Integration in the Field of Unitary Patent Protection?'(2011) 42 *International Review of Intellectual Property and Competition Law* 879; S Luginbuehl, *European Patent Law—Towards a Uniform Interpretation* (Cheltenham, Edward Elgar, 2011) 185–92.

[4] Convention on the Grant of European Patents of 5 October 1973 (EPC).

patents to be established and coexist in different EU territories, based on national, EU and international law.

In this context, the role of the Court of Justice of the EU (CJEU) is very controversial. In the long debate that preceded the adoption of the new system, one of the major obstacles concerned the role of the CJEU. There were many voices from industry and national governments favouring a limited role of the CJEU, alleging this would safeguard the efficiency of patent litigation.[5] The compromise that was reached aims to safeguard an effective and efficient system of patent protection, whilst respecting the foundational role of the CJEU within the EU legal order. Nevertheless, the parallel but interrelated existence of different types of patents, which are partly based on common rules, makes the identification of the limits of the CJEU's jurisdiction difficult. More importantly, the establishment of the UPC as a special patent litigation system in parts of EU territory established under an international agreement perplexes the determination of the CJEU's jurisdiction in patent cases. In fact the long negotiations before the final adoption of the UPC Agreement were concerning directly or indirectly the delimitation of the CJEU's jurisdiction over patent matters and the relation between the two courts.[6] However, despite the compromise reached with the conclusion of the UPC Agreement in early 2013, it seems that the role of the CJEU in patent matters is still unclear. This is particularly so, in light of the CJEU's judgment in the *Daiichi Sankyo*[7] case, where the Court found that EU exclusive competence under Article 207 TFEU confers jurisdiction on it to interpret the patent provisions of the TRIPS Agreement.

Within this framework, this chapter aims to identify the limits of the CJEU's jurisdiction in patent matters, focusing in particular on the implications of the CJEU interpretative jurisdiction over the TRIPS. In that respect, it looks first at the scope of the CJEU's jurisdiction after the introduction of the EPUE and the conclusion of the UPC Agreement, examining the scope of the CJEU's jurisdiction over different types of patents. Following this, the CJEU's judgment in *Daiichi Sankyo* is analysed, identifying the scope and nature of the CJEU's jurisdiction to interpret the TRIPS Agreement. Finally, the implications of a CJEU interpretative jurisdiction over TRIPS are examined, identifying how it affects the patent litigation system envisaged after the conclusion of the UPC Agreement.

[5] On the debates regarding the role of the CJEU in the new patent system see for example the discussions at the UK House of Commons European Scrutiny Committee<http://www.publications.parliament.uk/pa/cm201012/cmselect/cmeuleg/uc1799ii/uc1799ii.htm≥.

[6] Opinion 1/09 [2011] ECR I-1137.

[7] Case C-414/11 *Daiichi Sankyo and Sanofi-Aventis Deutschland* [2013] ECR I-0000.

II. The (Limited) Scope of the CJEU's Jurisdiction under the New European Patent System

Patent law is no stranger to the CJEU. Being the ultimate judicial authority of the EU, the CJEU has established jurisdiction on numerous cases dealing directly or indirectly with patent law. The obligation of the CJEU to ensure the unity and effectiveness of EU law, which translates into a jurisdictional monopoly over the application and interpretation of EU law,[8] has enabled the CJEU to establish jurisdiction and decide cases concerning patent protection that are directly or indirectly linked to EU law. Without entering into a detailed analysis of the patent-related jurisprudence of the CJEU, it is worth sketching the different avenues used for engaging the CJEU and the scope of its jurisdiction over patent matters, in order to identify how, and when, the CJEU is expected to interfere with patent law.

A. EU Patent Law and the CJEU

As the CJEU enjoys a jurisdictional monopoly to apply and interpret EU law, the most important avenue for engaging the CJEU in patent protection is through the establishment of EU rules on patents. Although a specific legal basis on IP harmonization was introduced for the first time under the Lisbon Treaty,[9] the EU had long before adopted secondary EU rules on IP. Based on the internal market provisions, whenever it was necessary to attain the objectives of the internal market, significant aspects of IP law were harmonized, from trademarks and designs to aspects of copyright.[10] However, the protection of patents was the least harmonized within the EU. Taking into consideration the existence of the EPC and a number of political complexities relating in particular to languages and translations,[11] the EU was very cautious in developing common rules on patents.[12]

[8] TEU, Art 19(1).

[9] TFEU, Art 118 confers powers on the Union to create European intellectual property rights, aiming to provide 'uniform protection of intellectual property rights throughout the Union'.

[10] See Directive 89/104/EEC on the approximation of the laws of the Member States relating to trade marks, OJ L40/2 (11 February 1989).

[11] National interests with regard to official languages, translations and jurisdictional arrangements have in the past stopped the efforts towards an EU patent. On the failed initiatives to establish an EU patent see further below.

[12] Given the economic significance of patents and the problems that arise from the current regime, it is not surprising that an EU patent system has been debated since the 1960s. What is surprising is that all the proposed plans had foundered due to disagreements over translations and jurisdictional arrangements. Indicatively see the comments of the Max Planck Institute for Intellectual Property, Competition and Tax Law on the 2009 Commission Proposal for the Establishment of a Unified Patent Judiciary (2009) 40 *International Review of Intellectual Property and Competition Law* 81; T Jaeger, 'The EU Patent: Cui Bono et Quo Vadit?' (2010) 47 *CML Rev* 63; H Ullrich, 'Patent Protection in Europe: Integrating Europe into the Community or the Community into Europe' (2002) 8 *European Law Journal* 433.

Instead of following its practice in other areas of IP law, the EU adopted a rather partial and subject-specific attitude towards patent harmonization. The EU focused its attention on new and controversial aspects of patent protection, leaving general questions on validity and infringement outside EU law.[13] In that respect, harmonization focused on new technological and ethical questions of patent law, such as on protection of biotechnology,[14] or medicinal and plant protection products.[15] Moreover, EU secondary norms were established with regard to the enforcement of IP rights, including patents.[16]

Adding to these specific types of norms, the CJEU has recently expanded the scope of its jurisdiction over patents with the establishment of the EPUE. The adoption of the Unified Patent Protection Regulation (UPPR), which entered into force on 1 January 2014, marks the first EU patent harmonization instrument that establishes common rules for different types of patents in the EU. Nevertheless, the scope of the EPUE, which gives rise to CJEU jurisdiction, is rather limited. First of all, as the UPPR was concluded only by 25 Member States,[17] the EPUE partitions the EU into three separate territories. In addition to the questions of legality concerning the procedure of enhanced cooperation,[18] since two Member States are excluded from the scope of the enhanced cooperation the CJEU has limited jurisdiction over patents in Italy and Spain.

More importantly, significant issues are left outside the scope of the UPPR.[19] It does not address the issues of prior user rights, or the unitary patent as an object of property (assignments, voluntary licenses),[20] nor compulsory licenses and government use.[21] These exceptions question the usefulness of the EPUE, as for

[13] C Wadlow, 'The Impact of General European Union Law on Industrial Property Law' in A Ohly and J Pila (eds), *The Europeanization of Intellectual Property Law* (Oxford, Oxford University Press, 2013) ch 6.

[14] Directive 98/44/EC of the European Parliament and of the Council of 6 July 1998 on the legal protection of biotechnological inventions, OJ L213 (30 July 1998).

[15] Regulation (EC) No 2100/94 of 27 July 1994 on Community plant variety rights, OJ L227/1 (1 September 1994); Regulation 469/2009 of the European Parliament and of the Council of 6 May 2009 concerning the supplementary protection certificate for medicinal products, OJ L152/1 (16 June 2009); Regulation (EC) No 1610/96 of the European Parliament and of the Council of 23 July 1996 concerning the creation of a supplementary protection certificate for plant protection products, OJ L198/30 (8 August 1996); Directive 2001/83/EC of the European Parliament and of the Council of 6 November 2001 on the Community code relating to medicinal products for human use, OJ L311/262 (28 November 2001).

[16] Directive 2004/48/EC of the European Parliament and of the Council of 29 April 2004 on the enforcement of intellectual property right, OJ L195/16 (2 June 2004).

[17] Italy and Spain opted-out of the enhanced cooperation for creating the EPUE, but they may join whenever they wish to do so.

[18] The legality of the process of enhanced cooperation is the subject matter of a challenge pending in front of the CJEU in Joined Cases C-146/13 & C-147/13 *Spain v European Parliament and Council* (pending). See also Lamping (n 3) 884; Jaeger (n 3) 290–92.

[19] For an elaborate analysis, see H Ullrich, 'Harmonizing Patent Law: The Untamable Union Patent' in M Jannsens and G Van Overwalle (eds), *Harmonization of European IP Law. From European Rules to Belgian Law and Practice* (Brussels, Bruylant, 2012) 243–94.

[20] UPPR, Art 7.

[21] UPPR, Recital 10.

example it would be practically impossible to obtain compulsory licenses covering the territory of enhanced cooperation, given that interested market actors would have to go through different national systems.[22]

But even with regard to the subject matters covered under the UPPR, the scope of the CJEU's jurisdiction is unclear. Although the UPPR contains rules on the unitary effect of the patent,[23] and the principle of exhaustion,[24] it is controversial whether the legal effects of EPUEs are defined in the UPPR, and thus, whether they are subject to the jurisdiction of the CJEU. In the initial Proposal of the UPPR the legal effects of the EPUE were defined in Articles 6–8, and thus, substantive patent rules were part of the EU legal order. The European Council though, on 28/29 June 2012 suggested that Articles 6–8 be deleted and their substance be part of the UPC Agreement. In the final adopted version, Article 5(3) UPPR defines the acts infringing the EPUE and the applicable limitations by referring to a specific national law as determined by Article 7 UPPR. However, the applicable national law is not the law of a Member State, but rather the substantive patent law defined in Articles 24–30 UPC Agreement. As a result, the substantive law concerning the effects of EPUEs and which the UPC will have to apply and interpret, is located in the UPC Agreement, while the Regulation refers only in Article 5(2) to the uniform application of the rules across the territory where EPUEs are protected. In that respect, it is at least controversial what is the scope of the CJEU's jurisdiction to interpret the effects of EPUEs, as Article 5(2) may be viewed as an indirect invitation to the CJEU to interpret Articles 24–30 UPC Agreement.[25]

Consequently, the scope of the CJEU's jurisdiction over secondary EU patent law is limited even after the introduction of the EPUE. The UPPR has not been able to achieve substantial harmonization in the field of patent law; on the contrary it has created ambiguities as to the scope of EU secondary rules in the field and the extent of the CJEU's jurisdiction.

B. National Patent Law and the CJEU

Although substantive patent protection remains to a large extent outside EU law, this does not mean that it will necessarily avoid the scrutiny of the CJEU. Adhering to the principle of primacy of EU law, the CJEU will examine any rule of national law that may conflict with EU law and set it aside. In that context, the Court has systematically expanded its jurisdiction in the field of national patent law, despite the lack of IP rules in either primary or secondary EU law.

Since the early days of the common market, the Court examined the compatibility of national IP rules with EU law, focusing in particular on their impact on

[22] Ullrich (n 19) 280–81.

[23] UPPR, Art 3.

[24] UPPR, Art 6.

[25] On this debate, see W Tilmann, 'The Compromise on the Uniform Protection of EU Patents' (2013) 8 *Journal of Intellectual Property Law and Practice* 78.

the exercise of the free movement of goods and competition rules.[26] The CJEU formulated the theory of core rights, holding that rules concerning the existence of IP rights could not infringe EU rules, while the exercise of these rights may in certain circumstances do so, so that the exercise of IP rights could be the subject of EU rules.[27] In that respect, the CJEU has developed a vast jurisprudence as to whether and under what circumstances patent protection is a restriction to free movement and competition rules. However, when an issue of substantive protection of patents arose in the past, the Court carefully avoided setting any substantive rules concerning patent protection, paying deference to national law.

As a result, the CJEU has limited jurisdiction in matters concerning substantive patent protection based on national law. This holds true despite the existence and proliferation of European-wide patents, which are still regulated under the EPC and national law. In fact, in addition to the EPUE, there are three other types of patents within the EU, namely national patents, the 'old' European patents granted by the EPO, from which the parties obtained a bundle of national patents,[28] and future European patents granted by the EPO, which do not have a unitary effect.[29] Considering the limited territorial and substantive scope of the EPUE, this makes clear that the CJEU only has a very limited say in patent protection throughout the EU.

C. The UPC and the CJEU

The jurisdictional monopoly that the CJEU enjoys regarding the application and interpretation of EU law is not threatened or undermined by the establishment of the UPC. On the contrary, the UPC, being a court of EU Member States, contributes to the proper application of EU law and safeguards the role of the CJEU. Nevertheless, this does not mean that the CJEU becomes an appeal court, able to hear cases decided by the UPC. It is only with regard to EU law matters, as defined above, that the CJEU holds jurisdiction.

Indeed, the role of the CJEU in patent litigation was one of the major reasons that resulted in the current multi-layered system of patent protection in the EU, the long negotiations, and the partial scope of the UPPR. As the CJEU's involvement in patent litigation was regarded as resulting in delays, increase of litigation costs, legal uncertainty and unpredictability, there have been efforts to minimize its role in patent litigation. In fact, the re-positioning of the provisions on infringement

[26] Case C-30/90 *Commission v UK* [1992] ECR I-892.

[27] Case 24/67 *Parke Davis v Probel* [1968] ECR 55. For an analysis of the existence versus exercise doctrine, see U Immenga and J Mestmäcker, *EG-Wettbewerbsrecht: Kommentar*, *Band II*, 4th edn (Munich, Beck, 2007) 15–43.

[28] See UPC Agreement, Art 83(3), which establishes an opt-out route for European patents existing at the time of the entry into force of the Agreement.

[29] These patents consist of territorially fragmented national rights, which are harmonized as to the conditions of their grant, the substance and the scope of exclusivity they confer upon their owner.

from the UPPR to the UPC Agreement,[30] is the result of a political compromise reached to accommodate the concerns of various Eurosceptics that warned against the perils of the CJEU having jurisdiction in patent disputes. However, the exclusion of CJEU involvement in patent litigation does not strip the CJEU from the jurisdiction it holds to apply EU law and assess the compliance of Member State law with EU law. The fact that the UPC was adopted as a pan-European court to apply national, EU and EPC law does not necessarily undermine the role of the CJEU. Without entering into a detailed analysis of the features of the relationship between the UPC and the CJEU, for the purposes of this contribution suffice it to highlight only how the UPC may interfere with the CJEU's jurisdiction to apply and interpret EU law and the measures taken in order to prevent such interferences.

More specifically, the UPC Agreement, being an agreement concluded by EU Member States, has to respect the primacy and autonomy of EU law. The CJEU has discussed at length the obligation of Member States to respect the primacy and preserve the autonomy of Union law, when they conclude international agreements between themselves or with third countries.[31] This obligation requires Member States, among others, to respect the exclusive jurisdiction of the CJEU to determine and interpret all issues that fall within the scope of EU law. As the Court has repeatedly emphasized, its exclusive jurisdiction, which is based on Article 19(1) TEU, prohibits any third court from offering a binding interpretation of EU rules without the possibility of review by the CJEU.[32] Given that the UPC applies EU (patent) law and also that questions of compatibility of national patent law with EU law may arise at the outset of proceedings, if these matters could not be decided by the CJEU, that would amount to a violation of the CJEU's jurisdiction and, thus would render the UPC incompatible with EU law. To avoid such incompatibilities, the UPC Agreement provides explicitly in Article 21 that questions such as the one mentioned above will be referred for a preliminary ruling to the CJEU in accordance with the preliminary reference procedure under Article 267 TFEU.[33]

Preserving the autonomy of EU law means, not only protecting the exclusive jurisdiction of the CJEU, but also safeguarding the role of national courts as European courts. It is in that respect that the first UPC draft agreement was found

[30] Above n 19.

[31] Case C-10/61 *Commission v Italy* [1962] ECR 1, 23; Case C-235/87 *Matteucci* [1988] ECR 5589. Indicatively, see J Klabbers, *Treaty Conflict and the European Union* (Cambridge, Cambridge University Press, 2009) 120–26; M Cremona, 'Defending the Community Interest: The Duties of Cooperation and Compliance' in M Cremona and B De Witte (eds), *EU Foreign Relations Law—Constitutional Fundamentals* (Oxford, Hart Publishing, 2008) 144–52.

[32] Case C-459/03 *Commission v Ireland (Sellafield)* [2006] ECR I-4635, [123]; Opinion 1/91 (EEA Agreement) [1991] ECR I-6079, [35]; Opinion 1/00 (Common Aviation Area) [2002] ECR I-3493, [11], [12].

[33] On the preliminary reference mechanism under UPC Agreement, Art 21 see N Jääskinen, 'The Future of European Intellectual Property Courts: Intellectual Property and the European Judicial Architecture' in Ohly and Pila (n 13) ch 12.

incompatible with EU law in Opinion 1/09.[34]As the UPC, in its original form was going to be an international court, laying outside the national judicial system, it affected both the powers of national courts of EU Member States to interpret and apply EU law, and the power to request a preliminary ruling from the ECJ and its own power to reply.[35] The Court emphasized also that the EU legal order has established a 'complete' system of legal procedures and remedies in order to guarantee the judicial review of the acts of EU institutions and Member States, which the UPC, by being an international court, avoided.[36] Remedying these incompatibilities, the revised UPC Agreement renders the UPC a court 'common' to EU Member States,[37] thus ensuring the full application of, and respect for, Union law and the judicial protection of individuals' rights under EU law, especially since the conduct of the UPC is directly attributable to the Member States.

Nevertheless, the subordination of the UPC to the CJEU in matters of EU law does not mean that the CJEU has jurisdiction to hear all cases litigated in the UPC. Rather than turning the CJEU into an appeals court, the UPC has an obligation to make a reference for a preliminary ruling only if EU law is at stake. And this would be the case, when the UPC is applying EU patent law, national law that may conflict with EU law, or, as explained below, EU or national patent law, the interpretation of which may conflict with TRIPS or any other international agreement on patent protection concluded by the EU.

D. International Agreements on Patent Protection and the CJEU

In addition to EU and national patent law, the CJEU holds jurisdiction over international agreements on patent protection concluded by the EU. Of particular interest is the WTO Agreement on Trade Related Aspects of Intellectual Property Rights (TRIPS), which presents the most comprehensive international agreement on patent protection concluded by the EU. It is in this context that the Court's ruling in the *Daichii Sankyo* case adds a new dimension to the role of the CJEU in the formation and application of patent law in the EU.

Considering first the scope of TRIPS, suffice it to mention that 'the result [for the patents provisions of the TRIPS Agreement] is impressive, in that the scope and coverage of the section are comprehensive, and makes TRIPS the most important multilateral statement in this field'.[38] Indeed, TRIPS defines patents and patentability, introduces a non-discrimination principle and establishes the

[34] [2011] ECR I-1137. For a thorough analysis of the case and how it affected the new UPC Agreement see, R Baratta, 'National Courts as "Guardians" and "Ordinary Courts" of EU Law: Opinion 1/09 of the ECJ' (2011) 38 *Legal Issues of Economic Integration* 297.

[35] [2011] ECR I-1137, [77].

[36] Ibid, [87], [88].

[37] UPC Agreement, Art 1(2).

[38] D Gervais, *The TRIPS Agreement, Drafting History and Analysis* (London, Sweet & Maxwell, 2010) 336–37.

scope of protection of patents by providing for specific exceptions.[39] For example, TRIPS introduces a general exception[40] and a list of specific exceptions (compulsory licences)[41] to the exclusive rights of patent owners. The extent of patent protection provided in TRIPS becomes even more important given that TRIPS incorporates by reference many of the provisions of the Paris Convention.[42]

Despite the broad scope of patent protection granted in TRIPS, the Court was until recently hesitant to apply and interpret the TRIPS patent provisions. Unlike trademarks,[43] in a series of cases the CJEU clarified that the interpretation of the substantive patent provisions of TRIPS lies outside its jurisdiction.[44] However, this case law was found to be no longer relevant in *Daiichi*. In that regard, in order to identify the scope and nature of the CJEU's jurisdiction over TRIPS, it is necessary to explain briefly the rules concerning the jurisdiction of the CJEU over international agreements concluded by the EU.

Based on Article 216(2) TFEU, which provides that EU international agreements are binding on EU institutions and on Member States, the Court recognised international law norms as an important source of EU law.[45] In that respect, international agreements concluded by the EU present a benchmark for the assessment of the legality of EU secondary and national law.[46] The basic test for reviewing the legality of EU and Member State measures was formulated by the Court in *International Fruit Company*,[47] subjecting judicial review in light of Union agreements to a two-prong test. The first prong requires that an international agreement is binding on the EU, while the second prong requires that the provision of the international agreement has direct effect.[48]

Applying both prongs of this test to TRIPS is problematic. First, the CJEU has established over a number of cases that none of the WTO Agreements, including TRIPS, has direct effect, since 'having regard to their nature and structure, the WTO Agreements are not in principle among the rules in the light of which

39 TRIPS, Art 29.

40 TRIPS, Art 30.

41 TRIPS, Art 31.

42 TRIPS, Art 2(1) incorporates the Paris Convention for the Protection of Industrial Property, Arts 1–12 and 19. However, the Paris Convention did not set a harmonized supranational set of norms and principles. With the exception of compulsory licensing requirements, it was restricted to basic principles for securing readier access to the patent systems maintained by different contracting parties (principle of national treatment, principle of priority and principle of independence).

43 Case C-245/02 *Anheuser Busch* [2004] ECR I-10989.

44 Case C-431/05 *Merck Genéricos Produtos Farmacêuticos* [2007] ECR I-7001.

45 Case 181/73 *Haegeman* [1974] ECR 449.

46 Recent jurisprudence (Case C-308/06 *Intertanko* [2008] ECR I-4057) indicates the nature and structure of a Union agreement has become an independent condition for the judicial review of EU acts, while it is not necessary for the judicial review of Member States' acts. See M Mendez, 'The Legal effect of Community Agreements, Maximalist Treaty Enforcement and Judicial Avoidance Techniques' (2010) 21 *European Journal of International Law* 83.

47 Joined Cases 22/72, 23/72 & 24/72 *International Fruit Company* [1972] ECR 1219.

48 P Eeckhout, *External Relations of the European Union: Legal and Constitutional Foundations*, 2nd edn (Oxford, Oxford University Press, 2011) 300–02.

the Court is to review the legality of [Union or Member State] measures'.[49] The failure of the WTO Agreement, due to its nature and structure, to satisfy the conditions for direct effect, thus deprives individuals and Member States of the possibility to rely on WTO rules so as to challenge the legality of national or Union law measures.[50] However, the CJEU established an alternative way for relying on WTO provisions in order to review the legality of EU and Member States measures. WTO norms can be relied upon in order to review measures that are meant to execute a particular obligation undertaken under the WTO,[51] or if the Union act explicitly refers to specific provisions of the WTO Agreements.[52] More importantly, the review of the legality of EU and national legislation is possible, as the latter have to be interpreted in consistency with the provisions of EU agreements. The primacy of EU international agreements over provisions of secondary Union law and national law means that 'such provisions must, as far as possible, be interpreted in a manner that is consistent with those agreements'.[53] In that respect, the principle of consistent interpretation presents an efficient method for reviewing the legality of national and, to a lesser extent, secondary EU law in light of WTO rules.[54]

Secondly, even if WTO rules can be relied upon in front of the CJEU, this is only possible if they satisfy the first prong of the *International Fruit* test, namely that they are binding on the EU. This question has been particularly relevant for TRIPS. As the WTO Agreement was concluded jointly by the EU and its Member States as a mixed agreement, and given that mixed agreements 'have the same legal status in the [Union] legal order as purely [Union] agreements insofar as the provisions fall within the scope of [Union] competence',[55] the determination of EU competence over the TRIPS patent provisions has been crucial for the determination of the CJEU's jurisdiction over them. Without entering into details, suffice it to mention that until the entry into force of the Lisbon Treaty, the CJEU had found that the patent provisions of TRIPS fell outside the scope of EU exclusive competence, hence the CJEU had no jurisdiction to apply and interpret them.[56]

[49] Case C-149/96 *Portugal v Council* [1999] ECR I-8385, [47].

[50] On the nature and structure of the WTO Agreement and its failure to satisfy the conditions for judicial review see indicatively, P Kuipjer and M Bronckers, 'WTO Law in the European Court of Justice' (2005) 42 *CML Rev* 1313; F Snyder, 'The Gatekeepers: The European Courts and the WTO' (2003) 40 *CML Rev* 313.

[51] Case C-69/89 *Nakajima All v Council* [1991] ECR I-2069.

[52] Case 70/87 *Fediol III* [1989] ECR 1805.

[53] Case C-89/99 *Schieving-Nijstad* [2001] ECR I-5851. On the exceptions to direct effect see Eeckhout (n 48) 355–65.

[54] Kuipjer and Bronckers (n 50) 1326, 1328–29.

[55] Case C-239/03 *Commission v France (Etang de Berre)* [2004] ECR I-9325, [25].

[56] In Opinion 1/94 [1994] ECR I-5267, the Court ruled that the majority of TRIPS provisions were outside the scope of the Common Commercial Policy, and thus [EC] exclusive competence, as their primary purpose was not the regulation of trade but the harmonization of IP rights protection. Following Opinion 1/94, the Intergovernmental Conference in Nice expanded the scope of the Common Commercial Policy to trade-related aspects of IP. Despite the establishment of express powers over commercial aspects of IP, EC Treaty, Art 133 did not confer exclusive competence to the EU, thus keeping the ruling of Opinion 1/94 valid as regards the question of which parts of the TRIPS Agreement fell under the scope of exclusive EC competence. For a critical analysis of the development of EU competence over IP until the Lisbon Treaty, see C Hermann, 'Common Commercial Policy after Nice: Sisyphus would have done a Better Job' (2002) 39 *CML Rev* 26.

The rule was confirmed and clarified in *Merck Genericos*, where the CJEU dealt with the interpretation of Article 33 TRIPS on the minimum term for patent protection. After considering that the Union had not yet exercised its powers in the sphere of patents, the Court concluded that Member States remained principally competent and could choose whether or not to give direct effect to that provision and how to interpret it, thus excluding them from the scope of CJEU jurisdiction.[57]

III. The CJEU's Jurisdiction over TRIPS

The entry into force of the Lisbon Treaty and the establishment of EU exclusive competence in the field of the Common Commercial Policy affected drastically the scope of the CJEU's jurisdiction over TRIPS. In *Daiichi Sankyo* the CJEU had the opportunity to clarify its jurisdiction, and in essence established another layer of substantive patent rules over which it holds jurisdiction to apply and interpret. In order to understand fully the implications of this new patent jurisdiction of the CJEU for the European patent system, it is necessary to explain first the scope and the limits of the new EU exclusive competence under Article 207 TFEU, and hence, the CJEU's jurisdiction.

A. The Nature of EU Exclusive Competence

The exact scope and the nature of EU competence in the fields covered by the Common Commercial Policy has been ambiguous since the creation of the WTO. In order to offer clarity and enhance legal certainty, the Lisbon Treaty provides explicitly for the exclusive character of Union competence in the field of commercial aspects of IP. Article 3(1)(e) TFEU clearly stipulates that the Common Commercial Policy falls under the exclusive competence of the Union, while Article 2(1) TFEU integrates the principle that express powers are of a priori exclusive nature.[58]

[57] *Merck Genéricos Produtos Farmacêuticos* (n 44) [46]–[48]. For a critical reading of this case, see R Holdgaard's case note in (2008) 45 *CML Rev* 1233.

[58] TFEU, Art 207 does not distinguish between the different fields of the Common Commercial Policy in terms of the nature of competence, nor does TFEU, Art 3 limit its scope to trade in goods. On the author's views on impact of the Lisbon Treaty on the scope of the Commercial Policy, see A Dimopoulos, 'The Common Commercial Policy after Lisbon: Establishing Parallelism between Internal and External Economic Policy' (2008) 4 *Croatian Yearbook of European Law and Policy* 102. See also, M Krajewski, 'The Reform of the Common Commercial Policy' in A Biondi et al (eds), *European Union Law after the Treaty of Lisbon* (Oxford, Oxford University Press, 2012) 292–311. Besides, TFEU, Art 207 does away with EC Treaty, Art 133(5)(4), which retained the right of the Member States to maintain and conclude agreements with third countries. See also, J Ceyssens, 'Towards a Common Foreign Investment Policy?—Foreign Investment in the European Constitution' (2005) 32 *Legal Issues of European Integration* 259, 286–87.

In that respect, the CJEU explicitly recognized in *Daiichi Sankyo* that 'the question of the distribution of the competences of the European Union and the Member States must be examined on the basis of the Treaty now in force'.[59] Opinion 1/94 and *Merck* cannot be applied any longer with regard to TRIPS, although they remain relevant for determining the legal effects of mixed agreements in other fields of shared competence.

As a result, to the extent that the TRIPS patent provisions fall under exclusive EU competence, they generate EU law effects and hence the CJEU has jurisdiction to interpret them. Although TRIPS remains an international agreement that was concluded as a mixed agreement prior to EU competence becoming exclusive, what matters for the determination of the EU legal effects of the TRIPS Agreement is the *current* scope and nature of EU competence. Without prejudice to the international responsibility of Member States under the WTO,[60] the direct effect and interpretation of TRIPS within the EU legal order are dependent on the time EU competence becomes exclusive, rather than the time when the relevant international agreement was concluded.

B. The Scope of EU Exclusive Competence

According to Article 207 TFEU, the EU holds exclusive competence over commercial aspects of IP. Whether the CJEU has jurisdiction to interpret the patent provisions of TRIPS, depends on whether the latter are covered under EU exclusive competence, namely whether they are 'commercial aspects of IP'. This was one of the most controversial questions raised in *Daiichi Sankyo*. According to the CJEU, the essential criterion for determining whether international rules on IP fall under the 'commercial aspects of IP' is whether they exhibit a specific link to international trade.[61]Applying this criterion to TRIPS, the CJEU found that the entirety of the TRIPS provisions, including those on patents, exhibit such a link to international trade, as TRIPS is an integral part of the WTO.[62] Considering that the primary objective of TRIPS is to 'reduce distortions of international trade by ensuring the effective and adequate protection of IP rights',[63] the CJEU found that TRIPS provisions on the availability, scope and use of patents fall under EU exclusive competence.

The broad interpretation of the term 'commercial aspects of IP' is consistent with the previous case law of the CJEU and reflects the relationship between the WTO and the EU's Common Commercial Policy so far. The scope of EU com-

[59] *Daiichi Sankyo* (n7), [48].

[60] P Kuijper and E Paasivirta, 'Further Exploring International Responsibility: The European Community and the ILC's Project on Responsibility of International Organizations' (2004) 1 *International Organizations Law Review* 111, 134.

[61] *Daiichi Sankyo* (n 7), [52].

[62] Ibid, [53] and [54].

[63] Ibid, [58].

petence under the Common Commercial Policy reflects the scope of the WTO Agreements, as the CJEU explicitly ruled in Opinion 1/08. As the term 'trade in services' in Article 207 TFEU is not limited to services as they are defined under the internal market, but reflects the similar term found in the WTO Agreements,[64] it is only logical to conclude that the term 'commercial aspects of IP' is meant to reflect the scope of IP protection expressed in the WTO Agreements.[65]

Moreover, the broad interpretation of EU exclusive competence under Article 207 TFEU does not undermine the scope or the nature of the EU's internal competence to harmonize IP law under Article 118 TFEU, which is shared with the Member States. At first sight it may look as if the broad scope of EU external competence results in a type of 'indirect' harmonization of patent law in the EU via the conclusion of international agreements, whilst such harmonization has been explicitly rejected internally. However, contrary to the arguments raised by AG Cruz Villalon, the coexistence of exclusive 'external' competence alongside a shared 'internal' competence does not lead to a dead end.[66] Indirect harmonization via TRIPS is possible under Article 207 TFEU and does not affect the internal shared competence found in Article 118 TFEU.

First of all, the possibility of external competences exceeding internal competences is explicitly recognized in Article 207(6) TFEU.[67] This provision precludes the Union from taking external action under the Common Commercial Policy only in fields where EU competence in the internal market is limited. However, this does not mean that the *lack of exercise* of Union internal competences poses a limitation on the existence or the exercise of external competence, even at the procedural level.[68] Considering that harmonization in the field of patent protection is now explicitly allowed under the TFEU, the lack of common rules on patents does not present an impediment to the existence or exercise of EU external competence. Moreover, Article 207(6) TFEU limits the exercise of Union external powers in fields where harmonization is excluded. This means that the Common Commercial Policy cannot be used for the adoption of Union measures in fields in which other treaty provisions exclude harmonization. However, harmonization in the field of patent protection, or IP harmonization in general, is not excluded under the EU Treaties.[69]

[64] Opinion 1/08 [2009] ECR I-11129, [119]; M Cremona, 'Balancing Union and Member State Interests: Opinion 1/2008, Choice of Legal Basis and the Common Commercial Policy under the Treaty of Lisbon' (2010) 35 *EL Rev* 678, 683–84.

[65] Ibid.

[66] Opinion of AG Cruz Villalon, *Daiichi Sankyo* (n 7), [60].

[67] TFEU, Art 207(6) provides that 'the exercise of the competences conferred by this Article in the field of the common commercial policy shall not affect the delimitation of competences between the Union and the Member States, and shall not lead to harmonization of legislative or regulatory provisions of the Member States insofar as the Treaties exclude such harmonization'.

[68] W Shan and S Zhang, 'The Treaty of Lisbon: Half Way toward a Common Investment Policy' (2010) 21 *European Journal of International Law* 1049, 1064–65.

[69] Exclusion of harmonization is provided in TFEU, Arts 149(2), 153(2)(a), 165(4), 166(4), 167(5) and 168(4).

More importantly, the existence of exclusive external competence under the Common Commercial Policy does not affect the exercise of Member State internal concurrent powers in the field of IP protection.[70] Even though the EU can adopt international agreements on a specific subject matter, this does not signify that the EU obtains exclusive powers to regulate in this field in the internal market. Indeed, as the CJEU explicitly stated in *Daiichi Sankyo*,

> it remains altogether open to the European Union, after the entry into force of the FEU Treaty, to legislate on the subject of intellectual property rights by virtue of competence relating to the field of the internal market. However, acts adopted on that basis and intended to have validity specifically for the European Union will have to comply with the rules concerning the availability, scope and use of intellectual property rights in the TRIPs Agreement.[71]

C. The Effects of EU Exclusive Competence on the CJEU

The recognition that EU exclusive competence over commercial aspects of IP covers the TRIPS patent provisions has far-reaching consequences. As the entire scope of TRIPS falls now under EU exclusive competence, the CJEU has jurisdiction to determine its legal effects, including the entirety of its patent provisions. In that regard, the CJEU can decide whether EU secondary law or national law can be interpreted consistently with TRIPS patent provisions.

The importance of the principle of consistent interpretation and the broad powers it confers to the Court in matters of patent law is clearly illustrated by the second and third questions asked in *Daiichi Sankyo*. In case the Court found it had jurisdiction, the national court asked the CJEU to determine the temporal scope of patent protection under the TRIPS Agreement and to identify what is the extent and content of that protection, in particular in light of Article 70 TRIPS.[72] In that regard, the CJEU had to interpret Article 27 TRIPS, one of the core provisions of patent law concerning patentability and the prohibition of discriminatory treatment of patent rights as regards fields of technology. The

[70] M Cremona, 'A Constitutional Basis for Effective External Action? An Assessment of the Provisions on EU External Action in the Constitutional Treaty' EUI Working Paper 2006/30 <http://cadmus.eui.eu/bitstream/handle/1814/6293/LAW_2006-30.pdf?sequence=1%20> 32.

[71] *Daiichi Sankyo* (n 7), [59].

[72] 'Under Articles 27 and 70 of the TRIPS Agreement, do patents covered by the reservation in Article 167(2) of the 1973 Munich Convention which were granted before 7 February 1992, that is to say, before the above agreement entered into force, and concerned the invention of pharmaceutical products, but which, because of the aforementioned reservation, were granted solely to protect their production process, fall within the protection for all patents pursuant to the provisions of the TRIPS Agreement and, if so, what is the extent and content of that protection, that is to say, have the pharmaceutical products themselves also been protected since the above agreement entered into force or does protection continue to apply to their production process only or must a distinction be made based on the content of the application for grant of a patent, that is to say, as to whether, by describing the invention and the relevant claims, protection was sought at the outset for the product or the production process or both?'

CJEU had no difficulty in interpreting Article 27 TRIPS. Without engaging with the most ambiguous elements of patentability, such as what constitutes technology, it reached a non-controversial conclusion, namely that while pharmaceutical products are patentable subject matter under Article 27 TRIPS,[73] a patent granted for a process of manufacturing such a product does not extend to the pharmaceutical product as such.[74] Nevertheless, the fact that the Court had no difficulty in interpreting the substantive patent provisions of the TRIPS Agreement marks the beginning of a new era in the CJEU's involvement with the application and interpretation of substantive patent law rules.

D. Fitting the CJEU's Jurisdiction over TRIPS into the European Patent System

The interpretative jurisdiction of the CJEU over the TRIPS patent provisions presents a unique opportunity for the CJEU to have for the first time a say in patent protection. More interestingly, the CJEU's TRIPS jurisdiction can be very far-reaching, enabling the Court to interpret and apply substantive national and international IP rules. However, there are limits to its jurisdiction. Rather than becoming a new last instance court on patents, the CJEU's jurisdiction over TRIPS allows for harmony, conformity and consistency of patent courts' rulings.

i. The Far-reaching Scope of the CJEU's Jurisdiction

The CJEU can use its TRIPS jurisdiction to establish common minimum rules applying to different patents. The EU has a broad interest in the application of the provisions of TRIPS that fall within the scope of EU law; hence their legal effects are determined by EU law, irrespective of whether their interpretation concerns in a given case the judicial review of EU law or national law provisions.[75] As the Court held in its landmark decisions in *Hermes*[76] and *Dior*,[77]

> where a provision can apply both to situations falling within the scope of national law and to situations falling within the scope of [Union] law, it is clearly in the [Union]

[73] *Daiichi Sankyo* (n 7), [67]–[68].

[74] Ibid, [81]–[82]. More specifically, the national court had to identify the scope of protection offered to pharmaceutical patents granted in Greece before 7 October 1992, the duration of which is stretching after the expiry of the reservation provided for in EPC, Art 167(2)(a). In other words, in cases where the patent was filed to protect the invention of a pharmaceutical, but because of the time of the filing of the application, it protected only the process of manufacture of the pharmaceutical, the question arises whether after the adoption of TRIPS, the patent also protects the pharmaceutical product.

[75] Cremona (n 31) 147–48, 152–53; P Koutrakos, 'Interpretation of Mixed Agreements' in C Hillion and P Koutrakos (eds), *Mixed Agreements Revisited* (Oxford, Hart Publishing, 2010) 116, 123–25.

[76] Case C-53/96 *Hermes International* [1998] ECR I-3603.

[77] Joined Cases C-300/98 & C-392/98 *Parfums Christian Dior* [2000] ECR I-11307.

> interest that, in order to forestall future differences of interpretation, that provision should be interpreted uniformly, whatever the circumstances in which it is to apply.[78]

In fact, the Court had the opportunity to interpret TRIPS provisions in a number of disputes concerning national trademarks,[79] since these provisions could affect the interpretation of the corresponding Union rules on Community trademarks.

Of course, the UPPR does not contain many substantive patent law rules, as the effects of EPUEs are determined by the UPC Agreement. However, the fact that the EPUE, as such, is part of Union law brings its protection within the scope of EU law. Therefore, for the purposes of its TRIPS jurisdiction, the CJEU has an interest to ensure the uniform interpretation of the TRIPS provisions, as they apply to the standards of protection of EPUEs. The CJEU can assess the consistency with TRIPS of all substantive rules applying to EPUEs, regardless of whether the latter are found in the UPPR, the UPC Agreement or national law. As a result, the CJEU can use its TRIPS interpretative jurisdiction to assess national patent rules, in order to ensure uniform application of TRIPS under different patent protection systems in the EU.

The exercise of the CJEU's interpretative jurisdiction to ensure consistency between the different types of patents is justified by the need to preserve the effectiveness and coherence of EU law. What explains the Court's interference with patents other than EPUEs is that a common interpretation is needed in order to forestall future differences between similar EU norms and national norms, which might jeopardise the effectiveness of EU law. As ensuring the effective application of EU law is a primary task of the CJEU, the exercise of its interpretative jurisdiction over TRIPS does not amount to judicial activism, but falls squarely within the well-defined and established limits of the CJEU's powers. Moreover, the effectiveness of EU law explains why the CJEU can use its interpretative jurisdiction over TRIPS to determine even issues that are not part of secondary EU law, such as the UPPR. Although the link to EU law is not apparent in this case, the fact remains that TRIPS per se is an integral part of EU law,[80] and consequently falls within the CJEU's jurisdiction.

ii. The Limits of the CJEU's Jurisdiction

Despite the broad scope of the CJEU's interpretative jurisdiction over TRIPS, which may contribute towards coherence and consistency in the application of patent rules in the EU, the use of the CJEU's powers does not result in de facto harmonization of patent law in the EU. The extent to which the CJEU can employ

[78] Ibid, [32].

[79] Case C-245/02 *Anheuser Busch* [2004] ECR I-10989; *Hermes International* (n76), [24]–[33]. See also, M Karayigit, 'Why and to What Extent a Common Interpretative Position for Mixed Agreements?' (2006) 11 *European Foreign Affairs Review* 445.

[80] Above n 45.

its jurisdiction over TRIPS to harmonize patent law is limited by the nature and content of TRIPS as an international agreement.

Starting from the nature of TRIPS as an international agreement, it is important to bear in mind that TRIPS, like other WTO Agreements, lacks direct effect.[81] Consequently, the CJEU cannot rely directly on TRIPS patent provisions to create new patent rights, or even set aside national patent law. The lack of direct effect of TRIPS provisions requires the Court to review national patent norms only with regard to their consistent interpretation with TRIPS. What the CJEU can do is to assess whether patent rules that apply in the EU are in conformity with TRIPS patent provisions.

Turning to the content of TRIPS, it is important to bear in mind that TRIPS is a minimum standards agreement that aims at harmonizing national laws of the WTO members, yet without establishing uniform rules.[82] Many provisions are drafted rather openly, leaving discretion to national legislators as to how they can comply with them. For example, Article 27(1) TRIPS states that

> [p]atents shall be available for any inventions, whether products or processes, in all fields of technology, provided they are new, involve an inventive step and are capable of industrial application

without defining 'novelty', or what constitutes 'technology'. As a result, when the CJEU exercises its interpretative jurisdiction, it can only identify the limits provided in TRIPS provisions and set out the general principles for their implementation, while respecting the flexibilities that are contained therein. Drawing a parallel to the interpretation of minimum harmonization legislation, the CJEU's role is to indicate the limits and offer guiding principles that guarantee the effective application of the relevant rules and define the degree of discretion granted to individual Member States.[83]

Of course, this does not negate the great impact that the CJEU's interpretative jurisdiction may play, as it can result in a number of instances of harmonization. For example, TRIPS contains specific rules on prior users' rights and exceptions, including in particular compulsory licenses, which are subject matters left outside the scope of the UPPR.[84] Consequently, the CJEU's interpretative jurisdiction over TRIPS can constitute a significant tool in the process of promoting coherence and consistency in the EU patent system.

[81] See above n 49.

[82] TRIPS, Art 1(1).

[83] S Weatherill, 'Competence and Legitimacy' in C Barnard and O Odudu (eds), *The Outer Limits of European Union Law* (Oxford, Hart Publishing, 2009) 1, 18–20.

[84] See above nn 38–41.

E. Reconsidering the Role of the EU and the CJEU in Patent Protection

In addition to the CJEU's interpretative jurisdiction over TRIPS, the recognition of EU exclusive competence over commercial aspects of IP can have much wider implications for the future development of patent protection in the EU. The consideration of the 'specific link to international trade' as the criterion for determining whether an international IP agreement, such as TRIPS, falls under 'commercial aspects of IP' has significant repercussions for defining the EU's role in future patent regulation. Although the link to international trade may have resulted in a correct outcome with regards to TRIPS, however, it is unclear what it means for the conclusion of future patent agreements by the EU and its Member States.

More specifically, following a narrow interpretation of the Court's approach in *Daiichi Sankyo*, IP rules that are similar to TRIPS but included in a non trade-related international agreement would not fall under EU exclusive competence. However, by relying solely on the trade links of an international IP agreement, the CJEU in essence strips Article 207 TFEU of its substantive content, contrary to how the scope and definition of the Common Commercial Policy has evolved so far.[85] Such reliance on the objectives of international agreements contradicts the very foundations of EU external competence, which is determined not only by the object of an international agreement, but also by its substantive content.[86] Moreover, given the focus on the trade linkages of IP and the lack of clarity as to the substantive IP rules covered under Article 207 TFEU, the danger of manipulation of Articles 118 and 207 TFEU by the Commission or the Member States becomes immediately apparent. It is, at least, paradoxical to enable EU institutions and Member States to abuse or circumvent the EU Treaties, merely by deciding whether an IP agreement will be concluded as part of a broader trade agreement or independently.

Instead of using an objectives test, the CJEU could have approached the concept of 'commercial aspects of IP' from a substantive law perspective. Since this term was introduced in Article 207 TFEU to reflect developments in the WTO, it would be logical to argue that the substantive issues covered under TRIPS fall within the EU's exclusive competence. However, a strict reliance on TRIPS could result in a 'compartmentalization' of IP rights, which as the AG Cruz Villalon correctly identifies in his Opinion, would negate the effectiveness of Article 207 TFEU.[87]

[85] Since Opinion 1/78 [1978] ECR 2151, the Court has endorsed a broad and instrumental approach to the concept of the Common Commercial Policy, so that any type of trade measures would fall under its scope. See Case 54/86 *GSP Commission v Council* [1987] ECR 1493.

[86] P Koutrakos, 'Legal Basis and Delimitation of Competence in EU External Relations' in Cremona and DeWitte (n 31) 172–74; M Cremona, 'Defining Competence in EU External Relations: Lessons from the Treaty Reform Process' in A Dashwood and M Maresceau (eds), *Law and Practice of EU External Relations* (Cambridge, Cambridge University Press, 2008) 34, 39–40.

[87] Opinion of AG Cruz Villalon in *Daiichi Sankyo* (n 7), [66]–[70].

Nevertheless, rather than finding the provision to be only declaratory in nature, or relying solely on the objectives of an agreement, the Court could have indicated which aspects of IP rights protection are not commercial, or more specifically, whether patent rules are non-commercial aspects of IP. In that respect, TRIPS offers important hints. As the only area of IP excluded from TRIPS are moral rights under copyright law,[88] and given that most WTO members are signatories to the Berne Convention, which protects moral rights, the exclusion of moral rights from TRIPS presents a clear category of IP rights that are not trade-related, that is 'commercial' for the purposes of the EU Common Commercial Policy.

In any case, the existence of EU exclusive competence to conclude any 'trade-related' IP agreement means that any TRIPS-Plus provisions included in EU bilateral trade agreements would be covered under EU exclusive competence. Given that bilateral EU FTAs go beyond TRIPS, providing more concrete obligations for the parties,[89] it becomes immediately apparent how the CJEU can use its interpretative jurisdiction to assess whether national patent laws comply with the bilateral FTAs. More importantly, since bilateral EU FTAs have been found so far to have direct effect,[90] the implications of EU exclusive competence become far greater, since individuals would be able to rely directly on their IP provisions and question the validity and applicability of national IP laws.

IV. Conclusions

The CJEU holds a key role in the EU patent litigation system, as in any EU-related system. The CJEU cannot be excluded from the application and interpretation of EU patent rules, nor from assessing the compatibility of national patent rules with EU law. Its jurisdiction cannot be threatened by the creation of the UPC. As the CJEU rendered clear in Opinion 1/09, it would be at least naïve to consider that the UPC takes over any patent related disputes, thus rendering the CJEU's jurisdiction obsolete. The only option available to Member States wishing to minimize the CJEU's involvement in patent litigation is not to use Article 118 TFEU to harmonize patent law in the EU, but rather to rely on extra-EU legal frameworks.

[88] The TRIPS Agreement does not incorporate Art 6 *bis* of the Berne Convention which requires the signatory states to protect moral rights. See M Killian, 'A Hollow Victory for the Common Law? TRIPS and the Moral Rights Exclusion' (2003) 2 *J Marshall Review of Intellectual Property Law* 321.

[89] On the scope of TRIPS-Plus obligations under EU FTAs, see M Aleman, 'Impact of TRIPS-Plus Obligations in Economic Partnership and Free Trade Agreements on International IP Law' in J Drexl et al (eds), *EU Bilateral Trade Agreements and Intellectual Property: For Better or Worse*, MPI Studies on Intellectual Property and Competition Law vol 20 (Munich, Springer, 2014) 61–85.

[90] On the direct effect of EU trade agreements, see indicatively F Jacobs, 'Direct Effect and Interpretation of International Agreements in the Recent Case Law of the European Court of Justice' in A Dashwood and M Maresceau (eds), *Law and Practice of EU External Relations* (Cambridge, Cambridge University Press, 2011) 19–21.

But even then, CJEU involvement could be significant, especially since the CJEU has jurisdiction to interpret not only EU secondary law, but also any international agreement concluded by the EU.

Within this framework, it is the CJEU's jurisdiction to apply and interpret international IP agreements falling under EU exclusive competence that enables the Court to play a significant role in patent litigation. The establishment of EU exclusive competence over commercial aspects of IP under Article 207 TFEU brings TRIPS patent provisions within the CJEU's jurisdiction. As the CJEU clearly recognized in *Daiichi Sankyo*, it can determine the legal effects of the TRIPS patent provisions, thus deciding whether EU or national patent law are in conformity with TRIPS. In that respect, the CJEU can use its jurisdiction to enhance coherence and consistency in the application of different types of patents and patent rights in the EU. However, the power to interpret TRIPS is not a panacea, as, due to the nature of TRIPS as a minimum standards agreement, it cannot result in the establishment of uniform substantive rules.

Whether the CJEU will utilize its new jurisdiction sparingly and how it will affect the efficiency and costs of patent litigation in Europe remains to be seen. What is clear for now though is that the CJEU holds a key constitutional function within every legal system that is even marginally tied to the EU legal order and it cannot be undermined.

6

A Constitutional Perspective

TUOMAS MYLLY[*]

I. Introduction

Before being fully born, the unitary patent package (UPP) is facing an identity crisis. Its Union law identity is called into question by the controversial removal of most substantive patent law provisions from Regulation 1215/2012 (EPUE Regulation)[1] to the Unified Patent Court Agreement (UPCA).[2] The latter is an instrument supposedly governed by international law only. The tight linkage of the UPP to another international law measure, the European Patent Convention (EPC) and the decisions of its administrative organ, the European Patent Office (EPO), had already made the regime a chimera of international and Union law.

The decision to transfer most substantive patent norms from the EPUE Regulation to the UPCA was motivated by the desire of European patent experts to avoid the jurisdiction of the Court of Justice of the European Union (CJEU) to interpret the patent norms especially as regards direct and indirect patent infringement. Their concerns related to the time lags resulting from references

[*] LLD, LLM Eur, Professor of European Economic Law, Faculty of Law, University of Turku, Finland. This chapter has been written in the framework of the research project 'ECoherence—Reconciling Economic and Non-economic Values in a Multi-polar Society', financed by the Academy of Finland.

[1] Regulation (EU) No 1257/2012 of the European Parliament and of the Council of 17 December 2012 implementing enhanced cooperation in the area of the creation of unitary patent protection, OJ L361/1 (31 December 2012). Translation arrangements are regulated by Regulation (EU) No 1260/2012 of 17 December 2012 implementing enhanced cooperation in the area of the creation of unitary patent protection with regard to the applicable translation arrangements, OJ L361/89 (31 December 2012).

[2] Agreement on a Unified Patent Court, OJ C175/1 (20 June 2013). The UPCA was signed by 25 EU Member States on 19 February 2013. Although it is not a Union measure, it has been published as a notice from EU institutions in OJ C175/1 (20 June 2013). The removed patent norms are Arts 6–8 of the draft EPUE Regulation and Arts 25–27 of the UPCA. On the European Parliament's initial reaction before reaching a compromise, see 'EU Unitary Patent: Council Move would Infringe EU Law, says EP Rapporteur' (10 July 2012) <http://www.europarl.europa.eu/news/en/news-room/content/20120709IPR48484/html/EU-unitary-patent-Council-move-would-infringe-EU-law-says-EP-rapporteur>.

to the CJEU and the lack of expertise of the CJEU in patent matters.[3] It is also feasible that the CJEU's emerging patent case law did not please substance-wise the interests of the European patent community, typically in favour of strong patent protection. The CJEU's *Monsanto* and *Brüstle* judgments,[4] in particular, could be interpreted as limiting the potential expansion of patent law in the area of biotechnology, even though the exact effects of these judgments are yet to be clarified.[5] These judgments, both decided in 2011, likely encouraged the limitation of the CJEU's role in the unitary patent package. The transfer of these patent law norms to the UPCA signifies a step towards intergovernmentalism in the unitary patent framework.

Is the European patent with unitary effect (EPUE) then a *sui generis* Union right with typical Union law effects subject to the interpretative powers of the CJEU? Or is it an international law instrument, the EPUE Regulation and other Union law merely applying to limited issues where EU law and the CJEU could not in any case be avoided? Could the CJEU unionise the international law parts of the unitary patent package?

The hovering between intergovernmentalism and supranationalism is as such nothing new in the context of intellectual property (IP). As Pila has demonstrated, it has been practiced thoroughly during the 65 or more years' history of trying to give birth to a European unitary patent.[6] The ambiguity of IP being regulated, institutionally separated but functionally linked to the Union, has been present from the entry into force of the European Economic Community (EEC). These ambiguities were also present in the Community Patent Convention of 1975:[7] an international treaty equipped with common market objectives, and intended to give new competences to some of the EEC institutions.[8]

This chapter argues that significant constitutional tensions are built into the unitary patent package. Some of these tensions will be addressed by the CJEU

[3] See J Smits and W Bull, 'The Europeanization of Patent Law: Towards a Competitive Model' in A Ohly and J Pila (eds), *The Europeanization of Intellectual Property Law. Towards a European Legal Methodology* (Oxford, Oxford University Press, 2013) 39, 52; J Brinkhof and A Ohly, 'Towards a Unified Patent Court in Europe' in Ohly and Pila (ibid) 199, 201; H Alps et al, *The EU Patent Package Handbook. A Practitioner's Guide* (Hoffman, Eitle, 2014) 12182.

[4] Case C-428/08 *Monsanto Technology LLC v Cefetra BV* [2009] ECR I-98 (*Monsanto*); Case C-34/10 *Oliver Brüstle v Greenpeace eV* [2011] ECR I-9821 (*Brüstle*).

[5] On *Monsanto* see G Van Overwalle, 'The CJEU's Monsanto Soybean Decision and Patent Scope—As Clear as Mud' [2011] *International Review of Intellectual Property and Competition Law* 1; on *Brüstle* see MI Schuster, 'The Court of Justice of the European Union's Ruling on the Patentability of Human Embryonic Stem-Cell-Related Inventions (Case C-34/10)' [2012] *International Review of Intellectual Property and Competition Law* 626. As Schuster notes (at 626, 633–40), the CJEU sets more limitations on the patentability of stem cell research than the decisions of the EPO.

[6] See J Pila, 'The European Patent: An Old and Vexing Problem' (2013) 62 *ICLQ* 917; also T Jaeger, 'The EU Patent: Cui Bono et Quo Vadit?' (2010) 47 *CML Rev* 63, and the discussions by Justine Pila and Christopher Wadlow in chs 2 and 3 of this volume.

[7] Convention for the European Patent for the Common Market 76/76/EEC (15 December 1975).

[8] See, eg V Scordamaglia, 'The Legal Framework of the Legislative Activity Concerning Intellectual Property Rights at European Regional Level' in C Geiger (ed), *Constructing European Intellectual Property. Achievements and New Perspectives* (Cheltenham, Edward Elgar, 2013) 61, 62–66.

when it hears two cases challenging the legality of the unitary patent package.[9] New challenges may later emerge in preliminary references. The CJEU has already twice evaluated the constitutionality of the previous proposals. In Opinion 1/09 it found that by establishing the European and Community Patents Court, as an international court with exclusive jurisdiction to hear patent cases and powers to apply EU norms directly, the draft agreement was problematic from the perspective of the autonomy of the European Union legal order. Moreover, it restricted the Member State courts' ability to utilise the preliminary ruling procedure.[10] The draft agreement was thus not acceptable. The Union, its Member States and any third countries being parties to the EPC would have been signatories to the agreement. In another case of constitutional significance the CJEU authorised the use of enhanced cooperation for the creation of the EPUE.[11]

The present chapter will not address these rulings in detail, as others have discussed them.[12] Nor will it evaluate the constitutionality of the unitary patent package from the perspective of Member States' constitutions. As such, the position of the Unified Patent Court (UPC) is interesting from this perspective. It has *sui generis* character as a Member State court, with its own procedural norms, sources of law doctrine, language regime, and composition of international judges. In contrast to typical Member State specialised courts, it is detached from the legal order of any particular Member State. It does not interact with other domestic courts, nor has it at its disposal general doctrines of law anchored in the legal order of any particular Member State. Moreover, it lacks a background constitution and a system of national fundamental rights. This trans-national court specialised solely in European patent law is thus cut loose from the chains of any Member State background legal order and its constitutional framework.

The chapter submits that the CJEU could hold the unitary patent package to be unconstitutional. It has good reason for doing so. Yet the political pressure to save the unitary patent package negotiated for decades from being unconstitutional is significant. Provided the CJEU bends to these political pressures, it might save the package by simultaneously discovering unexpected constitutional safeguards, and its own competence to evaluate the UPCA and perhaps also other intergovernmental parts of the package. Nevertheless, such a solution could also entail constitutional problems.

The chapter proceeds as follows. First, two competing approaches to the unitary patent package will be introduced. This will be followed by considering the unitary patent package from the perspective of Union fundamental rights law. The focus will be on the question of how Union fundamental rights might provide the CJEU with jurisdiction in respect of the intergovernmental parts of the unitary

[9] Joined Cases C-146/13 & C-147/13 *Spain v European Parliament and Council* (pending).
[10] Opinion 1/09 [2011] ECR I-1137, [73]–[87].
[11] Joined Cases C-274/11 & C-295/11 *Spain v Council* (16 April 2013).
[12] See, eg S Peers, 'The Constitutional Implications of the EU Patent' (2011) 7 *European Constitutional Law Review* 229; T Lock, 'Taking National Courts more Seriously? Comment on Opinion 1/09' (2011) 36 *EL Rev* 576.

patent package. After this, the focus will shift to the question of whether some of the constitutional problems underlying the package could give the CJEU cause to quash the whole package. The analysis will be limited to the question of whether the participating Member States had the competence to conclude the UPCA without the EU and whether the de facto delegation of decision-making power to the EPO to grant EPUEs without access to Union courts was acceptable.

II. Two Visions of the Unitary Patent Package

The premises from which we start to construct the EPUE largely determine its character, which in turn greatly affects its treatment under EU constitutional law. Hence, before going to the constitutional challenges facing the EPUE in more detail, two competing visions of the EPUE will be introduced. Both can be anchored in the norms regulating EPUEs, and even in the language of a single source such as the EPUE Regulation.

The *first vision* emphasises the accessory nature of unitary effect by building on the *transformation approach*: unitary effect is merely an ancillary feature attached to a granted European patent and applying within the geographical area of the participating Member States. The legal basis of the unitary effect would be Article 142 of the EPC, which permits special agreements for any group of EPC Contracting States to provide that a European patent granted for those states has a unitary character throughout their territories. In the words of Recital 6 to the EPUE Regulation:

> This Regulation constitutes a special agreement within the meaning of Article 142 of the EPC.[13]

From this perspective, what takes place at the EPO when processing patent applications would not concern Union law.[14] Moreover, as the UPCA is an agreement concluded under international law to the exclusion of the Union, its interpretation and application would similarly be outside the reach of EU law and the CJEU.

Recital 7 of the EPUE Regulation reflects the transformation approach by noting that unitary patent protection is achieved by attributing unitary effect to European patents *in the post-grant phase* by virtue of the Regulation in respect of all the participating Member States. It specifically mentions that the unitary effect

[13] Yet for a Union act like the EPUE Regulation to constitute an agreement under EPC, Art 142 could require the accession of the Union to the EPC. See T Jaeger, 'Shielding the Unitary Patent from the ECJ: A Rash and Futile Exercise' [2013] *International Review of Intellectual Property and Competition Law* 389, 389.

[14] See T Jaeger, 'Back to Square One?—An Assessment of the Latest Proposals for a Patent and Court for the Internal Market and Possible Alternatives' [2012] *International Review of Intellectual Property and Competition Law* 286, 291, distinguishing between the transformation and delegation approach. The latter characterises the earlier attempt to create a true *sui generis* EU right (EU patent), whereby the EPO would have been formally delegated powers over the EU Patent.

should have an *accessory nature* and should be deemed not to have arisen to the extent that the basic European patent has been revoked or limited. Articles 9(1)(g) and 3(3) of the EPUE Regulation provide that the request for unitary effect can be submitted within one month after the mention of the grant is published in the *European Patent Bulletin*, and that the unitary effect shall be deemed not to have arisen to the extent that the underlying European patent has been revoked or limited. In accordance with Article 4(1) EPUE Regulation, the unitary effect will be retroactive as of the date of publication of notice of grant in the *EPO Official Bulletin*. The EPO would thus grant EPUEs in the same way as European patents; by ensuring that they satisfy the same requirements of the EPC as any European patent application.

This vision is demonstrated in the argument that the EPUE is best conceptualised as a European patent being validated as a single patent for a group of countries, the difference to national validation being a quantitative one: 'the supra-national EPUE will cover many states and a large territory, but it would still remain a part of the classic European "bundle" patent'.[15] The Regulation could thus be seen as merely endowing the European patent granted by the EPO with an additional quality of unitary effect, but being subject to the grant and continued existence of the underlying European patent.[16] From this perspective, the EPUE would not be an independent Union right, but wholly dependent on the fate of the underlying European patent and the interpretation and application of the EPC. It would differ in this respect significantly from the unitary EU trade mark and design rights, which are independent *sui generis* rights.[17]

The other vision builds on the unitary character, uniform protection and equal effect of the EPUE as its overarching primary objectives, confirmed in Articles 3(2), 5(2) and Recital 7 of the EPUE Regulation. In this view, the uniformity of EPUE protection is not confined to the EPUE being limited, transferred or revoked, or lapsed, only in respect of all the participating Member States.[18] The requirement of Article 5(2) of the EPUE Regulation that the scope of the EPUE and its limitations 'shall be uniform in all participating Member States in which the patent has unitary effect', could only be achieved by an integrative approach according to which the relevant parts of the EPC, UPCA and domestic laws of the participating Member States are seen as integral parts of the Union law-based EPUE.[19] This approach thus emphasises the Union law dimension of the EPUE, its market integration aim, and the need for coherent construction of all norms

[15] Alps et al (n 3) 975.

[16] See W Tilmann, 'Spain's Action against the EU Patent Package—Arguments and Counter-arguments in Case C-146/13' (2014) 36 *European Intellectual Property Review* 4, 5.

[17] See also M Haedicke, 'Rechtsfindung, Rechtsfortbildung und Rechtskontrolle im Einheitlichen Patentsystem' [2013] *Gewerblicher Rechtsschutz und Urheberrecht, Internationaler Teil* 609, 610.

[18] See EPUE Regulation, Recital 7.

[19] See, eg Haedicke (n 17).

applicable to EPUEs. Moreover, it sees the transformation approach as a legal fiction.[20]

The UPC and finally the CJEU should hence, according to this vision, advance a coherent view of the unitary patent package. Achieving coherence would be possible only provided the CJEU sees its interpretative competence broadly and provided the UPC actively refers questions to the CJEU.[21] For example, although key aspects of the EPUE, namely patentability and scope of protection, are regulated by the EPC,[22] the UPC and the CJEU should interpret these norms as part of the unitary patent package, equipped with overarching teleology connected to uniform and equal effects. The same approach would apply to the interpretation of the UPCA and national norms.[23] The CJEU does not have competence to interpret the EPC authoritatively or give preliminary rulings concerning it.[24] However, the UPC and the CJEU must give primacy to Union norms over the UPCA *and* the EPC.[25] The EPC and the UPCA should accordingly be interpreted against the teleology of the unitary patent package and—due to the primacy of Union law and duty of consistent interpretation with Union law—in conformity with related Union law, such as the IPR Enforcement and Biotechnology Directives,[26] as well as Union fundamental rights.

Similarly, the proponents of this vision argue that the application of the domestic laws of Member States should be avoided whenever possible, as this would be in tension with the underlying teleology of the unitary patent package. The national law of the participating Member States is then in practice a source of last resort, applied only if none of the other sources provides an answer.[27] When applicable, the EPUE Regulation would set interpretative constraints on the application of domestic norms. For example, compulsory licensing or prior user rights would interfere with the objectives of the unitary patent package related to uniformity and equal effects.[28]

[20] See, eg Jaeger (n 14) 291–92.

[21] Haedicke (n 17) 615, stresses the function of preliminary rulings in achieving the desired coherence of the unitary patent.

[22] In the absence of norms regulating the scope of patent protection in the UPCA or EU law EPC, Art 69 will largely determine the scope of protection.

[23] Haedicke (n 17) 610–11.

[24] The CJEU could interpret it, had the EU acceded to the EPC, as was planned in the court system of the previous proposal rejected by the CJEU in Opinion 1/09 (n 10).

[25] Haedicke (n 17) 612. However, the CJEU cannot review EPC decisions directly, as discussed below. To the extent that there are conflicting interpretations by the EPO Boards of Appeal and the CJEU, the UPC will have to decide in favour of the CJEU interpretation due to the primacy of Union law and the binding nature of CJEU decisions, as also confirmed in the UPCA.

[26] Directive 98/44/EC of the European Parliament and of the Council of 6 July 1998 on the legal protection of biotechnological inventions, OJ L213/13 (30 July 1998); Directive 2004/48/EC of the European Parliament and of the Council of 29 April 2004 on the enforcement of intellectual property right, OJ L195/16 (2 June 2004) (Enforcement Directive).

[27] See Brinkhof and Ohly (n 3) 212.

[28] See Haedicke (n 17) 611, arguing that the applicability of the national norms to the unitary patent should be interpreted restrictively. In case of doubt, a question of unitary patent law would presumptively be covered by the joint norms. See also, A Dimopoulos and P Vantsiouri, 'Of TRIPs and

Some scholars go further in arguing that the CJEU is required to interpret the unitary patent package coherently. Dimopoulos and Vantsiouri argue that the patent provisions of the TRIPS Agreement, now fully included in the interpretative competence of the CJEU, could provide the CJEU with the integrative tool needed to unionise the EPUE.[29] This position and the effects of the TRIPS Agreement are discussed below.

Moreover, an argument exists that the indirect reference in Article 5(3) of the EPUE Regulation to the definitions of protected acts and limitations of protection, removed from the EPUE Regulation to the UPCA, should establish CJEU competence to interpret the relevant Articles of the UPCA as 'Union law'.[30] The Legal Affairs Committee and Legal Service of the European Parliament reportedly believed in such a possibility after the compromise over the removal of the substantive patent law provisions from the EPUE Regulation to the UPCA was reached.[31]

The EPUE Regulation naturally had to refer to these norms somehow after they were removed from the EPUE Regulation to the UPCA. However, norms of *inter se* agreements concluded between Member States cannot be transformed into Union norms by simply indirectly referring to them in a Union law instrument.[32] Union norms with union law effects, and the competence of the CJEU to authoritatively interpret them as part of Union law, can only become established in the legislative procedures regulated by Union law and involving the participation of the Union institutions. The Union cannot outsource its own norm-production to Member States to be agreed in *inter se* agreements or otherwise.[33] The UPCA is formally an international agreement between the participating Member States. As such, its provisions cannot be declared Union law for preliminary ruling or any other purpose.

Traps: The Interpretative Jurisdiction of the Court of Justice of the EU over Patent Law' (2014) 39 *EL Rev* 210, 228, stating that any compulsory licence granted under national law could be at odds with the EPUE Regulation, 'as compulsory licenses affect the very essence of IP rights'.

29 Dimopoulos and Vantsiouri (n 28) especially 212, 228; also the discussion by Angelos Dimopoulos in ch 5 of this volume.

30 As EPUE Regulation, Art 5(3) states, Member State law defines the infringing acts and the limitations thereto. This law constitutes in practice the law of the EPUE Regulation and other EU norms, the UPCA and the EPC, other international agreements applicable to patents and binding on all the Contracting Member States, and finally of national laws of the participating Member States. See UPCA, Arts 20 and 24.

31 See V Metzler, 'Does Art 5 UPP Regulation Enable CJEU Jurisdiction over Substantive Patent Law?' (13 January 2013) <http://blog.ksnh.eu/en/2013/01/13/does-art-5-upp-regulation-enable-cjeu-jurisdiction-over-substantive-patent-law/>, who also seems to accept this possibility. According to this theory, EPUE Regulation, Art 5(3), by linking the EPUE Regulation with the UPCA, would extend the CJEU's competence to the linked norms transferred from the EPUE Regulation to the UPCA. The CJEU interpretation could thus satisfy the uniform protection requirement of TFEU, Art 118, 'as the CJEU is the only authority that can assure the required uniformity of patents'. Dimopoulos and Vantsiouri (n 28) 230, similarly accept (however without further developing the argument) that it would be possible to argue for both the CJEU involvement with, and exclusion from, these patent norms of the UPCA, and that simply 'it is left to the CJEU to decide on which of the two interpretations is in line with EU law'.

32 See also Haedicke (n 17) 616.

33 At least not without good reasons and without resorting to TFEU, Art 2(1).

It is another matter that the CJEU can check the conformity of the relevant UPCA norms against existing Union norms, as the norms of the UPCA related to unitary effect are treated for this purpose as Member State law, and Member State implementation of Union law for the purposes of the Union fundamental rights, as argued below. The primacy of Union law would thus fully apply to the UPCA even in the absence of an explicit provision in the UPCA recognising the primacy of Union law over the UPCA.

It is also another matter that some provisions of the UPCA constitute blueprints of EU norms and thus provide the CJEU competence to interpret them. This applies in particular to the Bolar exemption[34] and remedies as regulated in the IPR Enforcement Directive.[35] These provisions of the UPCA must be in conformity with the requirements of their model EU provisions, as interpreted by the CJEU.[36] Some EU Member States have implemented the Bolar exemption with a broader scope than the minimum level required by the Directive. Yet the UPCA only reproduces the minimum requirements of the Directive and hence seems to prevent the application of the Bolar exemption for studies and trials for innovative pharmaceutical products.[37] It might also be difficult for the UPC to broaden the minimum level remedies copied from the IPR Enforcement Directive. The minimum level required by these Directives thus seems to become the applicable floor *and* ceiling for the UPC. In the context of the Bolar exemption, this might broaden the patent monopoly by excluding broader domestic variations. In the context of remedies, it seems to work in the opposite direction.

The first vision characterised above largely represents the views of European patent law experts not trained in general Union law. It seeks to insulate the unitary patent package from Union law and the CJEU and to construct the EPUE predominantly as an international law measure. The second vision represents the views of scholars content and familiar with EU integration and Union law. It emphasises the role of the CJEU. Whereas the former approach suffers from formalism and the denial of any effects of Union norms,[38] the latter approach suffers from the drive to unionise the unitary patent package and make it coherent at the expense of other considerations.[39] For example, it does not pay attention to the fact that unionising the UPCA would set a dangerous precedent: Union law with

[34] Bolar exemption enables generic manufacturers to prepare generic pharmaceuticals before the patent expiration, subject to limitations and conditions. See UPCA, Art 27(d); Directive 2004/27/EC amending Directive 2001/83/EC on the Community code relating to medicinal products for human use, OJ L136/34 (30 April 2004), Art 10(6).

[35] See, eg UPCA, Arts 63, 64 and 67; Enforcement Directive, Art 5.

[36] See also Alps et al (n 3) 3145; Haedicke (n 17) 612–16.

[37] See Alps et al (n 3) 846, 3042–62.

[38] Eg the transformation approach cannot justify the absence of EU court review from the EPO rejections of patent applications, as argued below. The CJEU might also be able to indirectly review and affect the intergovernmental and domestic parts of the unitary patent package to a greater extent than the proponents of this vision are prepared to accept.

[39] As the UPC has an exclusive competence with respect to EPUEs, it will in practice be the sole court competent to apply and interpret the totality of norms applicable to EPUEs, although for the EPUE Regulation and other applicable Union norms the final authoritative interpreter is the CJEU.

its typical effects could be created outside the legislative processes of the Union. Similar problems plague the idea of relying on the TRIPS Agreement to unionise the EPUE, as elaborated on below.

In the following, the UPC, EPC and the UPCA will be placed in the framework of Union law. The focus will be on the applicability of Union fundamental rights. Even without fully unionising the intergovernmental parts of the unitary patent package, Union law, and in particular its system of fundamental rights protection, will constrain all norms of the package, and thus affect their interpretation.

III. How will EU Fundamental Rights affect the Unitary Patent Package?

As the UPC is a court common to the participating Member States, it is already bound by the same Union law obligations as Member State courts. Yet the UPCA includes in its Chapter IV declaratory norms on the EU law obligations of the UPC. These must be interpreted in line with general Union law as developed by the CJEU.

Hence, the duty to apply Union law in its entirety and to respect its primacy (Article 20 UPCA),[40] and the duty to cooperate with the CJEU in the framework of the preliminary ruling procedure and to treat CJEU decisions as binding (Article 21 UPCA), are not dependent on these Articles, but emanate directly from Union law. The same is true with regard to liability for damages caused by infringements of Union law. By concluding the UPCA, Member States cannot lessen the Union law-based right to damages for breaches of Union law.[41] This means that Articles 22–23 of the UPCA cannot reduce Member State liability below the standards set by the CJEU.

Union fundamental rights bind the UPC whenever they bind Member State courts. Union fundamental rights apply to Member State action when Member States *implement* Union law under Article 51(1) of the Charter of Fundamental Rights of the European Union (EU Charter).[42] The EPUE Regulation, the UPCA,

Only the UPC may pronounce how these polycentric norms jointly produce the outcomes intended by the unitary patent package.

[40] To recognise that Union primacy also applies with respect to governments and parliaments, the UPCA could have clarified that to the extent its provisions conflict with Union law, or give rise to conflicts with Union law by reason of subsequent Union measures, the provisions of the UPCA shall not apply, and shall be modified by UPCA Member States as appropriate. This would have clarified the respective obligations of the participating Member States now based on the principles of primacy and loyalty only. Bruno de Witte (B de Witte, '"Old Flexibility": International Agreements between Member States of the EU' in G de Búrca and J Scott (eds), *Constitutional Change in the EU: From Uniformity to Flexibility* (Oxford, Hart Publishing, 2000) 31, 52) proposes that such a provision could be included in all *inter se* agreements between the Member States.

[41] Potential liability of the EPO (and its implementation in practice) for a breach of Union law is an interesting and many-sided question. However, it cannot be analysed in this context.

[42] Charter of Fundamental Rights of the European Union, OJ C364/1 (18 December 2000).

the EPC, decisions of the EPO, and finally Member State norms applicable to EPUEs should all be evaluated against this standard. The standard is *contextually determined*, rather than abstract.

The EPUE Regulation is Union law proper, and is fully subject to the effects and application of the EU Charter. The CJEU could review its conformity with Union fundamental rights standards in a direct action based on Article 263 of the TFEU, or review its validity in a preliminary ruling. As the CJEU can authoritatively interpret the provisions of the EPUE Regulation, it can also read fundamental rights into the substantive norms of the Regulation. When the UPC applies and interprets the Regulation, it acts within the scope of Union law and is bound by the EU Charter, as is clear from Article 51(1) of the EU Charter and for example the *Åkerberg Fransson* case: 'The applicability of European Union law entails applicability of the fundamental rights guaranteed by the [EU] Charter'.[43] The CJEU can thus check the EPUE Regulation and its application and interpretation against the EU Charter.

How Union fundamental rights apply to the UPCA, EPC, domestic laws and EPO decisions applicable to EPUEs is less obvious. The UPCA is not a Union agreement, but an *inter se* treaty between the participating Member States. The EPC is an international agreement involving not only all EU Member States, but also third European states. The EPO is not an organ or agency of the Union, even though it has in practice been entrusted with tasks and decision-making powers related to EPUEs. Domestic laws of the participating Member States define important features of EPUEs. With regard to all these categories of norms and decisions applicable to EPUEs, the CJEU could neither exercise direct judicial review under Article 263 of the TFEU, nor declare them invalid in preliminary rulings, as it could with regard to the EPUE Regulation.

Yet as the EPUE Regulation is not a stand-alone measure, but always involves the application of the provisions of the EPC, the UPCA, the EPO's decisions and in many situations also domestic norms of Member States, these categories of norms could constitute Member State implementation of Union law in the application of the EPUE Regulation. This would mean that Member States, and hence also the UPC, are bound by Union fundamental rights whenever EPUEs are adjudicated, and that the effects of Union fundamental rights would extend to all norms applicable to EPUEs. This would offer the CJEU ample opportunities to interpret all norms applicable to the EPUE—something the participating Member States tried to avoid. This is considered further below.

In *Åkerberg Fransson*, the CJEU stated that the Member State had acted within the scope of Union law and was thus bound by EU fundamental rights when it applied national procedural and penal provisions *not* adopted to fulfil Union obligations, on the ground that the substantive provisions applicable in the case derived from Union law, and Union law required the Member States to take effective

[43] Case C-617/10 *Åklagaren v Hans Åkerberg Fransson* (26 February 2013), [21].

and deterring measures to counter fraud to protect the financial interests of the Union, and in particular to adopt the same measures they take to counter fraud affecting their own interests.[44] The function—not the intention—of the domestic norms was thus decisive. The case confirmed that *implementation* referred to in Article 51(1) of the EU Charter is interpreted broadly so as to cover acting within 'the scope of application' of Union law.[45]

In other cases the CJEU has also accepted that when the Union law-based right to damages for breach of Union law is exercised, the decisions on costs and legal aid, as well as the norms defining the domestic court's jurisdiction, constitute implementation of Union law for the purposes of Article 51(1) of the EU Charter.[46] Such domestic norms must thus be in line with Union fundamental rights when the Union law-based right (to damages for breach of Union law) is exercised before Member State courts.

In *Siragusa* the Court clarified that for domestic norms to be caught by Article 51(1) of the EU Charter, there must be 'a certain degree of connection above and beyond the matters covered being closely related or one of those matters having an indirect impact on the other'.[47] The Court explained that the EU Charter has not applied to Member State legislation where the relevant Union norms in the subject area concerned have not imposed any obligation on Member States *in the circumstances of the case at hand*. The Court further connected the applicability of the EU Charter to the aim of protecting fundamental rights in the EU, 'which is to ensure that those rights are not infringed in areas of EU activity, whether through action at EU level or through the implementation of EU law by the Member States' (at [31]).

The CJEU concluded in *Pringle* that Member States did not implement Union law for the purposes of Article 51(1) of the Charter when they established the European Stability Mechanism (ESM) through an *inter se* agreement.[48] The CJEU connected its conclusion to the fact that the TEU and the TFEU did not confer any specific competence on the Union to establish such a mechanism. This left unanswered whether the EU Charter binds Member States when they have concluded an *inter se* agreement in an area of shared competence. Peers has argued that extending the applicability of the EU Charter to such agreements would not constitute a plausible interpretation of Article 51(1), as in such a case Member States do not implement Union law. Only the Union institutions would

[44] Ibid, [26]–[28].

[45] See also, D Sarmiento, 'Who's Afraid of the Charter? The Court of Justice, National Courts and the New Framework of Fundamental Rights Protection in Europe' (2013) 50 *CML Rev* 1267, 1279.

[46] Case C-279/09 *DEB Deutsche Energiehandels- und Beratungsgesellschaft mbH v Germany* [2010] ECR I-13849; Case C-199/11 *Europese Gemeenschap v Otis NV* [2012] ECR I-684. The latter case ([45]) indicates that the whole legal process leading to the court's final judgement constitutes 'implementation' within the meaning of the EU Charter, Art 51(1). See also, Sarmiento (n 45) 1283–84.

[47] Case C-206/13 *Cruciano Siragusa v Regione Sicilia—Soprintendenza Beni Culturali e Ambientali di Palermo* [2014] ECR I-126, [24].

[48] Case C-370/12 *Thomas Pringle v Government of Ireland, Ireland and the Attorney General* [2012] ECR I-756, [180].

be bound by the Charter in the context of such *inter se* treaties, provided they have been entrusted a role in their operation.[49] However, answering this question is not necessary with regard to the UPCA, as those of its provisions related to the EPUE involve an implementation of Union law within the meaning of Article 51(1) of the EU Charter for other reasons, as argued below.

Finally, the much-debated *Kadi* ruling demonstrates that there are substantive constitutional filters on how far international norms may interfere with the fundamental principles underlying the EU Treaties.[50] The case confirmed that UN resolutions could not override fundamental rights as protected in the EU legal order when the CJEU exercises judicial review over secondary Union law.

The UPCA as an *inter se* agreement is treated as 'Member State law' for the purposes of Article 51(1) of the EU Charter.[51] As an *inter se* treaty, it cannot derogate from Union law and is fully subject to its primacy. The CJEU has not distinguished between infringements of Union law caused by a state's internal laws and infringements caused by that state's international agreements.[52] Such *inter se* agreements cannot be invoked to derogate from the principle of primacy of Union law in any circumstances.[53] Thus, to the extent that the UPCA involves an implementation of EU law, the CJEU may also check its conformity with Union fundamental rights. The same is true with regard to domestic norms applicable to EPUEs, such as prior use right and compulsory licensing provisions, as well as domestic norms defining the property law aspects of EPUEs.

The UPCA defines the substantive characteristics of the EPUE formally established with the EPUE Regulation. Articles 25–26 of the UPCA define direct and indirect patent infringement and thus determine the core substantive content of patent rights within the framework of the EPUE Regulation. The UPCA is for these parts directly connected to the EPUE Regulation; its norms operate in the scope of Union law. The same applies to the UPCA provisions defining limitations to patents.[54] Procedural norms of the UPCA similarly satisfy the case law

49 S Peers, 'Towards a New Form of EU Law? The Use of EU Institutions Outside the EU Legal Framework' (2013) 9 *European Constitutional Law Review* 37, 52. See also P Craig, '*Pringle* and the use of EU Institutions outside the EU Legal Framework: Foundations, Procedure and Substance' (2013) 9 *European Constitutional Law Review* 263, 281–82.

50 Joined cases C-402/05 P & C-415/05 P *Yassin Abdullah Kadi v Council* [2008] ECR I-6351.

51 Actually the UPCA is a specific *inter se* agreement: see EPUE Regulation, Recitals 9 and 11, Art 18, which connect the entry into force of the Regulation to the entry into force of the UPCA. The tight connection between the UPCA and the EPUE Regulation speaks in favour of extending the application of Union fundamental rights norms to the UPCA provisions whenever applicable to EPUEs.

52 See J Klabbers, *Treaty Conflict and the European Union* (Cambridge, Cambridge University Press, 2009) 209; B de Witte and T Beukert, 'The Court of Justice Approves the Creation of the European Stability Mechanism outside the EU Legal Order: *Pringle*' (2013) 50 *CML Rev* 805, 829.

53 This is confirmed by TFEU, Art 351(1) and related case law. See also A Rosas, 'The Status in EU Law of International Agreements Concluded by EU Member States' (2011) 34 *Fordham International Law Journal* 1304, 1319–20.

54 They also constitute exceptions to Union norms, thus being under the *ERT* case law (based on case C-260/89 *Elliniki Radiophonia Tileorassi v Dimotiki*, [1991] ECR I-2925) and hence under the effects of Union fundamental rights also on this basis. Case C-390/12 *Robert Pfleger et al* (30 April 2014) demonstrates that the *ERT* case law is still valid under the EU Charter, Art 5(1). Hence, Member

requirements concerning Article 51(1) of the EU Charter. Similar arguments speak in favour of applying Union fundamental rights to Member States' domestic norms when applied to EPUEs. The CJEU could thus, for example, pronounce on whether some aspects of the Rules of Procedure of the Unified Patent Court satisfy the requirements of effective judicial protection under Article 47 of the EU Charter, or whether a compulsory licence based on Member State law is in conformity with the protection of property ownership under Article 17 of the EU Charter.

The CJEU would likely also be able to indirectly review EPC interpretations and EPO decisions applicable to EPUEs. Formally, the EPC is an international agreement binding not only EU Member States, but also third European states. As the EU is not a contracting party to the EPC, it does not constitute 'an integral part' of Union law, as international treaties signed by the EU do. Union conclusion of the EPC would change the position in this respect and give the CJEU competence to interpret its provisions and define their effects within the Union.[55] Most EU Member States have acceded to the EPC *after* their accession to the EU. In line with Article 351(1) of the TFEU, these Member States cannot derogate from Union norms based on the EPC. On the other hand, with regard to EU Member States that have acceded to the EPC *before* their EU membership, third states and their nationals could in theory invoke the EPC to justify derogation from Union norms.[56] This makes the position of the EPC interesting from the perspective of Article 351(1) of the TFEU.[57]

Yet the EPC forms an integral part of the unitary patent package. Its norms define patentability and the scope of protection for EPUEs. The EPO applies EPC norms when processing European patent applications leading to EPUEs, and the UPC applies them post-grant in patent litigation. Leaving such core norms of EPUE protection outside the Union fundamental rights safeguards would be unacceptable. As *Kadi* demonstrates, potentially conflicting international norms and decisions by international bodies do not prevent fundamental rights review of Union secondary acts.

States act in the scope of Union law also when they seek to rely on exceptions to Union norms. Such norms have typically been exceptions to fundamental freedoms, but could also constitute, for example, exceptions to IP rights defined on the Union level. Exceptions to EPUE defined in the UPCA or domestic laws can thus be reviewed under the Union standard of fundamental rights protection.

[55] See also Peers (n 12) 254.

[56] Such countries include at least Austria, Croatia, Bulgaria, Cyprus, Czech Republic, Estonia, Hungary, Latvia, Romania, Slovakia, Slovenia and Sweden. I have not addressed the situation of EU Member States that have acceded to both during the same year. Moreover, changes made to the EPC might again change the situation and render the EPC a posterior treaty in relation to the EU membership. An amendment is treated as a new agreement. See Klabbers (n 52) 198.

[57] Thus, to take an example, a patent owner from Switzerland could in theory invoke the EPC in Sweden to enable setting aside a conflicting Union norm, for example a provision of the Biotechnology Directive. On the other hand, as the EPUE is supposed to have uniform effect in all participating EU Member States, the UPC could not override EU norms due to conflicting EPC obligations in some participating Member States only. The position of Union law in such a situation is yet unknown. See also Case C-812/79 *Attorney General v Burgoa* [1980] ECR 2787; Klabbers (n 52) 126–226.

The indirect review of the EPO's grant decisions against Union fundamental rights (or other Union norms) in preliminary rulings would not be problematic from the perspective of the immunity of the EPO either,[58] as finding a conflict between a granted EPUE and Union fundamental rights would not overrule the EPO's grant decision, but would merely abolish the EPUE's unitary effect, attached to the European patent automatically by the EPUE Regulation if the conditions for it are fulfilled. Hence, the CJEU would not formally overrule EPO decisions, but could pronounce that unitary effect in the participating Member States is not possible whenever the EPUE is in breach of Union fundamental rights (or other Union norms).

Although such indirect fundamental rights review of the EPO's decisions is not sufficient, it is important given that the European Court of Human Rights (ECtHR) has been unwilling to review the EPO's decisions or challenge their immunity from domestic court review.[59] The German Constitutional Court has adopted a similar approach.[60] The Boards of Appeal of the EPO have admittedly accepted that fundamental rights and the European Convention *acquis* affect the interpretation of the EPC.[61] However, fundamental rights have not played a significant role in their decisions. There are no guarantees that they would even try to follow the fundamental rights standards set by the EU Charter and the CJEU.

Another question is the applicable fundamental rights standard. A combined reading of *Åkerberg Fransson* (referred to above) and *Melloni*,[62] given the same day, confirms that whenever Union acts require domestic implementation measures, national authorities and courts remain free to apply national standards of protection of fundamental rights, provided the Union fundamental rights standard is not higher, and provided the domestic fundamental rights standard does not compromise the primacy, unity and effectiveness of Union law.[63] Hence, where Union norms only partially determine the question at hand and thus leave

[58] The immunity of the EPO's decisions is discussed below in more detail.

[59] *Rambus Inc v Germany* Appl no 40382/04 (16 June 2009); *Lenzing AG v Germany* Appl no 39025/97 (9 September 1998).

[60] See BVerfG, 2 BvR 1458/03 vom 3.7.2006, Absatz-Nr (1–25), and previous case law referred to there. In order to succeed, the complainant should be able to substantiate a claim that there was *a structural deficit* in the EPC system as far as legal protection was concerned. The German Constitutional Court could exercise its jurisdiction in the area of the supranational powers of an international organisation upon condition that the persons affected substantiate their claim *that the absolutely necessary protection of fundamental rights cannot generally be provided within the organisation.* The German Constitutional Court has in its previous case law determined that the system of legal protection in the European Patent Convention corresponds essentially to the standards of the Basic Law.

[61] The EPO Board of Appeal has accepted in T377/95 *Herpes simplex virus/UNIVERSITY PATENTS INC* [1999] OJ EPO 11, [36] that 'The overall acceptance of the ECHR as guidance is shown by the fact that all member states to the EPC adhere to the ECHR'. See also G3/98 *Six-month period/UNIVERSITY PATENTS* [2001] OJ EPO 62; D11/91 *Disciplinary penalty* [1995] OJ EPO 721, [3.3] (recognising the ECHR rules as expressions of general principles that form part of the legal system of the EPO and which must therefore be observed).

[62] Case C-399/11 *Stefano Melloni v Ministerio Fiscal* [2013] ECR I-107.

[63] *Åkerberg Fransson* (n 43), [29]; *Melloni* (ibid), [60].

scope for domestic variation, more effective fundamental rights protection based on domestic norms is possible.[64]

In the context of the unitary patent package, this likely means that the CJEU could subject the UPCA, the EPC and the domestic norms applicable to the EPUE only under the minimum level requirements set by Union fundamental rights.[65]

In theory, the UPC could thus resort to more extensive protection based on the European Convention on Human Rights (ECHR) and Member State basic rights norms. However, as the UPC is detached from any Member State system of fundamental rights, it could not in practice do this. Hence, what should constitute the minimum standard becomes the maximum standard for the UPC in the absence of a higher standard based on Member State fundamental rights norms. Moreover, as the ECHR establishes minimum standards, it is likely that the UPC could not introduce higher standards based on its provisions in most instances.

Although the CJEU likely has jurisdiction to indirectly review the norms of the unitary patent package from the perspective of fundamental rights, the transfer of most substantive patent norms from the EPUE Regulation to the UPCA still shields these norms from the CJEU's fundamental rights review. Unlike with the EPUE Regulation, there could be no direct fundamental rights challenge of the UPCA, and even less so with the EPC or decisions of the EPO. Their content could in practice be challenged only indirectly through preliminary rulings initiated by the UPC. The scope for the CJEU to use Union fundamental rights to interpret the EPUE will thus depend on the willingness of the UPC to refer questions to the CJEU.

In the following, the focus will shift to the question whether the package could be considered unconstitutional as a whole. The analysis will be restricted to two questions: were Member States able to validly conclude the UPCA without the EU, and could the position of the EPO amount to the delegation of decision-making powers to an organ outside the Union framework without sufficient remedies and Union law safeguards?

IV. Could Member States Conclude the UPCA without the Union?

Enhanced cooperation under the EU Treaties on one hand, and international treaties between the Member States only on the other hand (*inter se* agreements), are often considered two alternative tracks a group of Member States can follow when

[64] See also Sarmiento (n 45) 1289–95; A Ward, 'Article 51' in S Peers et al (eds), *The EU Charter of Fundamental Rights. A Commentary* (Oxford, Hart Publishing, 2014) 1413, 1419.

[65] A theoretical possibility exists that the CJEU might consider resorting to higher standards of Member State fundamental rights protection as jeopardising the uniformity intended by the EPUE Regulation. However, this would be unlikely, as the EPUE Regulation clearly does not settle all the questions related to the unitary patents, but explicitly leaves room for national implementation.

all EU Member States are unable to agree on a course of future Union measures.[66] Yet with the unitary patent package we have both: enhanced cooperation *and* the UPCA, concluded between a group of Member States, and including subject matter earlier intended to exist in the EPUE Regulation enacted in the mode of enhanced cooperation.

The EU was dropped as a contracting party from the UPCA, because the intention was to avoid the problems related to the unity and primacy of EU law identified in the CJEU's Opinion 1/09 by making the UPC a court common to the participating Member States, subject to the same obligations under Union law as any domestic court of a participating Member State. Having the EU as a contracting party, together with EU Member States and third states belonging to the EPC, would have given the European Parliament the right to veto the conclusion of the UPCA in line with Article 218 of the TFEU. Moreover, the UPCA would have constituted 'an integral part of EU law', followed by the broad interpretative powers of the CJEU, as well as the normal EU law effects applicable to EU international agreements.[67] This was also something that the key drivers of the unified patent package wanted to avoid.

The exclusion of the EU from the UPCA raises the question whether the Member States could validly conclude it without the Union's participation or authorisation under Article 2(1) of the TFEU, which states that Member States may adopt legally binding acts within the area of the Union's exclusive competence 'only if so empowered by the Union or for the implementation of Union acts'.

Competence issues previously prevented the Member States from entering the proposed European Patent Litigation Agreement (EPLA) without Union participation.[68] The UPCA differs from the EPLA in many respects, especially in that the former involves only EU Member States. Yet its conclusion without EU participation might be problematic due to the Union's existing exclusive competence with regard to civil jurisdiction, as well as its internal and external regulation of IP and patent law. In addition to the Union's internal regulation of IP and patent law, IP norms are now typically included in its trade agreements.[69] Moreover, the TRIPS Agreement now belongs to the Union's exclusive Common Commercial Policy (CCP) competence, as discussed below. The transfer of substantive patent norms to the UPCA might also infringe enhanced cooperation and the legal basis of the EPUE Regulation in Article 118 of the TFEU.[70]

66 See, eg de Witte (n 40) 56–57; Craig (n 49) 274.

67 On these effects, see T Mylly, 'Constitutional Functions of the EU's Intellectual Property Treaties' in J Drexl et al (eds), *EU Bilateral Trade Agreements and Intellectual Property: For Better or Worse* (Munich, Springer, 2014) 241–64.

68 See also Jaeger (n 6) 104; Peers (n 12) 259. The Union's external competence as regards civil jurisdiction is exclusive. The Union also has external competence for example as regards the enforcement of IP because of its Enforcement Directive.

69 On their effects in EU law see Mylly (n 67).

70 Jaeger (n 13) 390.

Inter se agreements differ in many respects from the more traditional external agreements, where also third states are parties. Peers has noted that through the proliferation of such agreements we might be witnessing a new form of EU law.[71] The CJEU, sitting in full court, accepted in *Pringle* one such agreement, namely the ESM, as the EU Treaties did not confer on the Union a specific competence to establish a permanent stability mechanism such as the ESM, and the arrangement was substantively compatible with EU law.[72]

Yet many questions still remain unanswered as regards such agreements. In particular, *Pringle* did not definitively settle the question whether *inter se* agreements are permissible also where the Union enjoys specific non-exclusive competence, or whether they would be strictly restricted to situations like the ESM, where the Union did not possess a specific legal basis in the treaties to act. Furthermore, the CJEU ruling did not address the issue to what extent *inter se* agreements can be utilised once enhanced cooperation has been authorised for a group of Member States.

Beukert and de Witte have opined that *inter se* agreements are in principle permissible in areas falling outside the Union's exclusive competence. They argue that if Member States have preserved the competence to make domestic law within a given sphere, they can within the limits of Union law's primacy 'logically also exercise that competence together, by concluding an international agreement between themselves'.[73] Peers has similarly argued that Member States retain their power to conclude treaties with each other outside the Union's exclusive competence or areas where the Union has exercised its shared competence to the extent that it has pre-empted Member States' action within the meaning of Article 3(2) of the TFEU.[74] Being outside the scope of the Union's exclusive competence would thus be decisive.

Inter se agreements might impede Union policy making in the absence of substantive conflicts. Hence, the doctrine of pre-emption, being about impediments rather than existing conflicts, also governs the acceptability of such agreements.[75] Like the transformation of EU regulations into domestic law, the inclusion of internal EU norms into *inter se* agreements could affect the status of the EU norms and restrict CJEU supervision over their application. In other words,

[71] Peers (n 49) 39. See, however, Craig (n 49), expressing concerns regarding the proliferation of such agreements.

[72] Case C-370/12 *Thomas Pringle v Government of Ireland, Ireland and the Attorney General* [2012] ECR I-756 ('*Pringle*'), [105], [168]. As Peers (n 49) fn 47 notes, 'specific competences' likely referred to all of the EU's competences other than the residual power based on TFEU, Art 352.

[73] See de Witte and Beukert (n 52) 829.

[74] See Peers 48, fn 49. See also in this respect Craig (n 49) 274. The CJEU stated in *Pringle*, [101] that it follows from TFEU, Art 3(2) that Member States are prohibited from concluding an *inter se* agreement when this 'might affect common rules or alter their scope'. Peers ((n 12) 263–64) has argued that Member States are not prevented from concluding *inter se* agreements even in spheres where EU competence is exclusive by exercise, unless they infringe the principle of primacy of Union law by contradicting their EU obligations or the principle of loyal cooperation.

[75] De Witte (n 40) 41.

Member States could in effect interfere with the operation of internal EU norms through international agreements devoid of EU law character and effects. Thus, to the extent that pre-emption precludes domestic regulation by Member States, it logically also precludes the conclusion of international agreements on the same topics between several Member States.

Adam and Mena Parras argue that as the CJEU in *Pringle* concluded that the Union did not possess a specific competence to establish the ESM, it did not have to settle the question of under what conditions Member States may act outside the Union law framework. The *Pringle* judgment would thus not automatically mean that it is permissible to use *inter se* agreements in areas characterised by the Union's non-exclusive competence and pre-emption.[76] Judge Rosas of the CJEU has also stressed that *inter se* agreements could sometimes be considered as efforts to circumvent the Union's legislative and other procedures established by the EU Treaties. This could be the case also in areas of shared competence where the principle of pre-emption applies.[77] When acting under international law instead of Union instruments, Member States control the negotiation process to the exclusion of the Union institutions. *Inter se* agreements could thus be seen as problematic even when the Union has not occupied the whole field with its internal norms overlapping with the intended agreement.

Before being able to evaluate the position of the UPCA from the above perspectives, it is necessary to address the effect of the CJEU's newly found competence to interpret the whole TRIPS Agreement on the unitary patent package and the UPCA. The Union's CCP competence now fully covers 'commercial aspects of intellectual property'. The Lisbon Treaty included it, together with trade in services and foreign direct investment, explicitly under the exclusive CCP legal basis in Article 207(1) of the TFEU.[78] The CJEU interpreted this concept in *Daiichi Sankyo*.[79] It concluded that the whole TRIPS Agreement is included within this concept, as it fulfils the criterion of relating 'specifically to international trade in that it is essentially intended to promote, facilitate or govern trade and has direct and immediate effect on trade' (at [51]).

This means that the Union enjoys an exclusive competence under Article 3(1) of the TFEU over the whole TRIPS Agreement, including its patent provisions. The competence is exclusive *by nature*. The CJEU thus possesses full jurisdiction to interpret the TRIPS Agreement and to define its effects for the whole EU.

[76] S Adam and FJM Parras, 'The European Stability Mechanism through the Legal Meanderings of the Union's Constitutionalism: Comment on *Pringle*' (2013) 6 *EL Rev* 848, 862. The CJEU thus mostly concentrated on the question whether the Member State action was *substantively consistent* with EU law. *Inter se* agreements must naturally respect the primacy of Union law.

[77] Rosas (n 53) 1319.

[78] The CCP as a whole belongs to the exclusive competence of the Union, as confirmed by TFEU, Art 3(1)(e).

[79] Case C-414/11 *Daiichi Sankyo and Sanofi-Aventis Deutschland* [2013] ECR 520. On this decision, and its potential significance for the unitary patent, see Dimopoulos and Vantsiouri (n 28); the discussion by Angelos Dimopoulos in ch 5 of this volume; Mylly (n 67) 245–51 (before the CJEU's decision in *Daiichi Sankyo*).

Member State infringement of TRIPS obligations would trigger the responsibility of the Union under international law. Member States have a Union law-based obligation to comply with TRIPS.

The legal basis of the EPUE Regulation in Article 118 of the TFEU falls within the ambit of the functioning of the internal market, which is a shared competence in accordance with Article 4(2) of the TFEU.[80] The judgment in *Daiichi Sankyo* will not transform this internal competence of the Union into an exclusive one.[81] However, secondary legislation based on Article 118 will naturally have to comply with EU external agreements, be they under exclusive or shared competence.

This is also significant from the perspective of the UPCA. The Commission could initiate infringement proceedings against Member States participating in the unitary patent package and allege that the UPCA, or practices under it, infringe the TRIPS Agreement. The exclusion of direct and judicial review effects from the WTO Agreements only prevents the direct invocation of TRIPS before Member State and EU courts and the use of TRIPS for the judicial review of EU acts, such as the EPUE Regulation.[82] However, the EU law obligation to interpret secondary EU law and all Member State law in conformity with TRIPS[83] could also be invoked before the UPC and extend to the UPCA.

Dimopoulos and Vantsiouri have suggested that the fact that the CJEU had no difficulty in interpreting the substantive patent provisions of TRIPS in *Daiichi Sankyo* would signify 'the beginning of a new era in the CJEU's involvement with the application and interpretation of substantive patent law rules'.[84] This may be so, but there are fewer reasons to agree with their proposal that in the context of the unitary patent package, the CJEU should through its newly found competence to interpret the patent provisions of TRIPS 'ensure coherence and consistency in the interpretation of the different regimes of patent infringement rules'.[85]

TRIPS requires minimum harmonisation in favour of IP owners. The CJEU could not use it as a springboard for all-things-considered interpretations of patent law, but rather could only use it to identify international minimum standards in favour of patent owners. In most cases, the minimum standards would have no impact on interpretations of the EPC, the UPCA or the applicable domestic norms. What TRIPS demands must basically be required from all 159 members

[80] This was confirmed by the CJEU in Joined Cases C-274/11 & C-295/11 *Spain v Council* (16 April 2013), [25].

[81] The Union's external exclusive IP competence is thus now broader than the EU's internal exclusive competence to legislate IP. See more closely Mylly (n 67) 250.

[82] See, more closely, Mylly (n 67) 252–59.

[83] For instances where the interpretative effect of the TRIPS Agreement has been applied, see Case C-53/96 *Hermes International v FHT Marketing Choice BV* [1998] ECR I-3606; Case C-306/05 *Sociedad General de Autores y Editores de Espana (SGAE) v Rafael Hoteles SA* [2006] ECR I-11519, [35]; Case C-275/06 *Productores de Música de Espana (Promusicae) v Telefónica de Espana SAU* [2008] ECR I-271, [60]; Case C-431/05 *Merck Genéricos—Produtos Farmaceuticos Lda v Merck & Co Inc, Merck Sharp & Dohme Lda* [2007] ECR I-7001, [35]. See more closely Mylly (n 67) 259–60.

[84] Dimopoulos and Vantsiouri (n 28) 224. See also the discussion by Angelos Dimopoulos in ch 5 of this volume.

[85] Dimopoulos and Vantsiouri (n 28) 230. See also Dimopoulos ibid.

of the WTO. European patent laws, including their diverse interpretations, are typically in line with the requirements of the TRIPS Agreement. Hence, TRIPS should not much affect the interpretation or application of the patent provisions of the unitary patent package, especially as the standard of protection followed by the UPC will likely reflect the majority views of participating Member States.

Thus, I find it difficult to agree with Dimopoulos and Vantsiouri that the competence of the CJEU to interpret the whole TRIPS Agreement would 'provide the CJEU with the opportunity to establish uniform rules on patent protection in the European Union',[86] as diverse existing and potential patent norms in Europe satisfy the minimum standards of TRIPS.[87] A coherent and consistent patent system would certainly be preferable over a fragmented and partially harmonised one. However, if the EU policy makers can only achieve the latter, the CJEU could not legitimately transform this regime into a coherent and uniform one by force, be it by recourse to the TRIPS Agreement or to teleological interpretation ignoring the incompletely harmonised, fragmented reality.

Yet, even in the absence of apparent conflicts between the UPCA and TRIPS, the question remains whether Member States could conclude the UPCA validly as an *inter se* agreement, without EU authorisation under Article 2(1) of the TFEU.

The UPCA differs significantly from other *inter se* agreements regulating special fields. For example, the Schengen instruments and the Prüm Convention were originally designed as interim arrangements waiting Union measures.[88] Moreover, the ESM Treaty, accepted by the CJEU in *Pringle*, was in practice the only available solution for Member States in the Union hit by the euro crisis, and in the absence of a specific EU legal basis to act. Hence, its creation was strongly in the Union's interest.[89] Its creation did not involve an 'intergovernmental plot' through which the respective governments sought to avoid the constraints set by Union law, and sought to exclude the Commission and the European Parliament from decision-making.[90]

Similar factors, making the UPCA appear as a more integration-friendly solution than the alternatives, are not present. Quite the opposite: the last-minute removal of substantive patent norms from the EPUE Regulation to the UPCA due to the open distrust of CJEU decision-making makes the arrangement look like an intergovernmental plot, although the Union legislature also apparently approved it by enacting the EPUE Regulation.[91] Substantive patent law with regard to the EPUE is not only rendered (partially) outside the reach of the CJEU, but in practice

[86] Dimopoulos and Vantsiouri (n 28) 228.

[87] For a thoughtful account of TRIPS emphasising the need for flexibility and contextuality, see GB Dinwoodie and RC Dreyfuss, *A Neofederalist Vision of TRIPS: The Resilience of the International Intellectual Property Regime* (Oxford, Oxford University Press, 2012).

[88] See also de Witte (n 40) 42 and Rosas (n 53) 1318–19.

[89] See also Craig (n 49) 268.

[90] De Witte and Beukert (n 52) 847–48.

[91] However, EU secondary law cannot authorize derogation from the treaty-based division of competences between the Union and its Member States. Therefore, to the extent that the UPCA covers subject matter belonging to the Union's exclusive competence (by nature or through pre-emption), the silent 'approval' of the EU legislator cannot be decisive.

also outside the Union's legislative processes and the intellectual property policy of the Commission. It is obvious that the removal was not intended to be temporary, but a permanent feature of the unitary patent package. Still, the substantive and procedural norms of the UPCA constitute core parts of EPUEs established by the EPUE Regulation in the mode of enhanced cooperation. Nothing in the creation of the UPC necessitated the removal of the substantive patent norms from the EPUE Regulation to the UPCA.

The UPCA contains provisions overlapping with the TRIPS Agreement and likely also with the EU's Free Trade Agreements falling under its exclusive CCP competence. The EU's exclusive CCP competence as regards commercial aspects of IP should not affect the internal division of competence to legislate between the EU and Member States, nor their competences to conclude international agreements including IP norms outside the EU's CCP competence.[92] Yet, the exclusivity of the EU's competence over TRIPS and other IP trade measures emphasises the need to apply the remaining Member State competences loyally to avoid conflict with the CCP competence.

The Union also enjoys an exclusive competence within the scope of the Brussels Regulation on jurisdiction and the recognition and enforcement of judgments in civil and commercial matters.[93] The EU has also harmonised substantive patent law to some extent, for example through the Biotechnology Directive. It has also harmonized remedies in IP law through the IPR Enforcement Directive. Although, for example, the changes in the domestic court systems and many of the procedural rules required by the UPC require involvement of the participating Member States, the inclusion of subject matter in the UPCA falling under the Union's exclusive competence appears to be problematic.

As enhanced cooperation was permissible among the participating Member States and Article 118 of the TFEU enabled full recourse to Union instruments (except for the creation of the UPC), the large-scale switching from the Union law track to the international law track could have been avoided. Staying predominantly on the Union law track would have connoted fuller engagement of the Union legislature and judicature with regard to the unitary patent package, as well as fuller EU law effects and legal safeguards covering more aspects of unitary patent protection. Both the use of enhanced cooperation and reliance on Article 118 of the TFEU as the UPP's legal basis functioned as strong arguments in favour of Union measures.[94]

92 See more closely Mylly (n 67).

93 Regulation (EC) No 44/2001 of 22 December 2000 on jurisdiction and the recognition and enforcement of judgments in civil and commercial matters, OJ L12/1 (16 January 2001).

94 There were concerns during the negotiations that the transfer of the key substantive patent provisions outside the EPUE Regulation could result in infringement of the Regulation's legal basis in TFEU, Art 118. See, eg Haedicke (n 17) 614. The editorial, 'What do we want? "Flexibility! Sort-of..." When do we want it? "Now!" Maybe...' (2013) 50 *CML Rev* 673, 679, discusses the possibility—although unlikely—that when a specific treaty legal basis to act is available, the availability of enhanced cooperation could prevent recourse to *inter se* agreements as an alternative. Moreover, the decision authorising enhanced cooperation could be infringed, as removing the substantive patent provisions to the UPCA does not further the objectives, protect the interests and reinforce the integration process of the Union, as required from enhanced cooperation.

Article 118 confers an explicit power to establish *uniform protection* of IP *throughout the Union*. As has become evident, the EPUE Regulation does not achieve uniformity of protection in practice. Nor is protection equal throughout the participating Member States, as for example some important exceptions are left to domestic law.

It is thus possible that Member States lacked the competence to conclude the UPCA without the Union's participation or authorisation under Article 2(1) of the TFEU for the parts falling under exclusive Union competence. Similarly, the package could have been based predominantly on the EPUE Regulation. The exceptions and limitations could have been included fully in it to enable the uniformity of protection required by Article 118 of the TFEU. If this is what Union law ultimately requires, the unitary patent package as a whole would be unconstitutional and we would have to go back to square one. But, alas, the constitutional challenges of the unitary patent package do not stop here, as the discussion below seeks to demonstrate.

V. The Role of the EPO and the Shadow of *Meroni*

The status of the EPO in the granting and administration of EPUEs is another constitutional problem related to the unitary patent package. The conferral of decision-making powers on the EPO against the so-called *Meroni* doctrine of Union law constitutes one of the main grounds of Spain's challenge of the unitary patent package.[95] The *Meroni* case was concerned with the sub-delegation of the High Authority's (now the European Commission's) powers *to a private law body* outside what is now the Union structure.[96] Only clearly defined executive powers could be delegated, provided the exercise of such powers was subject to strict rules based on objective criteria. Discretionary powers involving extensive freedom of judgment could not be delegated. It can be concluded from the *Meroni* judgment that the absence of EU Court supervision could jeopardise the conformity of the body's decision-making with Union law and hence the autonomy of EU law and the EU rights of affected individuals.

[95] For a critical account of Spain's arguments, see Tilmann (n 16).

[96] Case C-9/56 *Meroni & Co, Industrie Metallurgiche, SpA v High Authority of the European Coal and Steel Community* [1958] ECR English special edition 133. M Chamon, 'EU Agencies between *Meroni* and *Romano* or the Devil and the Deep Blue Sea' (2011) 48 *CML Rev* 1055, emphasises the importance of the less-often mentioned *Romano* case (Case 98/80 *Giuseppe Romano v Institut national d'assurance maladie-invalidité* [1981] ECR 1259), especially when the agencies have been delegated their powers through a legislative measure. However, the CJEU argumentation in the *Romano* case is very scant. The Advocate General emphasised more clearly the significance of judicial review and availability of appropriate remedies as conditions affecting the legitimacy of delegation. The *ESMA* case treated below does not give weight to the *Romano* judgment.

The CJEU re-evaluated the *Meroni* doctrine in the recent *ESMA* case.[97] The Court accepted that the powers granted to the European Securities and Markets Authority (ESMA) through a legislative measure were precisely delineated and amenable to judicial review in the light of the objectives established by the delegating authority. Hence, the powers of ESMA complied with the requirements laid down in the *Meroni* case. The CJEU emphasised the fact that the measures adopted by the EU financial agencies were subject to judicial review under Article 263 (4) of the TFEU. Otherwise the judgment enables agencification by admitting that Articles 290 and 291 of the TFEU do not prevent the conferral of powers upon agencies, especially where the conferral takes place in the context of an overall legislative framework. Finally, the internal market powers of the Union, and possibly by analogy other legal bases, do not prevent the delegation of powers to agencies to adopt legally binding measures.[98]

The EPUE Regulation relies in practice on the administrative services of the EPO. The conferral of powers is based on Member State action within the framework of the EPC, as mandated by the EPUE Regulation. The Regulation requires that core administrative functions related to unitary effect be transferred to the EPO: among other things, it will administer requests for unitary effect and the register for unitary patent protection, as discussed more fully below. The EPUE Regulation builds on the EPO as the sole administrative organ granting European patents capable of becoming EPUEs. The EPO will make binding decisions affecting the applicant and third parties when it grants or refuses to grant a European patent for which the applicant requests unitary effect.

In spite of constitutionally relevant differences to the *Meroni* case, the mutual concern in both is the transfer of decision-making powers to a body operating outside the reach of the EU institutions and Union law safeguards, and hence the negative effect on the autonomy of Union law and remedies for infringements of EU rights.[99] The EPO is an international organ outside the Union framework. It could breach Union law without aggrieved parties being able to challenge its decisions before EU courts, as explained in more detail below. This could threaten the autonomy, unity and primacy of EU law, as well as the EU rights of affected individuals.

Conferral of decision-making powers to a specialised agency within the area of patent law would have been possible for the administration of unitary patents by recourse to the legal basis of the EPUE Regulation, Article 118 of the TFEU.

[97] Case C-270/12 *United Kingdom and Northern Ireland v European Parliament and Council* (22 January 2014).

[98] See also M Costa, 'The EU's Financial Supervisory Authorities: Mind the Accountability Gap' (27 January 2014) <http://eulawanalysis.blogspot.fi/2014/01/the-eus-financial-supervisory.html>.

[99] It has been argued that the requirement concerning a system of effective judicial protection constitutes the core insight of the *Meroni* judgment for today, rather than its arguments related to institutional balance. See Chamon (n 96) 1060. On the constitutionally significant distinction between sub-delegation and conferral of powers through legislative measures, see HCH Hofman and A Morini, 'Constitutional Aspects of the Pluralisation of the EU Executive through "Agencification"' (2012) 37 *EL Rev* 419, 441–42.

Patent law is an area requiring specific expertise. As the examples of the Office for Harmonization in the Internal Market (OHIM) and the Community Plant Variety Office (CPVO) demonstrate, such EU agencies could enjoy the power to adopt individually legally binding decisions having *erga omnes* effects.[100]

The CJEU implicitly accepted in *Schräder* the powers of the CPVO to make externally binding decisions under Union law, even though the decisions of the Board of Appeal of the CPVO are only subject to limited judicial review by EU Courts.[101] The CPVO Board of Appeal decision was subject to EU General Court review as regards the application of Union law by that Board, as well as the question of whether there had been a manifest error in the assessment of distinctiveness of the plant variety in question.[102] After the internal complaint procedure is exhausted, the EU courts may thus review measures passed by the OHIM and the CPVO, such as the General Court review of the final decision of the Board of Appeal of the CPVO in *Schräder* demonstrates.[103]

Although the nature of the EPUE differs from the EU trade mark, design and plant variety rights in several respects, the EPO can *in practice* make legally binding decisions affecting third parties with regard to EPUEs. However, the EPO is not a Union agency, and the unitary patent package does not establish any mechanism of appeal from its decisions to Union courts. There is access to *no* court—Union or Member State—after the EPO rejects a European patent application which could also have become EPUE.[104]

In fact, Article 3(1) of the Protocol on Privileges and Immunities of the European Patent Organisation prevents judicial court review of EPO decisions.[105] The aggrieved applicant can only appeal to the EPO Boards of Appeal, which are organs internal to the EPO. There are no courts capable of requesting preliminary rulings from the CJEU.[106] The first instance tribunal at the EPO, the Opposition Division, does not constitute a true judicial panel. For example, it contains the examiner who was involved in granting the patent. The system of appeal, in turn, is largely treated as an additional first instance tribunal, with liberal rules regarding

[100] The OHIM and the CPVO thus constitute 'genuine decision-making agencies' with the capacity to enact legal instruments binding on third parties. For the related taxonomy of agencies, see S Griller and A Orator, 'Everything under Control? The "Way Forward" for European Agencies in the Footsteps of the *Meroni* Doctrine' (2010) 35 *EL Rev* 3, 14.

[101] Case C-38/09 P *Schräder v Community Plant Variety Office* [2010] ECR I-3209.

[102] Ibid, [76]–[77]. See also Hofmann and Morini (n 99) 428; Chamon (n 96) 1059–60.

[103] The decision rejected the registration of a plant variety. The measures of EU agencies must also comply with the EU Charter. See Ward (n 64) 1427.

[104] As Jaeger (n 6) 81 notes, the possibility of appeals to Union courts was dropped in the proposal published in 2000 seeking to establish a specialised Community Intellectual Property Court (CIPC). The subsequent proposals have not re-introduced appeals to Union courts from EPO decisions. The change was motivated by the desire to retain unified treatment of Community and European patents.

[105] Protocol on Privileges and Immunities of the European Patent Organisation of 5 October 1973.

[106] See G2/08 *Use of embryos/WARF* [2009] OJ EPO 306 (*Warf*), where the EBA declined a request to make a reference for a preliminary ruling due to the absence of any legal and institutional link between the EPO and the Union, as well as the absence of any mechanism for making a reference to the CJEU. Moreover, the CJEU would not in any case accept a reference, as the EPO Boards of Appeal do not constitute a Member State court for the purposes of TFEU, Art 267.

the admission of evidence and fresh arguments.[107] Hence, access to the Boards of Appeal of the EPO does not equate to independent court review.[108]

According to Article 263 of the TFEU, the CJEU has jurisdiction to review, among others, the legality of acts of bodies, offices or agencies of the Union intended to produce legal effects vis-à-vis third parties. The CJEU has jurisdiction with regard to them also for example through Article 265 (failure to act) and Article 267 (preliminary rulings) of the TFEU. Judicial control over administrative acts affecting Union rights of individuals constitutes a core aspect of the rule of law in the EU, and the CJEU's related supervisory functions.[109] Article 47 of the EU Charter secures, among others, the right to an effective remedy for violations of rights or freedoms guaranteed by EU law.[110] The position of the EPO thus seems problematic from the perspective of the norms and principles governing the conferral of powers to bodies outside the Union framework and the requirement of judicial review before EU courts.[111]

Yet, according to the official mantra, the Union has not delegated powers or administrative functions to the EPO. Instead, in line with what was referred to as the transformation approach above, European patents granted by the EPO become transformed into unitary rights post-grant if the applicant so requests. Hence, the EPO would not apply the EPUE Regulation when processing European patent applications.

Tilmann argues along these lines. He maintains that as the EPUE Regulation does not govern the grant or rejection of European patents, but might only confer subsequent unitary effect on European patents, the Union has not transferred powers to the EPO.[112] The unitary effect produced by the EPUE Regulation would be wholly parasitic with regard to the underlying European patent granted by the EPO: it is attached 'to a European patent which is a non-EU title based on international law'. Not being able to challenge the rejection of a patent application would thus not constitute a problem as the Regulation 'has not yet taken effect'. Similarly, not being able to challenge the rejection of a third party's opposition would be acceptable, as the EPO's decision 'relates only to the patent's international title,

107 See, eg R Jacob, 'The Relationship between European and National Courts in Intellectual Property Law' in Ohly and Pila (n 3) 185–98.

108 Cf *Warf* (n 106), [4], noting that EPO Boards of Appeal have been recognized as being courts or tribunals.

109 TEU, Art 19(1).

110 EU Charter, Art 47 is discussed in more detail below.

111 Peers (n 12) 254, notes that it is arguable that as far as the unitary patent is concerned, it is necessary to ensure judicial review of the EPO's decisions. Yet he notes that the rights of those opposing the grant of a patent might also be adequately protected by the possibility of bringing an action for revocation or by making an invalidity claim as a defence in a patent infringement case. Peers also recognises that for an aggrieved applicant the position is different, but it is according to Peers' analysis still uncertain whether the CJEU would tolerate any possibility of the automatic application within the Union legal order of the decisions of bodies established by international treaties and not being subject to effective judicial review. Peers refers in this context to *Kadi* (n 50), discussed above.

112 Tilmann (n 16) 5.

and not to its unitary effect', as the unitary effect would disappear 'because it has lost its basis'.[113]

Furthermore, the argument proceeds that although Article 9(1) of the EPUE Regulation lists the EPO's tasks related to the administration of unitary effect, there would be no Union delegation here either.[114] This is because the EPUE Regulation orders *the participating Member States* to entrust these administrative tasks to the EPO, in line with Article 143 of the EPC. Article 143 enables the group of EPC Contracting States pursuing unified protection to give additional tasks to the European Patent Office, to be carried out by the EPO in accordance with its internal rules. The participating Member States must, among others, assign to the EPO the tasks of administering requests for unitary effect by proprietors of European patents, and maintaining the register for unitary patent protection within the European Patent Register. The participating Member States must ensure the governance and supervision of these activities in their capacity as Contracting States to the EPC.[115] They must ensure compliance with the EPUE Regulation in fulfilling their international obligations under the EPC, and they have an obligation to cooperate to that end. Hence, in line with this argument, the participating Member States—not the EU—would assign the EPO certain tasks for the administration of unitary patents.

Importantly, the participating Member States must also ensure effective legal protection before a competent court of one or several participating Member States against the decisions of the EPO, when the EPO carries out the administrative tasks assigned to it.[116] They have implemented this obligation through Article 32(1)(i) of the UPCA. The Article states that the UPC has exclusive competence in respect of actions concerning decisions of the EPO in carrying out the tasks referred to in Article 9 of the EPUE Regulation. The EPO will have to waive its immunity regarding all actions brought against it under this Article.[117] This enables UPC review of the EPO's decisions related to the administration of unitary patent protection. This review does not extend to the grant and opposition stages, nor does it equal direct EU court review.

To the extent that the UPC reviews the administrative decisions of the EPO, the preliminary ruling procedure enables indirect and partial CJEU control over EPO decisions.[118] The UPC may also refer questions to the CJEU about the Union law conformity of EPO decisions when adjudicating infringements of EPUEs.

[113] See ibid.

[114] Ibid.

[115] To that end, the participating Member States shall set up a Select Committee of the Administrative Council of the European Patent Organisation within the meaning of EPC, Art 145. The Select Committee consists of the representatives of the participating Member States and a representative of the Commission as an observer. Decisions of the Select Committee are to be taken 'with due regard for the position of the Commission' and in accordance with EPC, Art 35(2).

[116] EPUE Regulation, Art 9(3).

[117] See Tilmann (n 16) 7.

[118] See also M Eck, 'Europäisches Einheitspatent und Einheitspatentgericht—Grund zum Feiern?' [2014] *Gewerblicher Rechtsschutz und Urheberrecht: Internationaler Teil* 114, 117.

Should an EPO grant decision conflict with Union law, the UPC must invalidate the EPUE due to the primacy of Union law. This would not affect the fate of the European patent outside the Union but, to the extent that the conflict between the EPO decision and, for example, the Biotechnology Directive would be confirmed by the CJEU, it would also affect the status of the European patent in non-participating EU Member States. In contrast, opposition and appeal proceedings before the EPO could produce a different outcome, as the EPO considers that it is only bound by the EPC under international law, not by Union norms.

However, EPO rejections of European patent applications could not end up before the CJEU, as in such cases there is no access from the EPO to any courts capable of making a preliminary reference. This is problematic, among other things, from the perspective of the functions of the preliminary procedure, as emphasised by the CJEU in Opinion 1/09.[119] Neither the Boards of Appeal of the EPO nor any court could refer a question to the CJEU involving an interpretation or assessment of the validity of the provisions of Union law. If the EPO rejection of a patent application were to be in breach of Union law, that decision could not be the subject of infringement proceedings either. Nor could it easily give rise to Member State liability.[120]

Overall, a convenient juridical construction emerges. The EPO would not be bound by EU norms at any stage: grant, opposition, or administration of unitary effect. Unitary effect would emerge in the absence of *any* administrative act applying Union norms or capable of being challenged before EU Courts. As in a vanishing trick, all EPO decision-making over unitary patents would disappear from sight. Instead, unitary effect would emerge automatically by virtue of Article 3(1) of the EPUE Regulation, once the unitary effect of the European patent 'has been registered in the Register for unitary patent protection'.

The CJEU will likely be able to see through this juridical facade. The EPUE Regulation builds on the granting of European patents by the EPO, as well as on the administrative activities it performs with regard to unitary effect. Although the EPO does not necessarily exercise Union powers when deciding on the grant of European patents,[121] the EU legislator should have ascertained that European patent applications, for which unitary effect is being applied for, are treated in conformity with Union norms, and that there is access to Union courts from the EPO's administrative decisions.

As one of the most experienced judges of the CJEU has earlier emphasised, the availability of appropriate legal remedies against possibly illegal decisions of an international body which the Union has entrusted, is a bottom-line necessity in the Union founded on the rule of law. Without such availability, the Union could circumvent judicial review of its executive acts simply by acting through

[119] Opinion 1/09 (n 10) [83]–[84]. See also Hofmann and Morini (n 99) 433.

[120] The CJEU considered these factors to be significant problems with the European and Community Patents Court in Opinion 1/09 (n 10) [88].

[121] See, however, the subsequent discussion.

and delegating international bodies.[122] An Advocate General of the Court has also recently paid attention to the fact that the model adopted for the unitary patent package did not address the problem discussed by Advocates General (unpublished, in the context of Opinion 1/09) concerning the absence of judicial review from the EPO's decisions to issue EPUEs.[123]

The EPUE Regulation does not ensure EPO compliance with EU norms when deciding on whether to accept or reject a patent application. All the tasks assigned to the EPO concern the post-grant phase, related to the unitary effect to be attached to a granted European patent. Hence, the legal remedies secured in Article 9(3) of the EPUE Regulation do not abolish the problem of access to courts in cases where the EPO refuses to grant or revokes the underlying European patent in conflict with Union norms. Had the administration of unitary patents been left for an agency of the Union in line with the model provided for by the OHIM and the CPVO, the grant decisions would be subject to judicial review, as explained above. Why should the legislative conferral of de facto decision-making powers to a body outside the Union justify lesser remedies?

The fact that the EPC Contracting States have tolerated the absence of judicial review of the EPO's decisions is not relevant. Institutional practice should not be accepted as a sufficient argument to permit the Union legislator to entrust bodies outside the Union framework to take binding decisions without adequate legal safeguards.[124] The European Court of Human Rights (ECtHR) cannot review EPO decisions directly, as it has accepted the immunity enjoyed by the EPO against domestic courts, even where the processes before the EPO appear problematic from the perspective of fair trial rights.[125] This should speak in favour of EU courts' judicial review over EPO decisions.[126] In the absence of adequate protection under the ECHR or Member State constitutions, Union law should secure the applicants' access to courts from the EPO's decisions affecting EU rights.

The argument that the EPO would not apply Union norms and is therefore legitimately outside EU court review is not decisive. It is relevant to ask whether it is acceptable that the Union de facto assigns the granting of unitary patents to

[122] K Lenaerts, 'Regulating the Regulatory Process: "Delegation of Powers" in the European Community' (1993) 18 *EL Rev* 23, 39.

[123] N Jääskinen, 'The Future of European Intellectual Property Law Courts: Intellectual Property and the European Judicial Architecture' in Ohly and Pila (n 3) 217, 222.

[124] See also Hofmann and Morini (n 99) 426.

[125] The same applies to the German Constitutional Court. See BVerfG, 2 BvR 1458/03 vom 3.7.2006, Absatz-Nr (1–25). According to the *Rambus* admissibility decision of the ECtHR (referred to above), for holding the member of the European Convention liable for the EPO's actions, the applicant would have to establish that the protection of Convention rights afforded by the EPO system was 'manifestly deficient'. The ECtHR cannot review EPO decisions directly, as the EPO is an international organ.

[126] Cf Tilmann (n 16) 5, who argues that the ECtHR and the German Constitutional Court have accepted the appeals within the EPO as being in conformity with the principle of judicial review under the ECHR and the German Constitution. However, as already indicated, these courts have not entered into substantive analysis; they have rather accepted the immunity of the EPO's decision-making by resorting to an abstract presumption that the EPC system is in conformity with the European Convention.

an international body outside the Union, which is *not* obliged to apply Union law. Whether the EPO formally applies Union norms or not is not decisive. Either way, de facto decision-making over unitary effect outside the Union institutional structure and beyond the reach of the EU court review is a significant constitutional problem that calls into question the validity of the EPUE Regulation.

It should also be noted that the participating Member States had to be involved in the delegation of administrative powers to the EPO, as the Union is not a contracting party to the EPC. The Union could not by itself transfer the tasks to the EPO within the framework of Article 143 of the EPC.[127] Based on the principle of Union loyalty, the Member States have in such situations a duty to act in the interest of the Union even in the absence of an explicit provision to that effect.[128] The EPUE Regulation makes this obligation explicit and detailed for the participating Member States.

The impossibility resulting from the EPC context of exercising Union competence directly does not affect the existence of the Union's exclusive competence over the administration of unitary effect. The involvement of the participating Member States simply could not be avoided in the achievement of the Union's tasks. Through the EPUE Regulation the Union—with the assistance of the participating Member States—thus de facto transfers administrative decision-making powers over unitary effect to the EPO. The argument that the EPO merely acts as an international body to which the participating Member States have transferred certain tasks based on Article 143 of the EPC[129] thus does not stand critical scrutiny. Behind the participating Member State action is legislative delegation under the exclusive competence of the Union.[130]

The CJEU might assume competence to interpret the agreement between the participating Member States and the EPO: it is possible to treat it as part of Union

[127] See also Jaeger (n 13) 389, who notes that the EU legislator cannot partake in an agreement regulated in EPC, Art 142, as the Union has not concluded the EPC.

[128] See E Neframi, 'The Duty of Loyalty: Rethinking its Scope through its Application in the Field of EU External Relations' (2010) 47 *CML Rev* 323, 351–52, and on the principle of loyalty in EU law in general, M Klamert, *The Principle of Loyalty in EU Law,* Oxford Studies in European Law (Oxford, Oxford University Press, 2014).

[129] Tilmann (n 16) 5. Tilmann's argument would mean that the UPC could review EPO administrative decisions in the light of what has been agreed between the participating Member States and the European Patent Organisation, and not in the light of the EPUE Regulation. These EPO tasks would thus essentially be international law obligations within the framework of the EPC. The UPC could therefore seek a preliminary ruling from the CJEU on the question whether the participating Member States have complied with their obligations under EPUE Regulation, Art 9, but not on the question whether the EPO has complied with Union norms, as in Tilmann's analysis the EPO would not apply the EPUE Regulation and the agreement reached between the participating Member States and the EPO would not constitute Union law, but pure international law under the EPC. Hence, there would be no administrative authority responsible for the unitary effect, whose decisions could be subject to judicial review before EU courts.

[130] EPUE Regulation, Recital 6 states that the Regulation 'constitutes a special agreement within the meaning of Article 142 of the EPC'. From this perspective, too, it would be odd to argue that the grant of tasks to the EPO under EPC, Art 143 by the participating Member States would not involve the exercise of Union competence.

law operating under the Union's exclusive competence.[131] In any case, the CJEU may evaluate the EPO's administrative actions related to unitary effect indirectly through the participating Member States' responsibility to ensure compliance of the EPO's actions with the EPUE Regulation, as well as through a fundamental rights review of Member States' implementation of Union law. To the extent that the participating Member States have assigned the EPO its tasks related to Article 9 of the EPUE Regulation, they have done so while giving effect to Union law obligations. This renders Article 32(1)(i) of the UPCA, the agreement between the participating Member States and the EPO regarding the EPO's administrative tasks, *and* even the EPO's performance of these tasks, subject to CJEU fundamental rights review in line with Article 51(1) of the EU Charter. These norms and the EPO's decision-making regarding unitary effect would then be subject to CJEU fundamental rights review as part of Member States' implementation of EU law.[132] The participating Member States would hence be responsible under the EPUE Regulation and Union fundamental rights law for the EPO's actions related to unitary effect. The EPO's decisions could be reviewed indirectly in preliminary rulings.

However, even though such indirect EU court review of EPO administrative decisions related to unitary effect is feasible, this neither equals direct judicial review of EPO decisions before Union courts, nor compensates for the absence of any court review of EPO rejections of European patent applications for which unitary effect was also requested. The CJEU could on this basis quash the EPUE Regulation, as it did with the Data Retention Directive in *Digital Rights Ireland*.[133] The de facto conferral of administrative decision-making powers to the EPO questions the autonomy, unity and primacy of Union law, as well as the availability of remedies for individuals before courts for breaches of their Union rights. Like the CJEU emphasised in its Opinion 1/91 (EEA), the autonomy of the Union legal order is jeopardised by the de facto allocation of judicial decision-making powers over Union-based rights to bodies outside the Union, where those bodies have neither an obligation to follow the judgments of the CJEU, nor are subject to direct effect and primacy of Union law. Article 47 of the EU Charter requires the right to an effective remedy before a tribunal for any violation of rights or freedoms guaranteed by Union law. It also applies in administrative proceedings and covers any right conferred by EU law.[134]

[131] Analogous to Case C-439/01 *Libor Cipra Vlastimil Kvasnicka and Bezirkshauptmannschaft Mistelbach* [2003] ECR I-745. See also *Neframi* (n 128) 352. The EPO would thus apply this Union law.

[132] Union fundamental rights thus bind the participating Member States in securing judicial review according to EPUE Regulation, Art 9(3) and UPCA, Art 32(1)(i). EU Charter, Art 47 (discussed below) requires the right to an effective remedy before a tribunal for any violation of rights and freedoms guaranteed by the law of the Union. The rules must not make it 'impossible or excessively difficult' to have the UPC review EPO decisions within the scope of the EPUE Regulation, Art 9(1)–(2).

[133] Joined Cases C-293/12 & C-594/12 *Digital Rights Ireland Ltd* (8 April 2014).

[134] Opinion 1/91, *Draft agreement between the Community, on the one hand, and the countries of the European Free Trade Association, on the other, relating to the creation of the European Economic Area* [1991] ECR I-6079. On the EU Charter, Art 47 in this respect see DC Shelton, 'sources of Article 47 Rights' in S Peers et al (eds), *The EU Charter of Fundamental Rights. A Commentary* (Oxford, Hart Publishing, 2014) 1200, 1210.

Intellectual property ownership as a fundamental right, protected under Article 17(2) of the EU Charter, might also be infringed. Under the ECtHR case law, applications for intellectual property protection also enjoy protection under Article 1 of Protocol 1 to the ECHR. The Grand Chamber of the ECtHR stated in *Anheuser-Busch* that a trade mark *application* is protected as a possession.[135] The impact of this ruling likely extends beyond trade mark applications. The general criteria used by the ECtHR when finding that a trade mark application constitutes a possession equally apply to patents. The ECtHR could thus review domestic court and administrative agency decisions refusing the registration of patents.[136] The same premise likely applies to Article 17(2) of the EU Charter. Hence, the absence of judicial remedies for rejection of a European patent application for which unitary effect is also requested might be contrary to a combined reading of Article 17(2) and Article 47 of the EU Charter.

As long as the EPUE is tightly connected to European patents and related EPO granting practice, securing access to Union courts would be difficult in practice, especially as regards EPO rejections of European patent applications. Although the EPO could subject itself to EU court review by waiving its immunity, the reviewing Union court could not simply overrule the EPO decision for infringing EU law. The EPC Contracting States would not accept EU court control of EPO decisions and the subjection of the EPO to a strict obligation to comply with Union law in the granting of European patents. The EPO sees itself essentially as an international body. Non-EU Contracting States to the EPC cannot be presumed to have conferred interpretative jurisdiction on the CJEU over EPO decision-making.[137] As the enlarged Board of Appeal stressed in its *WARF* decision, Article 23(3) of the EPC provides that in their decisions the members of the Boards shall not be bound by any instructions and shall comply only with the provisions of the EPC. Hence, no Board of Appeal of the EPO has 'the power to bind itself to follow a ruling of the [CJEU]' on the interpretation of an EU norm and apply this to a provision of the EPC. Hence, even where the EPC provisions are worded identically with the provisions of the Biotechnology Directive, the Boards of Appeal apply the provision 'because it is law under a specific Rule of the Implementing Regulations to the EPC, and not because the Directive is a source of law to be applied directly'.

As unitary effect has an accessory nature, the reviewing court could not create it independently, in the absence of a related European patent. Access to Union courts following EPO rejections of patent applications would thus be meaningless. With regard to granted EPUEs, access to Union courts could lead to the abolishment of EPUE protection if it was in conflict with Union norms. Yet the Union court decision could not affect the validity of the underlying European patent outside the Union.

The above means that the problem could not be easily remedied. An alternative regime could perhaps separate the granting of European and EPUEs at the EPO

[135] *Anheuser-Busch Inc v Portugal* (Grand Chamber, 11 January 2007) [73]–[78].

[136] See also LR Helfer, 'The New Innovation Frontier? Intellectual Property and the European Court of Human Rights' (2008) 49 *Harvard International Law Journal* 1, 24–26.

[137] *Warf* (n 106), [5]. See also R Fritt, 'New Guidance on the Patentability of Embryonic Stem Cell Patents in Europe' (2009) 27 *Nature Biotechnology* 338.

so that unitary patent protection would be established independently of European patents. Under such a regime, the EPO would be able to apply Union rules to the unitary patent application from the start, and Union courts could review EPO rejections of unitary patent applications without the problems described above. Such a design would differ significantly from the current unitary patent package. Another alternative would be to amend the EPC so as to enable judicial review of all EPO decisions before Union courts.[138] This option is even more unrealistic, as the EPC is not restricted to Union Member States, but covers 38 European states.

VI. Conclusions

The creation of the EPUE by recourse to Union law is not without consequences. It is not possible to treat the operation of the international law instruments and organs, and the Union law instruments and organs, as two neatly separated worlds. Instead they intertwine, with each placing demands on the operation of the other. Rephrasing Koskenniemi's words about international law to fit the Union law context, you 'cannot just take one finger out of [the EU legal order] and pretend it is alive. For the finger to work, the whole body must come along'.[139] Accordingly, the CJEU may find its way to indirectly review the intergovernmental parts of the unitary patent package thought to lie outside its reach. For example, it was argued above that the CJEU could indirectly review the conformity of the UPCA, EPC and EPO decisions related to EPUEs with the Union's fundamental rights norms.

However, the CJEU should *not* try to mend the fragmented and incompletely harmonised unitary patent package through a combination of an extended competence to interpret and an all-embracing teleological method, supposedly leading to a coherent and complete whole. Neither should the CJEU seek to use its newly-found competence to interpret the whole TRIPS Agreement to reach such ends. Such strategies would be both unacceptable and unworkable. There are limits to what the CJEU should try to accomplish in areas where European policy makers have failed. The CJEU has admittedly been very active in patching and expanding the Union's copyright law based on fragmented Directives.[140] However, the democratic legitimacy of it doing so is questionable. Moreover, only the unitary patent package is based on polycentric regulation and administration. This would make CJEU activism more difficult.

[138] Or at least a court capable of making a request for a preliminary ruling to the CJEU.

[139] M Koskenniemi, 'The Fate of Public International Law: Between Technique and Politics' (2007) 70 *MLR* 1, 17.

[140] On this judicial activism, see PB Hugenholtz, 'Copyright in Europe: Twenty Years Ago, Today and What the Future Holds' (2013) 23 *Fordham Intellectual Property, Media & Entertainment Law Journal* 503.

The will of the European community to exclude the CJEU from the interpretation of the unitary patent has led to several constitutional problems. The unitary patent package constitutes a hybrid regime between international and European law, tailored to satisfy the wishes of European patent experts. The position of the UPCA as an *inter se* agreement is problematic, as it includes subject matter belonging to the Union's exclusive competence. The transfer of substantive patent norms from the EPUE Regulation to the UPCA could also have led to an infringement of enhanced cooperation norms and the legal basis of the EPUE Regulation in Article 118 of the TFEU.

Perhaps the most problematic aspect of the unitary patent package relates to the EPO's position in granting EPUEs. The EPO's decisions de facto constitute the EPUE: they decide the original title to the European patent capable of becoming an EPUE, and attach or deny unitary effect to that title. They may revoke the European patent in an opposition procedure, and as a corollary the unitary effect attached to that patent. The EPO will be the only administrative organ involved in granting EPUEs. The unitary effect intended by the EPUE Regulation thus cannot exist without the prior EPO decision to grant the underlying European patent and another decision to register its unitary effect.

To argue that unitary effect becomes established automatically through the direct effect of the EPUE Regulation only misses the significance of these constitutive administrative steps required for the unitary effect to take place. At any stage, the EPO might infringe Union law norms. The European patent might have been granted or rejected in conflict with Union law. Unitary effect might have been accepted or rejected contrary to Union norms, or the patent might have been rejected in an opposition procedure without due regard for EU norms. This means that decision-making power over the fate of unitary patents has in practice been transferred to the EPO without access to Union courts, and with regard to the rejection of patent applications, without access to any courts. This end result is based on the systemic design of the unitary patent package and the provisions of the EPUE Regulation. The transformation approach—the idea that the unitary effect is merely attached to granted European patents as an additional quality—does not abolish this systemic defect of the UPP and the absence of direct access to Union courts from the decisions of the EPO.

The inescapable effect of the adopted arrangements is that EPUE protection might not exist where, according to Union norms, it should exist, and might exist where, according to Union norms, it should not exist. Only in the latter case is *indirect* court review of the EPO grant decision possible before the UPC, and through the preliminary ruling procedure, before the CJEU. The unitary patent package hence builds administratively on a body external to the Union and acting under international law, without any guarantees that this body will apply Union norms, and without adequate judicial review of its decisions before Union or any other courts.

The foregoing analysis of the UPP suggests that there are no solutions to these problems that would not be problematic from the perspective of EU constitutional law. This is satisfying from the perspective of legal scholarship only.

7

A Competition Law Perspective I: Competition Law Aspects of European Patents with Unitary Effect

STEFAN ENCHELMAIER*

I. Introduction

This chapter considers competition law aspects of European patents with unitary effect ('European patents'). The Regulation creating the European patent, Regulation (EU) No 1257/2012,[1] provides in its Article 15 that

> [t]his Regulation shall be without prejudice to the application of competition law.

As a consequence, conduct permissible under the Regulation, it is not for that reason alone allowable under EU competition law.[2] It is, instead, a separate question whether a patentee's conduct is compatible with TFEU, Articles 101 and 102.

'Competition law' is here widely understood as all legal rules in the Treaty on the Functioning of the European Union (TFEU, formerly the Treaty Establishing the European Community, EC) that seek to enable goods and services to flow unhindered between Member States. Patents are creations of the law, and European patents are creations, at least in part, of European Union (EU) law.[3] The law that creates intellectual (and other) property rights is also an important part of any polity's economic law, and so it is appropriate to reflect briefly on the

* Dr iur (Bonn) habil (Munich), LLM (Edinburgh), MA (Oxon), Professor of European and Comparative Law, University of Oxford, and Fellow of Lincoln College, Oxford.

[1] Regulation (EU) No 1257/2012 of the European Parliament and of the Council of 17 December 2012 implementing enhanced cooperation in the area of the creation of unitary patent protection, OJ L361/1 (31 December 2012) (Regulation 1257/2012).

[2] See, eg Case C-457/10 P *AstraZeneca v Commission* (6 December 2012), [132]: 'the illegality of abusive conduct under Article [102 TFEU] is unrelated to its compliance or non-compliance with other legal rules and, in the majority of cases, abuses of dominant positions consist of behaviour which is otherwise lawful under branches of law other than competition law'.

[3] The reasons for the unusual mixture of Union law and international law need not be revisited here; see the discussion by Justine Pila (among others) in ch 2 of this volume.

foundations of the EU's legal system (section II). The focus will then be on the provisions on the free movement of goods (section III) and on competition law in the traditional, narrow sense (section IV). It will be seen that these rules cannot be considered in isolation: they complement each other. It will be concluded that the European patent does not raise any substantially new questions for this area of European Union law (section V).

II. The Creation of an Internal Market as the Primary Object of the EU

At its most basic, the EU is about the creation of the internal market. TFEU, Article 26 (ex EC, Article 14) thus provides,

1. The Union shall adopt measures with the aim of establishing or ensuring the functioning of the internal market, in accordance with the relevant provisions of the Treaties.
2. The internal market shall comprise an area without internal frontiers in which the free movement of goods, persons, services and capital is ensured in accordance with the provisions of the Treaties.

The 'relevant provisions of the Treaties' come in two guises, distinguished by their addressees: some apply to Member States, others to private economic operators ('undertakings' in the language of the Treaty). Nevertheless, in their objective (the creation of the internal market), these provisions complement each other.

TFEU, Article 26(2) lists the 'four freedoms' of the internal market: free movement of goods, freedom to provide services, free movement for employed and self-employed as well as for legal persons and free movement of capital. The removal of the 'internal frontiers' is achieved by prohibitions addressed to the Member States (that is, all bodies vested with, and exercising, powers of public law in the Member States). In the patent law context, the relevant prohibitions are the ones on free movement of goods and, in legislation and case law much less prominently, on freedom to provide services.

What is more, the Treaty addresses prohibitions to undertakings. These prohibitions are, however, not differentiated by the subject matter of the restriction (goods or services) but by the way the restriction arises, namely (simply speaking) by several undertakings forming a cartel, or by one undertaking abusing its dominant position.

Despite these differences, the two groups of provisions serve the same purpose of creating the internal market. This is highlighted by the opening words of the two prohibitions addressed to undertakings, 'prohibited as incompatible with the internal market'. In the same sense, the Court of Justice of the European Union

(CJEU or 'the Court') explained in one of its earliest judgments on the Treaty's competition provsions, *Consten and Grundig*, that

> [a]n agreement between producer and distributor which might tend to restore the national divisions in trade between Member States might be such as to frustrate the most fundamental objecti[ve]s of the [EU]. *The Treaty, whose preamble and content aim at abolishing the barriers between states, and which in several provisions gives evidence of a stern attitude with regard to their reappearance, could not allow undertakings to reconstruct such barriers.* Article [101](1) is designed to pursue this aim, even in the case of agreements between undertakings placed at different levels in the economic process. (Emphasis added)[4]

In a similar vein, the Court held that intellectual property rights (IPRs) form 'an essential element in the system of undistorted competition which the Treaty seeks to establish and maintain'.[5] Such rights allow undertakings to attract and to keep their customers by virtue, in the case of patents, of the unique and innovative technologies which their products or services embody. There is, hence, complementarity between IPRs, free movement, and competition law in the internal market.

This is not to say that there is no tension between, on the one hand, affording a proprietor the means, by granting him a patent, of temporarily excluding all others from free use of the protected invention and, on the other hand, the internal market's emphasis on free trade as well as competition law's misgivings about the creation and maintenance of positions of economic strength. Nevertheless, 'exclusivity' (which is a legal position) is not the same as 'monopoly' (a specific market formation). The balance between the proprietor's interest in the maintenance of his exclusivity, and the public's interest in free trade on open markets, is struck by the doctrine of exhaustion and by the corresponding principle that measures taken to protect the specific subject matter of IPRs are not per se anti-competitive; both are more fully explained below.

III. Free Movement of Goods

The main prohibition addressed to Member States with regard to the free movement of goods is TFEU, Article 34 (ex EC, Article 28), according to which,

> [q]uantitative restrictions on imports and all measures having equivalent effect shall be prohibited between Member States.

[4] Joined Cases 56/64 & 58/64 *Établissements Consten SàRL and Grundig-Verkaufs-GmbH v Commission of the European Economic Community* [1966] ECR 299, 340.

[5] Case C-10/89 *SA CNL-SUCAL NV v HAG GF AG* [1990] ECR I-3711, [13]; Case C-9/93 *IHT Internationale Heiztechnik GmbH and Uwe Danzinger v Ideal-Standard GmbH and Wabco Standard GmbH* [1994] ECR I-2789, [45].

An identically worded prohibition pertaining to exports is contained in TFEU, Article 35 (ex EC, Article 29), and a similar rule concerning the freedom to provide services in TFEU, Article 56 (ex EC, Article 49); below, goods and services will together be referred to as 'products'. The provision of Article 34 has been of paramount importance in the development of the law of the internal market through the case law it has generated, above all others the Court's judgment commonly referred to as *Cassis de Dijon.*[6] Here is not the space to deduce the entirely uncontroversial position that the national courts' upholding a proprietor's insistence on his IPR can amount to a measure having equivalent effect to a quantitative restriction.[7]

Provisions of the Treaty such as Article 34, because they operate by way of prohibition, bring about so-called 'negative'[8] integration (that is, market-opening) between Member States. With regard to virtually all these prohibitions, however, the Treaty contains exceptions. TFEU, Article 36 (ex EC, Article 30) is the relevant provision in the Treaty's chapter on the free movement of goods. It reads,

> [t]he provisions of Articles 34 and 35 shall not preclude prohibitions or restrictions on imports, exports or goods in transit justified on grounds of ... the protection of industrial and commercial property. Such prohibitions or restrictions shall not, however, constitute a means of arbitrary discrimination or a disguised restriction on trade between Member States.

This, and the other exceptions, allows Member States to pursue national policies on the grounds enumerated therein, subject to the requirement that Member States act proportionately. The requirement of proportionality is somewhat clumsily expressed in the second sentence of Article 36.[9] One of the elements of proportionality is that the restriction must not go further than is required to achieve its objective. This is the springboard for the Court's developing the doctrine of exhaustion of IPRs according to which,

> Article 36 only admits derogations from the fundamental principle of the free movement of goods within the [internal] market to the extent to which such derogations are justified for the purpose of safeguarding rights which constitute the specific subject-matter of such property; consequently, the owner of an industrial property right protected by the legislation of a Member State cannot rely on that legislation to prevent the importation or marketing of a product which has been lawfully marketed in another Member State by the owner of the right himself, with his consent, or by a person economically or legally dependent on him.[10]

[6] Case 120/78 *Rewe Zentral-AG v Bundesmonopolverwaltung für Branntwein* [1979] ECR 649, in particular [8] and [14].

[7] The Court in its judgments never discusses the matter but instead averts instantly to the question of justification discussed next in the text above.

[8] From Latin *negare,* to deny, to prohibit.

[9] Case 178/84 *Commission v Germany ('Beer purity')* [1987] ECR 1227, [43]; Case 40/82 *Commission v United Kingdom ('Newcastle poultry disease')* [1982] ECR 2793, [14]–[19].

[10] Case C-10/89 (n 4), [12], with further references.

The specific subject matter of an IPR (in fact, of *all* IPRs), therefore, is the right of first marketing. Once first marketing has occurred, the right is exhausted. It would go beyond this to grant the proprietor any protection against onward sales of the goods that he had marketed himself, or someone else with the proprietor's permission, certainly as long as the goods retain the condition in which they were on first marketing.[11] The same applies to services, to the extent that they are embodied in, say, a physical data storage medium such as a CD/DVD or similar.[12] Such protection against further commercialisation of the original products would be excessive, given that the proprietor, when he decided on the first marketing, was in full control over quantities, prices, distribution channels, and recipients. To allow him to invoke his IPR after exhaustion would, in other words, be disproportionate. It would, hence, not be covered by the exception. It would thus be established that invocation of the exhausted right falls foul of the prohibition in Article 34.

Article 6 of Regulation 1257/2012 adopts the doctrine of exhaustion for the European Patent in that it provides,

> Exhaustion of the rights conferred by a European patent with unitary effect
>
> The rights conferred by a European patent with unitary effect shall not extend to acts concerning a product covered by that patent which are carried out within the participating Member States in which that patent has unitary effect after that product has been placed on the market in the Union by, or with the consent of, the patent proprietor, unless there are legitimate grounds for the patent proprietor to oppose further commercialisation of the product.

The introduction of the European patent, therefore, does not entail any changes to this central area of European Union law: once products embodying a European patent have been put on the market *any*where in the internal market, they can be sold on *every*where in that market. In this respect, it does not matter that the rights of the patentee are uniform throughout the Member States: exhaustion continues to occur as with traditional patents. The specific subject matter of all types of patents, and indeed of all IPRs, is the same.

IV. Competition Provisions Addressed to Private Economic Operators

The second instrument of EU law for the creation of the internal market are the provisions on competition law, TFEU, Articles 101 and 102 (ex EC, Articles 81 and 82). Article 101 proscribes cartels, Article 102 abuses of dominant positions.

[11] Here is not the space to discuss, even only in outline, the question when repackaging is permissible; on this, see Case C-348/04 *Boehringer Ingelheim KG and Others v Swingward Ltd and Dowelhurst Ltd* [2007] ECR I-3391, with a summary of the case law.

[12] See Case C-128/11 *UsedSoft GmbH v Oracle International Corp* (3 July 2012).

Both provisions have a dual objective. First, as has been seen above, they aim at preventing private economic operators from re-erecting barriers to trade between Member States which the four freedoms oblige the Member States to remove. Secondly, they aim at (among others) technological progress.

The Treaty does not spell out what are the aims of its competition law provisions. These aims can, however, be deduced from the text of Article 101,[13] which has three paragraphs. The first stipulates the prohibition of cartels. The third lists the conditions for exemption (among them, as under Article 36, proportionality: 'not indispensable'). The second paragraph, finally ('pursuant to this Article', ie all the Article's paragraphs), makes provision for the nullity of agreements that are caught by the prohibition but fail to meet the conditions for exemption. A contribution to technological progress can justify, pursuant to Article 101(3), a cartel that falls under Article 101(1). There is no indication nor, in fact, any reason to think that prohibited conduct can be exempt from the prohibition if it achieves one set of goals (among them technological progress), while the prohibition itself pursues another set of goals. Article 101(3), therefore, describes the aims pursued by Article 101 in all its paragraphs. This is echoed in Article 101(1)(b), which gives as an example of a prohibited cartel one that limits, inter alia, technical development.

The same is true of Article 102.[14] The Court juxtaposes 'abuse' as prohibited by that prohibition with 'competition on the merits'[15] and additionally, when it gauges justifications, subjects the conduct in question to a test of proportionality. 'Merits' are, in everyday parlance, as much as for the purposes of competition law desirable outcomes intentionally achieved. Article 101(3) is about a cartel's merits, such as are capable of underpinning an exemption from the prohibition in Article 101(1). What is more, Articles 101 and 102 must, in the words of the EC, Article 3(1)(g), be understood as a 'system' to ensure undistorted competition, that is, as a coherent whole.[16] Article 102, therefore, also aims at fostering technological progress.

[13] '3. The provisions of paragraph 1 may, however, be declared inapplicable in the case of:
- any agreement or category of agreements between undertakings,
- any decision or category of decisions by associations of undertakings,
- any concerted practice or category of concerted practices,
which contributes to improving the production or distribution of goods or to promoting technical or economic progress, while allowing consumers a fair share of the resulting benefit, and which does not: (a) impose on the undertakings concerned restrictions which are not indispensable to the attainment of these objectives; (b) afford such undertakings the possibility of eliminating competition in respect of a substantial part of the products in question'.

[14] It reads: 'Any abuse by one or more undertakings of a dominant position within the internal market or in a substantial part of it shall be prohibited as incompatible with the internal market in so far as it may affect trade between Member States. Such abuse may, in particular, consist in: (a) ... (b) limiting production, markets or technical development to the prejudice of consumers; (c), (d) ....'

[15] See, most recently, *AstraZeneca* (n 2), [74], [75].

[16] Now Protocol No 27 on the internal market and competition, introduced by the Lisbon Treaty. The Protocol has the same wording as the old Article, and it has equal rank to the Treaty. Its content was spirited out of sight for reasons of political expedience, namely to placate French voters after the referendum (with negative outcome) on the draft Constitution for Europe in May 2005.

A. Prohibition of Restrictions of Competition by Agreements etc, TFEU, Article 101(1)

The 'technology bias' (as just described) of Article 101 has consequences for the treatment of patents under that provision as much as under EU competition law generally. As stated above, a patent gives the proprietor control over the production and marketing of goods and services embodying the protected invention. With regard to this particular invention, the proprietor can (if he so chooses) exclude all competition in the use of the protected technology. Nevertheless, the very development of that technology took place in competition with other competitors working on solutions to the same technological problem, and with those (if any) who had already found different solutions. Patent law rewards such development with a temporary, legally enforceable exclusivity, and competition law also looks on it favourably (see above).

Anything done in defence of this exclusivity, and any other exercise of the rights flowing from the patent, in particular the granting of licences, will therefore prima facie be compatible with the requirements of competition law. Nonetheless, as under Article 36 and in keeping with what was above said about Articles 101 and 102, anything that goes beyond this defence or other exercise will fall foul of the requirements of the Treaty. The proportionality of any action taken by the patentee is, hence, again of crucial significance.

Of particular relevance in this context are territorial restrictions imposed by the licensor on his licensees. Such restrictions, however, are specifically dealt with in the Block Exemption Regulations discussed below. Because of the limits that these Regulations impose on restrictions, patentees have been looking for legal alternatives. The search was for a means of controlling the quantities of pharmaceuticals that are exported from one group of Member States into another. In the first group are those (predominantly southern) Member States that impose price caps on medicines whose costs are reimbursable in the framework of those Member States' health care systems. In the second group are those (mostly northern) Member States that do not impose such caps.

Patentees found a solution in supply quotas that are imposed unilaterally by a manufacturer/proprietor on its distributors. These must be imposed unilaterally (against the will of the other side) because otherwise, if the quotas are met by the express or only tacit consent of distributors, there is an 'agreement' in the sense of Article 101(1). As the General Court (then the Court of First Instance) explained,

> [t]he right of a manufacturer faced … with [parallel imports from Member States with price caps undermining his prices in Member States without such caps] to adopt the solution which seems to him to be the best is qualified by the Treaty provisions on competition only to the extent that he must comply with the prohibitions referred to in Articles [101 and 102]. Accordingly, provided he does so without abusing a dominant position, and there is no concurrence of wills between him and his wholesalers, a manufacturer may adopt the supply policy which he considers necessary, even if, by the very

> nature of its aim, for example, to hinder parallel imports, the implementation of that policy may entail restrictions on competition and affect trade between Member States.[17]

Where an agreement between supplier and wholesaler had been found, however, patentees argued that such agreements did not restrict competition to the detriment of consumers and were, therefore, not prohibited under Article 101(1). This was because the restriction of parallel trade pursued the objective of ensuring sufficient profits for the financing of research and development (R&D). The General Court (then the Court of First Instance) was persuaded. It characterised the economic context of the problem as follows:

> [T]he medicines sector is characterised by the importance of competition by innovation. R&D is costly and risky. Its cost is simultaneously a fixed cost (it is not connected with the number of medicines sold), a joint cost (it is incurred upstream from production and distribution and, in part, is not linked with a particular medicine) and a global cost (it is not connected with a particular country). It is most frequently financed from an undertaking's own funds rather than from borrowing. It therefore requires an optimum flow of income. The optimisation of income may be ensured by adapting the prices of medicines to the preferences of final consumers, where those preferences differ. Price differentiation thus allows the cost of R&D to be recovered from the final consumers who are prepared to pay for it. That practice of differentiated prices, which is presented here in a simplified form, is known to economists as 'Ramsey Pricing'.[18]

The customers of parallel traders in medicines, however, are not patients but directly or indirectly (via doctors and pharmacists) the operators of the various health insurance schemes in the Member States, be they public or private. Because of the regulatory environment on the procurement market, price competition plays only a limited role: savings achieved by providers are not immediately passed on to patients, but only in the medium to long-term (if at all) through lower or stable insurance premia. With regard to parallel trade, therefore, the General Court found that it,

> has the effect of reducing [proprietors'] income, to an uncertain but real degree. That practice, which economists know as 'free riding', is characterised by the fact that the intermediary leaves the role which he traditionally plays in the value chain and becomes an arbitrageur and thus obtains a greater part of the profit. The legitimacy of that transfer of wealth from producer to intermediary is not in itself of interest to competition law, which is concerned only with its impact on the welfare of the final consumer. In so far as the intermediary participates in intra-brand competition, parallel trade may have a pro-competitive effect. In the medicines sector, however, that activity is also seen in a special light, since it does not bring any significant added value for the final consumer. … The fact that the profit is retained by the producer will in all likelihood give rise to a gain in efficiency by comparison with the situation in which the profit is shared with

[17] Case T-41/46 *Bayer AG et al v Commission et al* [2000] ECR I-3383, [176], confirmed in Joined Cases C-2/01 & C-3/01 P *Bundesverband der Arzneimittelimporteure v Commission ('Bayer/Adalat')* [2004] ECR I-23, [110], [122] and [123].

[18] T-168/01 *GlaxoSmithKline Services v Commission* [2006] ECR II-2969, [271].

> the intermediary, because a rational producer which is able to ensure the profitability of its innovations and which operates in a sector characterised by healthy competition on innovation has every interest in reinvesting at least a part of its surplus profit in innovation.[19]

The Court of Justice, however, saw things differently. In a brief rebuke, it held that,

> with respect to the [General Court's] statement that, while it is accepted that an agreement intended to limit parallel trade must in principle be considered to have as its object the restriction of competition, that applies in so far as it may be presumed to deprive final consumers of the advantages of effective competition in terms of supply or price, the Court notes that neither the wording of Article [101(1)] nor the case-law lend support to such a position. First of all, there is nothing in that provision to indicate that only those agreements which deprive consumers of certain advantages may have an anti-competitive object. Secondly, it must be borne in mind that the Court has held that, like other competition rules laid down in the Treaty, Article [101(1)] aims to protect not only the interests of competitors or of consumers, but also the structure of the market and, in so doing, competition as such. Consequently, for a finding that an agreement has an anti-competitive object, it is not necessary that final consumers be deprived of the advantages of effective competition in terms of supply or price.[20]

The argument derived from the wording of the Treaty is as uncontroversial as it is, perhaps, unsatisfying. The second of the ECJ's arguments, however, correctly exposes the weakness in the General Court's reasoning. It is competition as such that is the best guarantee that consumers' interests will ultimately prevail. The same follows from what was above said about Article 101(3): the benefit to consumers is in that provision stipulated as a condition for the legality of restrictions of competition precisely, so that the overall result is the same as if undistorted competition prevailed. In other words, the only difference between the first and third paragraphs of Article 101 is the restriction of competition, not the final outcome for consumers.

The importance of competition as the ultimate safeguard of consumers' interests is further highlighted in the last condition in Article 101(3), namely that competition must not be eliminated. If that were the result of an agreement, it would not be exemptible, despite any short-term benefits to consumers. The only reliable spur for undertakings not to lose sight of their customers' interests is the presence of alternative offers, actual or potential, on the market.

In this respect, it does not make a difference what type of patent is involved. The introduction of European patents does not, in other words, require any adaptation of existing competition law doctrines. In particular, the uniform effect of the patent does not mean equal conditions of competition on all the markets that are affected. Geographical subdivision of licences is already permissible. This is all

[19] Ibid, [273] and [274].

[20] Joined Cases C-501/06 P, C-513/06 P, C-515/06 P & C-519/06 P *GlaxoSmithKline Services et al v Commission et al* [2009] ECR I-9291, [62], [63].

that needs to be said under Article 101(1) in the space available here. In practice, undertakings will be more concerned whether their agreements for patent licences or transfers come within the ambit of one of the Block Exemption Regulations to be discussed next.

B. Block Exemption Regulations

TFEU, Article 101(3) is couched in rather general terms. It offers some guidance, but provides little legal certainty to undertakings who want to gauge the legality of a proposed or existing agreement that is caught by Article 101(1). Until 2004, undertakings had to notify all such agreements to the Commission if they sought an exemption. The Commission had the sole right to grant exemptions in application of Article 101(3) (then, successively, EC, Articles 85(3) EEC and 81(3)). Its personnel resources, however, were never sufficient to adopt more than a handful of individual exemptions for the thousands of notifications it received, in particular immediately after the introduction of the notification requirement. Since this requirement has been abolished and Article 101(3) has become directly applicable, national courts and competition authorities, but first and foremost the undertakings themselves, have to assess whether the conditions for an exemption are fulfilled.

To ease the Commission's workload under the old system, and to afford undertakings legal certainty under the new, the Council has authorised the Commission to adopt Regulations to exempt particular types of agreement *en bloc* from the prohibition in Article 101(1). The exemption will be automatic, without any granting by the Commission or other authority being required, as long as the conditions in the Block Exemption Regulation are fulfilled. These conditions are, in essence, more concrete renditions of the conditions for exemption in Article 101(3), tailored to the characteristics, and repercussions on competition, of specific types of agreements. As far as patents are concerned, the following two Block Exemption Regulations are of particular importance.

i. Block Exemption Regulation (EU) No 316/2014 for Technology Transfer Agreements

Article 3(2), third sub-paragraph of Regulation 1257/2012 provides that the European Patent

> may be licensed in respect of the whole or part of the territories of the participating Member States.

This is in keeping with national patent laws, which also allow the territorial subdivision of licences. Such divisions, however, have a tendency, if not the outright purpose, to create or maintain frontiers within the EU's internal market. The first Recital to the Regulation expressly invokes the creation of the internal market as one of its motivations and justifications.[21] For this reason, Article 3 of the Regulation does not (and cannot) set out of application the (other) provisions for the creation of the internal market, among them those discussed above, not least because a Regulation is inferior in rank to the Treaty. Accordingly, Article 15 of the Regulation provides that

> [t]his Regulation shall be without prejudice to the application of competition law.

In keeping with what was said above about EU competition law more generally, the Block Exemption Regulation for technology transfer agreements takes a positive view of such agreements. According to its fourth Recital,

> [t]echnology transfer agreements concern the licensing of technology rights. Such agreements will usually improve economic efficiency and be pro-competitive as they can reduce duplication of research and development, strengthen the incentive for the initial research and development, spur incremental innovation, facilitate diffusion and generate product market competition.

Nevertheless, Article 4 of the Regulation lists so-called 'hardcore' restrictions, whose presence excludes an agreement altogether from the benefit of the block exemption. In this provision, the Commission sets out in some detail which territorial restrictions in licences are permissible.

Here is not the place to discuss these rules in detail. Suffice it to say that the rules of the Block Exemption Regulation apply regardless of the type of patent, that is whether it has unitary effect or not. With regard to territorial subdivisions of licences, the Regulation defines autonomously what belongs to the irreducible core of patentees' rights with regard to EU competition law. Any restrictions that go beyond this fail the proportionality requirement in TFEU, Article 101(3), as spelled out specifically for technology transfer agreements in the Block Exemption Regulation.

ii. Block Exemption Regulation (EU) No 1217/2010 for Research and Development Agreements

The picture is similar with regard to the Block Exemption Regulation for research and development agreements. Such agreements may provide for the joint exploitation by the parties of the results of their joint research and development. Among these results, the Regulation envisages patents in particular. These can take any form, including that of European patents. Again, however, the specific arrangements with regard to their exploitation are subject to an autonomous assessment under the competition rules. As a consequence, the Regulation imposes substantial fetters on

[21] 'The creation of the legal conditions enabling under takings to adapt their activities in manufacturing and distributing products across national borders and providing them with greater choice and more opportunities contributes to the attainment of the objectives of the Union set out in Article 3(3) of the Treaty on European Union. Uniform patent protection within the internal market, or at least a significant part thereof, should feature amongst the legal instruments which undertakings have at their disposal'.

the power of the patentee to limit the use that licensees may make of the protected technology.

While the language is slightly different as between the two Block Exemption Regulations, the one on research and development also contains a list of clauses whose presence denies the entire agreement the benefit of exemption under the Regulation. Again, the details of the entries on this list are immaterial. As before, the Regulation establishes an autonomous regime that limits the rights flowing from any patent, including European patents.

C. Prohibition of Abuse of Dominant Position, TFEU, Article 102

IPRs grant exclusive control over the exploitation of the invention, reputation, design, and so on. This exclusive position bears some similarity with a monopoly, a market structure that Community competition law shuns. The prerogative of a patentee relates, however, only to the exploitation of one particular invention, and mutatis mutandis for the holders of other IPRs. It is a question for traditional market analysis whether this exclusivity amounts to a monopoly on the market for products like the one embodying that invention.[22] In other words, an undertaking is not dominant in the sense of Article 102 merely because it holds intellectual property rights.[23] From this, it follows that not every act to exploit or defend the right, including a refusal to license, is per se abusive.[24] This question, too, is determined in the same way as every other allegation of abuse under Article 102.

The first step in any assessment under Article 102 is the determination of the relevant market. This is subdivided into two: the relevant product market, and the relevant geographic market. The relevant product market consists of those goods and services that consumers consider interchangeable with regard to the products' characteristics, uses and price. The relevant geographic market comprises all those territories between which there are no barriers to market access. Such barriers can be of a legal or factual nature. Legal barriers to market access are, for instance, the requirement of import licences and, relevant for present purposes, IPRs. Patents, in particular, are territorial and remain so even after the introduction of the European patent—uniform is only the protection that it provides in the various Member States, Article 3(1), first sentence, and (2), first sentence and Article 5 of

[22] Case C-40/70 *Sirena v Eda* [1971] ECR 69, [16]; Case C-78/70 *Deutsche Grammophon v Metro-SB-Großmärkte* [1971] ECR 487, [16]. Action taken by the rightholder to enforce the intellectual property right constitutes no agreement or other proscribed conduct under Art 101(1), either: Case 24/67 *Parke, Davis v Probel* [1968] ECR 55, 71.

[23] *AstraZeneca* (n 2), [186]: 'although the mere possession of intellectual property rights cannot be considered to confer such a position, their possession is none the less capable, in certain circumstances, of creating a dominant position, in particular by enabling an undertaking to prevent effective competition on the market'.

[24] Case 102/77 *Hoffmann-La Roche v Centrapharm* [1978] ECR 1139, [16]; Case 238/87 *Volvo v Veng* [1988] ECR 6211, [8].

Regulation 1257/2012. The most important factual barriers to market entry are transport costs.

The second step in the assessment is to gauge whether the undertaking in question occupies a dominant position on the internal market or a substantial part of it. The Court has in this context developed a rather convoluted formula that boils down to defining a dominant position as insulation from the pressures of competition.[25]

Thirdly, the dominant undertaking's conduct must amount to an abuse of its position. In this respect, Article 102 contains a number of specific examples ('Such abuse may, in particular'), but prohibits abuse in general ('Any abuse'). The Court has emphasised that,

> 'abuse', for the purpose of Article [102], is an objective concept referring to the behaviour of an undertaking in a dominant position which is such as to influence the structure of a market on which, as a result of the very presence of the undertaking in question, the degree of competition is already weakened and which, through recourse to methods different from those conditioning normal competition in products or services on the basis of the transactions of commercial operators, has the effect of hindering the maintenance of the degree of competition still existing in the market or the growth of that competition.[26]

The 'objective' nature of the concept of 'abuse' means that a dominant undertaking has a special responsibility not further to weaken competition.[27] As a consequence, such an undertaking may find itself deprived of the right to adopt a course of conduct or to take measures which are not in themselves abuses and which would even be unobjectionable if adopted or taken by non-dominant undertakings.[28] Nevertheless, as has already been seen, the dominant undertaking may adduce justifications akin to those under Article 101(3) in order to fend off the accusation of having committed an abuse.

Lastly, the abuse must take place within the internal market 'or a substantial part of it', and it must be capable of affecting trade between Member States. The uniform effect of a European patent does not make a difference in this respect: according to Regulation 1257/2012, Article 3(2), third sub-paragraph, such a patent may be licensed in respect of the whole or part of the territories of the participating Member States. There is, therefore, no change to the position that for the purpose of determining whether a specific territory for which a licence is refused is large enough to amount to 'a substantial part of the internal market' the pattern and volume of the production and consumption of the product in question

[25] Case 85/76 *Hoffmann-La Roche & Co AG v Commission* [1979] ECR 461, [38]: 'The dominant position thus referred to relates to a position of economic strength enjoyed by an undertaking which enables it to prevent effective competition being maintained on the relevant market by affording it the power to behave to an appreciable extent independently of its competitors, its customers and ultimately of the consumers'.

[26] Case T-111/96 *ITT Promedia NV v Commission* [1998] ECR II-2937, [138].

[27] See, most recently, *AstraZeneca* (n 2), [134].

[28] *Promedia* (n 26), [139].

as well as the habits and economic opportunities of vendors and purchasers must be considered.[29]

As far as the required effect on trade between Member States is concerned, the Court held that when the holder of a dominant position obstructs acccss to the market by competitors, it makes no difference whether such conduct is confined to a single Member State as long as it is capable of affecting patterns of trade and competition on the common market.[30] The position is, hence, the same as under Article 101.

i. Quota and Dual Pricing

In a similar manner as under Article 101(1),[31] the ECJ had to deal under Article 102 with quota and dual pricing by a dominant supplier of patented medicines. The quota were imposed by the patentee on those of its wholesalers who were known to have ordered quantities for export (by way of parallel trade) from price-capped Member States to Member States with free(r) price formation. The Court's solution under Article 102 mirrors that under Article 101(1). The ECJ explained that,

> although a pharmaceuticals company in a dominant position, in a Member State where prices are relatively low, cannot be allowed to cease to honour the ordinary orders of an existing customer for the sole reason that that customer, in addition to supplying the market in that Member State, exports part of the quantities ordered to other Member States with higher prices, it is none the less permissible for that company to counter in a reasonable and proportionate way the threat to its own commercial interests potentially posed by the activities of an undertaking which wishes to be supplied in the first Member State with significant quantities of products that are essentially destined for parallel export.[32]

In other words, it is clear that a dominant supplier need not accede to its distributors' demands for ever increasing quantities whose marketing by the distributors would only go towards undermining the supplier's pricing policies in the various Member States. A freeze on quantities, therefore, seems a safe option. An outright refusal in future to supply any quantities at all to (part-time) parallel traders can with equal certainty be classified as abusive. The situation is less clear, however, with regard to any cuts to quantities supplied in the past, short of a complete cessation of supplies.

In that regard, the Court instructed the national court

> to ascertain whether [past] orders are ordinary in the light of both the previous business relations between the pharmaceuticals company holding a dominant position and the wholesalers concerned and the size of the orders in relation to the requirements of the market in the Member State concerned.[33]

[29] Joined Cases 40/73–48/73, 50/73, 54/73–56/73, 111/73, 113/73 & 114/73 *Suiker Unie et al v Commission* [1975] ECR 1663, [371]–[372].

[30] Case 322/81 *Michelin v Commission* [1983] ECR 3461, [103].

[31] See section IV.A.

[32] Joined Cases C-68/06–C-478/06 *Sot Lelos kai Sia EE et al v GlaxoSmithKline* [2008] ECR I-7139, [71].

[33] Ibid, [73].

While the Court does not explain the application of this formula any further, the point of reference is apparently the aggregate demand on the national market of the Member State in question. To fulfil any orders beyond what is necessary to satisfy this demand is, therefore, at the discretion of the patentee. As a consequence, the patentee can refuse to supply quantities commensurate with those which, on objective if necessarily often circumstantial evidence, have gone into parallel trade.

From this arises a problem: the total quantity sold on the home market is the sum of the quantities sold by individual wholesalers. Their respective market shares will fluctuate over time, if within certain bands. The quantities supplied by the former parallel traders will be able to grow only in line with overall demand, that is their market share will become static. These traders will no longer be able to expand their market share at the expense of other traders on the market. It is impossible to say whether the Court has envisaged this consequence. It could be argued that these traders have only themselves to blame. Nevertheless, this outcome sits uneasily with the Court's insistence that even in a highly regulated market such as pharmaceuticals, parallel trade has a beneficial function in maintaining at least remnants of competition on the markets targeted by such trade.[34]

ii. Dominant Proprietors' Refusal to License

It has been seen above that just as the holding of IPRs does not of itself confer on the proprietor a dominant position, neither does the exercise of the rights flowing from, say, a patent constitute without further an abuse, even where a dominant position has been found. In principle, therefore, the patentee is free to decide whether and to whom to grant licences. Nevertheless, proprietors are not by virtue of their IPRs immune from scrutiny under Article 102 either, and so the Court has in certain circumstances found a refusal to license to be abusive. Such tests as can be found in the case law are very much tailored to the specific circumstances of the case in hand.

Before the most recent leading case, *Microsoft*, it could be said that a refusal to license by a dominant proprietor is abusive if the refusal suppresses a new product for which there is potential consumer demand; if the refusal is not justified by objective considerations and if the refusal reserves the market for the proprietor by eliminating all competition on that market.[35] In *Microsoft*, the General Court summarised the position as follows:

> It follows from the case-law that the refusal by an undertaking holding a dominant position to license a third party to use a product covered by an intellectual property right cannot in itself constitute an abuse of a dominant position within the meaning of Article [102]. It is only in exceptional circumstances that the exercise of the exclusive right by

[34] See section V.A.

[35] Joined Cases C-241/91 & C-242/91 P *Radio Telefis Eireann et al v Commission* [1995] ECR I-743, [52]–[56]; Case C-418/01 *IMS Health v NDC Health* [2004] ECR I-5039, [28]–[29], [38], [44]–[46], [49].

> the owner of the intellectual property right may give rise to such an abuse. It also follows from that case-law that the following circumstances, in particular, must be considered to be exceptional:
>
> — in the first place, the refusal relates to a product or service indispensable to the exercise of a particular activity on a neighbouring market;
> — in the second place, the refusal is of such a kind as to exclude any effective competition on that neighbouring market;
> — in the third place, the refusal prevents the appearance of a new product for which there is potential consumer demand.
>
> Once it is established that such circumstances are present, the refusal by the holder of a dominant position to grant a licence may infringe Article [102] unless the refusal is objectively justified.[36]

It will be noticed that 'in particular' still leaves the door open for ad hoc tweaking of the test but at least there is now some measure of legal certainty. One thing that can be said without doubt, however, is that again the nature of the patent whose licensing is refused is immaterial.

iii. Abuses in the Obtaining of Intellectual Property Rights

As was emphasised above, the mere holding of IPRs does not without further place an undertaking in a dominant position. Where, however an undertaking holds a dominant position, this position imposes a special responsibility on the undertaking. This responsibility does not prevent the undertaking from adopting a strategy whose object it is to minimise the erosion of its sales and to enable it to deal with competition from generic products. The Court held that such a strategy is legitimate and is part of the normal competitive process, provided that the conduct envisaged does not depart from practices coming within the scope of competition on the merits, which is such as to benefit consumers.[37] By contrast, a dominant undertaking must not use regulatory procedures in such a way as to prevent or make more difficult the entry of competitors on the market, in the absence of grounds relating to the defence of the legitimate interests of an undertaking engaged in competition on the merits or in the absence of objective justification.[38]

As a consequence, the Court firmly rejected the notion that an undertaking in a dominant position, considering that it can lay claim to a right (*in casu*, a Supplementary Protection Certificate for a medicine whose patent protection was about to expire), may use any means to obtain that right, and even have recourse to highly misleading representations with the aim of leading public authorities into error. Such an approach was manifestly not consistent with competition on the merits and the specific responsibility on such an undertaking not to

[36] Case T-201/04 *Microsoft v Commission* [2007] ECR II-3601, [331]–[333].
[37] *AstraZeneca* (n 2), [129].
[38] Ibid, [134].

prejudice, by its conduct, effective and undistorted competition within the European Union.[39]

Again, however, the precise geographical extent of the IPR, and the nature of the protection (uniform or otherwise) that it enjoys in each territory in which it is granted, does not affect the abusive nature of the conduct described above.

iv. Vexatious Litigation

The European patent offers inventors yet another possibility of obtaining property rights, with the concomitant new court system for defending these rights. The multiplication of layers of protection enables proprietors to start multiple proceedings, using the various patent systems, against their competitors. Such multiplicity of litigation might financially exhaust smaller competitors, and deter others from challenging the proprietor's position on the market in the first place. The European patent thus adds to the possibilities for patentees to litigate their competitors into submission. It is, therefore, worth asking whether such litigation might be abusive under TFEU, Article 102. Presented with this question, the Court held that,

> the ability to assert one's rights through the courts and the judicial control which that entails constitute the expression of a general principle of law which underlies the constitutional traditions common to the Member States and which is also laid down in Articles 6 and 13 of the European Convention for the Protection of Human Rights and Fundamental Freedoms of 4 November 1950. As access to the Court is a fundamental right and a general principle ensuring the rule of law, it is only in wholly exceptional circumstances that the fact that legal proceedings are brought is capable of constituting an abuse of a dominant position within the meaning of Article [102].[40]

The Court establishes the presence of such wholly exceptional circumstances with the help of two criteria. These must be cumulatively fulfilled, but are each narrowly construed in view of the importance of the right of access to the courts. First, the action must, on an objective view, be manifestly unfounded. Secondly, the aim of the action must be to eliminate competition.

As a consequence, the mere bringing of an unfounded action is not in itself abusive. This will be the case only where proceedings are instigated specifically with the object of restricting competition. What is more, the action is 'manifestly unfounded', viewed *ex ante,* only if it cannot reasonably be considered to be an attempt to assert the rights of the undertaking concerned. Put differently, the question is whether such an action was intended to assert what that undertaking could, at that moment, reasonably consider to be its rights. Only where it is otherwise can it be assumed that the litigation could only serve to harass the opposing party. Conversely, if the action is (foreseeably) well-founded, the patentee acts within its rights and does commit an abuse by taking the competitor to court.

[39] Ibid, [98].
[40] *Promedia* (n 28), [60] (references omitted).

In this case, it does not matter if the resulting elimination or restriction of competition is anticipated and desired by the patentee.[41]

In this context, the taking out of a European patent and the bringing of an action based on this patent will be assessed under the same rules as just set out. These patents are available to everyone, and the choice of such a patent over other possible modes of protection is entirely neutral from the perspective of competition law. The same is true of any measures taken in defence of such a patent: these will be abusive only if the above criteria are fulfilled, not merely because the patentee has sought a European patent rather than, or in addition to, any other kind of patent.

V. Conclusion

European patents may or may not make a substantial contribution to the further development of the internal market as an area without internal frontiers in which the free movement of goods and services is guaranteed. This will depend on a multitude of factors that are explored in other chapters of this book. As far as competition law is concerned, however, it is safe to predict that the arrival of European patents will not require much, if any, adaptation to existing principles. As has been seen above, the Treaty's provisions on the free movement of goods and on competition (antitrust), as interpreted by the EU courts, are well equipped to accommodate the new type of intellectual property. With regard to the free movement of goods, the doctrine of exhaustion will apply to European patents as it does to all other patents. Concerning EU competition law, such territorial limitations as can be imposed on licensees of a European patent are already known from the existing patents, and mechanisms exist that prevent any illegitimate divisions of the internal market. By and large, a fair and workable compromise has been found between, on the one hand, proprietors' interest in the exploitation and defence of the exclusivity that the patent grants them and, on the other hand, the interest of consumers everywhere in being able to obtain the most technologically advanced products at the lowest price available anywhere.

41 Ibid, [56], [61], [72] and [73].

8

A Competition Law Perspective II: The Relationship between Patents and Competition Rules

STEVEN ANDERMAN*

I. Introduction

The introduction of the European patent with unitary effect raises the intriguing question whether it will affect the existing relationship between patents and the competition rules. Will the change from patent legislation based at national level to patent legislation based at European level change the patent/competition interface? Historically, the interpretation given to the relationship between patents and the competition rules appears to have been influenced by the position of patent laws as legislation of the Member States compared to the basis of competition law as rules in the EU Treaty. Could the new status of patents remove the trump card that subordinates the exercise of patent rights to the Treaty based competition rules?

The answer to this question is particularly important because the commercial practices and strategies of corporate patent owners in recent years have increasingly raised the profile of conflict of patent practices with competition law. For a long while the concerns of competition law with IPRs were focused on patent and know how licensing and patent settlement agreements with the occasional foray into refusals to supply copyright protected data. In 2005, the basis for a competition law remedy of compulsory licence was increased by the *Microsoft* case.[1] More recently, corporate strategies involving patents have resulted in competition cases involving the misuse of patents. The *AstraZeneca* case raised a new issue of competition law when the patent owning pharmaceutical company unlawfully extended the period of patent protection by giving misleading information to

* Emeritus Professor of Law, University of Essex and Visiting Professor of European Law, University of Stockholm.

[1] Case T-201/04 *Microsoft v Commission* [2007] ECR II-3601 (*Microsoft*).

obtain a Supplementary Protection Certificate.[2] The Pharmaceutical Sectoral Inquiry of the Competition Directorate of the EU Commission has resulted in dawn raids and investigation of the practices of several firms with expiring patents on blockbuster drugs making 'payments for delay' to generic competitors to delay their post-expiry entry.[3] In the context of industrial standards in high technology industries, some owners of standard essential patents (SEPs) have insisted upon higher than FRAND (fair, reasonable and non-discriminatory) payments despite a FRAND commitment.[4] Others have applied for injunctions to enforce standard essential patents against willing licensees while under a FRAND obligation.[5] Some patentees, including patent assertion entities who buy up patent portfolios from patentees, have made baseless and vexatious claims for patent infringement[6] and some IP owners have refused to licence an IPR to 'follow on' inventors.[7] These cases will be described in greater detail later in this chapter but they all indicate that patent owners are engaging in commercial strategies that give rise to conduct that is prohibited by the existing competition rules. Could a new European unitary patent system have an impact on the way EU competition law limits the commercial practices of patentees? Would the creation of a unitary patent system at European level affect the current 'accommodation' of the competition rules with the exercise of patent rights?

II. Understanding the Status of Patents in Relation to the Competition Rules

The effect of a unitary European patent on the relationship between patents and competition law will ultimately depend upon how the EU courts look upon the foundations of that relationship. For many years it seemed as if patents were limited by the competition rules, simply because the former were based upon national laws, whereas the latter were embedded in the EU Treaty. The Court of Justice regularly affirmed that the exercise of IPRs must in principle be compatible with the competition rules, Articles 101 and 102, as well as the rules of freedom of movement of goods, Articles 34–37.[8] In the *Parke Davis* case,[9] the Court upheld the entitlement of the patent holder to exercise the patent but only because it was

[2] Case C-457/10 P *AstraZeneca v Commission* (6 December 2012).
[3] *Lundbeck* IP/13/563 (19 June 2013) (pay for delay agreement resulting in fine for Lundbeck and generics).
[4] Case COMP/38.636 *Rambus*, OJ C30/17 (6 February 2010).
[5] See Case C-170/13 *Huawei v ZTE* (reference to the CJEU).
[6] See Case T-111/96 *ITT Promedia v Commission* [1998] ECR II-02937; Case T-119/09 *Protégé International v Commission* (13 September 2012).
[7] See *Microsoft* (n 1).
[8] Case 24/67 *Parke Davis & Co v Probel* [1968] ECR 55.
[9] Ibid.

not contrary to the competition rules in the Treaty. In *Consten and Grundig*[10] the Court was unwilling to allow the exercise of a trade mark under national law to 'frustrate' the competition rules in the Treaty.[11] The Court's judgments appeared to suggest that it was because the patent rules were based on national laws that they were subject to the Treaty based competition rules thus offering the possibility that if patent legislation ever achieved equivalent European wide status that would cause a rethink of the relationship between the two systems of law.

These cases also had to deal with TFEU, Article 345 (ex EC, Article 295) which provides that the Treaties 'shall in no way prejudice *the rules in the Member States* governing the system of property ownership'. This raised the question of the scope of EU competition law vis-à-vis patents as well as other IPRs. The Court dealt with this issue by limiting the scope of the patent legislative 'rules' to those that governed the *grant* of patents and treating the *exercise* of patent property rights as subject to the competition rules. As the Court stated in *Consten and Grundig*, to require the firm

> to refrain from using rights under national trade mark law in order to set an obstacle to parallel trade does not affect the grant of those rights but only limits their exercise to the extent necessary to give effect to the prohibition under Article [101(1)].[12]

However, to assume that the 'subordination' of the exercise of patent rights to the competition rules was due only to their foundation in national legislation at the time was to misread the actual basis for the Court's judgments. The thinking of the Court in making the grant/exercise distinction, sometimes called the existence/exercise distinction, was, and continues to be, an acknowledgement that since the patent laws, even at national level, are public laws, the grant of the patent is a decision of public law, based on legislation. From that point of view it matters little that the legislation which is the source of the grant is national or Community based. The crucial point about the grant/exercise distinction, is that while the grant of the patent right may be a matter of *public* law whatever the legislative source, the patent itself once granted is regarded as the *private* property of its owner.

This private property right is one that does not consist of an absolute right against state regulation of market behaviour.[13] It is subject to the public law regulation of the competition rules. Even in the USA where patents and copyright have a base in the US Constitution, as well as Federal legislation, the exercise of patents is subject to the limits provided by the antitrust rules.[14] As the US Court of Appeals Federal Circuit stated in *US v Microsoft*,[15] it was 'frivolous' to argue

[10] Joined Cases 56/64 & 58/64 *Consten and Grundig v Commission* [1966] ECR 299.
[11] Ibid.
[12] Ibid, [345].
[13] See the interesting discussion by T Kaseberg, *Intellectual Property, Antitrust and Cumulative Innovation in the EU and the US* (Oxford, Hart Publishing, 2012).
[14] See, eg *FTC Actavis Inc* 133 SCt 2223, 2238 (2013).
[15] *United States v Microsoft Corp* 253 F3d 34 (DC Cir 2001).

that the lawful ownership of an IP right gave an absolute and unfettered right of exercise not susceptible to antitrust liability. That is the same as arguing that 'use of one's personal property, such as a baseball bat, cannot give rise to tort liability'.[16] The Court added that 'Intellectual property rights do not confer a privilege to violate the antitrust laws'. Similarly, the rules in Articles 101 and 102 of the EU Treaty create a set of outer limits to the lawful exercise of patents which will continue even under a unitary patent regime.

III. Exploitation of Patents and the Competition Rules

The nature of the relationship between patents and the competition rules, therefore, can be summed up as an accommodation between the two systems of law *within the framework of the competition rules*. The basis for the accommodation is the reassurance regularly given by the Court of Justice to IP holders that the 'normal' exercise of a patent will not be restricted by the Treaty rules on competition.[17] Thus in *Volvo*, the Court of Justice stated that to be abusive there must be an 'additional factor' beyond the effect of the exclusionary right eliminating competition in the market for the IP protected product.[18] Later in *Magill*, the Court of Justice stated that only in 'exceptional circumstances' would an IP owner not be entitled to refuse to licence an IP right.[19]

These references by the Court to the 'normal exercise' of IPRs not being subject to Articles 101 and 102 seemed to some to hint at a core of lawful exploitation rights for each IP right under the competition rules. Some argued that there should be an immunity for the 'specific subject matter' or the 'essential function' of the IP from the competition rules. However, the Court of Justice's statements were meant only to reassure IP owners that the mere fact of exclusivity of the IPR and its exercise are not violations of the competition rules, that is, that a legal 'monopoly' created by the patent laws is not contrary to the competition rules nor is its normal exercise of making, using, selling, licensing, refusing to licence to competitors and bringing an action for infringement. As the Court explained as early as the 1968 case of *Parke Davis*,[20] the exercise of the rights arising under a patent in accordance with the legislation of a Member State does not of itself

[16] Ibid, [82].

[17] In the case of the competition rules there is no comparable Treaty provision to that provided by Art 36 on the freedom of movement of goods which provides that 'the protection of industrial property' can justify a prohibition of imports or exports between Member States in certain circumstances.

[18] Case C-238/87 *AB Volvo v Erik Veng (UK) Ltd* [1988] ECR 6211.

[19] Joined Cases C-241/91P & C-242/91P *RTE and ITV v Commission* [1995] ECR-I 485.

[20] *Parke Davis* (n 8).

constitute an infringement of the rules of competition laid down in the Treaty. However, it was clear that the Court's statements were not intended to suggest that the line between 'normal' exercise and 'exceptional circumstances' could be defined by reference to the logic of the patent rules. As we have seen, in *Parke Davis* the Court upheld the entitlement to exercise the patent only because it was 'not contrary to the rules of the Treaty'.

It could not be expected, for example, that the 'subject matter' of a patent or other IP right could be an assurance of acceptable commercial practice under the competition rules. In *Volvo*, the Court stated that 'it must also be emphasised that the proprietor of a protected design to prevent third parties from manufacturing and selling or importing without its consent, products incorporating the design constitutes the very subject matter of its exclusive rights' and therefore a refusal to licence *in itself* cannot constitute an abuse of a dominant position.[21] However, this was confined to protection against imitation in the manufacture of spare parts. In a two-market situation, the first consisting of design right protected spare parts manufacture and sales and the second consisting of car maintenance activity, the Court indicated that in certain circumstances, where the spare part was indispensible to the activity on the second market, the owner of a design right might have a responsibility under the competition rules not to arbitrarily refuse to supply its spare parts or not to fix excessive prices for its spare parts or otherwise face a charge of abuse under Article 102.[22]

Nor could the 'essential function' of the IP create an irreducible minimum of rights for an IP owner in relation to the competition rules. The Advocate General in the *Magill* case made this argument and it was rejected by the Court of Justice. Consequently, after the *Magill* judgment in 1995, it was indisputable that the test of normal and exceptional exercise of an IPR was to be defined by the logic of the competition rules and not by the logic of the essential function of the particular IP right. The Court first stated that the exercise of an exclusive right by the proprietor may in 'exceptional circumstances' involve abusive conduct and went on to offer three specific conditions under Article 102 to define those circumstances.[23] If an IP owner of an indispensible input refused to supply or licence, if necessary, that input to a competitor: (i) offering a new product for which there was demonstrable consumer demand; (ii) otherwise reserved the secondary market for themselves by excluding competitors; and (iii) had no objective justification for its refusal, that could be an offence under Article 102(b) and give rise to a competition remedy of compulsory licence of the IP protected input.[24]

The accommodation of patents within the EU competition rules consists of an acceptance of the concept that there must be a wide berth for the 'normal' exercise of IPRs because IPRs contribute to economic welfare by producing innovative

[21] *AB Volvo* (n 18), [8].
[22] Ibid, [9].
[23] *RTE and ITV* (n 19), [50].
[24] Ibid, [54]–[56].

activity.[25] This view is built into the very fabric of the competition rules and applied at the operational level by the Commission.

Thus, Article 101 creates considerable room to breathe for patent/know-how licensing agreements by defining anticompetitive objects of agreements to exclude many clauses that are necessary for licensing under Article 101(1) and creating a wide zone of immunity in the form of 'safe harbours' in its Technology Transfer Block Exemption Regulation and Guidelines under Article 101(3). However, Article 101 also restricts certain agreements in the Block Exemption Regulation on technology transfer and its accompanying Guidelines as well as making certain patent settlements and patent pools unenforceable as well as prohibiting collusion to fix the prices of patented products. [26]

Moreover, Article 102 makes it clear, as a general proposition, that achieving a dominant position itself can be lawful. It is accepted that if you have a system of competition it would be inconsistent to penalise the winners. Consequently, a firm can legitimately grow to a dominant position through internal growth owing to efficiencies of production and distribution, investment in research and development (R&D) and exploitation of IPRs including brands. There may be a limit to the acquisition of dominance by the process of merger or acquisition where it may create a substantial impediment to competition.[27] However, 'organic' or internal efficient growth to dominance is lawful. Hence, even if a patent coincides with an economic monopoly created by a successful commercial enterprise, that *in itself* is not unlawful.

Further, even though Article 102 is concerned to maintain effective competition in markets that are threatened by a dominant player, it does not prevent dominant firms from competing and driving out other firms from the market as long as the dominant firms 'compete on the merits'. This allows the already dominant firm to increase its profits and market share through the legitimate use of IPRs and innovation. For example, in *AstraZeneca*,[28] the Commission decided that AstraZeneca had abused its dominant position in the market for drugs acting as proton-pump inhibitors by providing misleading information to national regulatory authorities in order to obtain extended patent protection in the form of a Supplementary Protection Certificate. It had also withdrawn its registration of its authorisation for the capsule version of its product, thereby preventing generic competitors from using that authorisation as a basis for approval of their products. With respect to the second count, the CJEU made the point that it was legitimate for a dominant firm, as competition on the merits, to prepare and pursue a strategy to

[25] Commission Notice: Guidelines on the Application of Article 81 of the EC Treaty to technology transfer agreements, OJ C101/2 (27 April 2004), [7].

[26] For a more detailed analysis in relation to Article 101, see S Anderman and J Kallaugher, *Technology Transfer and the New EU Competition Rules: Intellectual Property Licensing after Modernisation* (Oxford, Oxford University Press, 2006). This article concentrates on Art 102.

[27] See Regulation (EC) No 139/2004 of 20 January 2004 on the control of concentrations between undertakings, OJ L24/1 (29 January 2004).

[28] *AstraZeneca* (n 2).

minimise the erosion of its sales and to enable it to deal with competition from generic products.[29]

On the other hand, when a particular commercial practice by a dominant patent holder clashes with the competition rules because it is not competition on the merits, it will be prohibited. For example, in *AstraZeneca* the CJEU held that the company's decision to deregister Losec in capsule form, without objective justification and after the expiry of its exclusive right to make use of the results of the pharmacological and toxicological tests and clinical trials, did not come within the scope of competition on the merits.[30]

Moreover, under Article 102, even though the legal monopoly conferred by a patent is no longer viewed automatically as a real monopoly, a firm owning patent protected products can find itself being assessed as being in a dominant position because of the narrow market determinations of the Commission and this in turn can create a platform for restriction of 'abusive' conduct. The competition assessments of the market power of patents start with an analysis of the existence of possible substitute products normally in a *product market*.[31] If there are substitute products available to consumers then it is necessary to measure the market shares of competitors and the relative market power of the patent protected product. If the market share of the patented product is low, or substitute products are freely available, it is unlikely that a patented product will be found to occupy a dominant position in that market.

However, in some cases the product market can be defined so narrowly that it coincides with the patented product, and the market is defined as a one-product market. In such a case, the assessment of dominant market power may be predetermined by the definition of relevant market. For example, again in *AstraZeneca*, the firm was found dominant because its blockbuster drug product Losec, a treatment for ulcers, was characterized as in a separate market for proton pump inhibitors (ATC 4 Class) and not in a general market for anti-ulcer drugs (ATC 3). One reason given was that the latter class contained products such as H2 blockers that were not substitutable for the same therapeutic indication. Another reason was that consumers were not tempted to switch away from Losec to other anti-ulcer drugs by the prospect of higher prices for Losec. However, this narrow market definition virtually decided the issue of the market power of the drug owner because there were no competing proton pump inhibitors and the patent stood as a barrier to entry of imitators.

Another example is offered by the *Rambus* case. *Rambus* was a case where a patent holder did not disclose certain patent applications from a technology pool even though it agreed to disclose all existing patents and license them on

[29] Ibid, [129].

[30] Ibid, [130].

[31] Patents can also be assessed in a technology market which is distinct from the product itself and refers to the technology licensed by the parties and any substitutes for that technology. See Guidelines (n 25), [22].

FRAND terms if selected for the purpose of creating the chosen technological product. When the technology was eventually chosen for the standard, it included patents owned by Rambus that had not been disclosed to the pool. Rambus then insisted on a higher than FRAND royalty for the use of those patents claiming that they were not bound by their FRAND obligation. When the case came to the Commission Rambus, as the owner of a standard essential patent, was held to be in its own product market consisting of the technology protected by the patent. In this case, the competition authorities chose to define the relevant product market as the market for the patent after it was selected for the standard. Once the Rambus patents were chosen as standard essential patents, the Commission could find it to be dominant because there were no substitutes.[32]

In the assessment of dominance itself there are no special concessions to patents. The market power of the patent owning firm is assessed by a factual analysis, assisted by economic reasoning, which is similar to the analysis of the market power of any other form of property ownership. The patent could be factually relevant to the market power of the firm, or be factually irrelevant, depending upon whether it creates real restrictions of competition in the form of barriers to entry. Most patents are merely legal monopolies that either have no market at all or, if in a market, have substitutes. They only rarely coincide with market power.

In making the factual assessment of market power, the innovative features of patents are less important than their contribution to market power. Indeed, if anything, the truly breakthrough patent can coincide with market power because it creates a market on its own. Consequently, even though there is no longer an assumption that a patent is automatically associated with market power, a patent in a rare case can be found as a matter of fact to be an asset that helps its owner enjoy dominance in a market.[33] Of course, as we know, a finding of dominance is not itself a finding of unlawful conduct. The conduct must be found to be abusive.

IV. Accommodation in the Form of Support for 'First Inventors' in the Competition Rules

It is in the assessment of abusive conduct that the competition rules contain their main forms of 'accommodation' to patents and other IPRs. The rules make certain major concessions to the contribution of IPRs to innovation and consumer welfare particularly by first inventors. That is not entirely surprising because the concept of 'competition on the merits' embraces a theory of dynamic competition which recognizes that IPRs offer a reward/incentive to invent new products which is complementary to the pressure on firms to innovate created by effective competition. Two good examples of this are TFEU, Article 102(b) refusals to

[32] See *Rambus* (n 4).

[33] See, eg *AstraZeneca* (n 2).

licence and TFEU, Article 102(a) unfair pricing. Thus under Article 102(b) the abuse of refusing to license an IPR is given special treatment. It requires 'exceptional circumstances' to be shown before an IP owner in possession of an 'essential input' who refuses a licence can be found to be infringing Article 102(b).[34] Under Article 102(a) the test of unfair pricing takes into account the costs and risks of investing in R&D and IPRs and the economic value of the product in determining whether or not the pricing of an IPR is unfair.[35]

On the other hand, when commercial practices involving the exercise of IPRs threaten to foreclose other competing inventors from markets, EU competition law sets relatively strict limits to the exercise of patent rights. This approach is viewed as an indirect protection for consumers, that is 'consumer welfare,' but the primary concern is focused on the protection of effective competition in the market by 'as efficient' competitors. The competition rules aim to ensure that such competitors are not eliminated from the market as a result of anticompetitive practices by dominant patent owners as well as other dominant firms. In principle, if certain types of conduct by a dominant firm, with or without a patent, result in a further weakening of 'as efficient' competitors in a market by means other than competition on the merits, that conduct can be found to be abusive. The finding that a firm engages in such conduct, without objective justification, will be sufficient to prove abuse as long as such conduct can be plausibly shown to be capable of having exclusionary effects.[36]

The latter dimension of patent law can be seen, for example, in the disclosure of information during the protected period of patents, experimental use exceptions and compulsory licences for non-use or blocking patents. The 'exceptional circumstances' in which competition law applies an external layer of regulation of the exercise of patents often offers support to this second dimension of the patent system. Let us look at each type of support in turn.

V. The Competition Rules and 'Follow On' Innovation

In so far as competition law aims to protect as efficient competitors from foreclosure, its norms have the effect of protecting 'follow on' or cumulative innovation. As we know, the patent system is not only designed to provide incentives to first inventors. It also assists follow on innovation by ensuring disclosure of information in the patent claim and particulars during patent period that might otherwise be left to trade secrets. It also facilitates licensing and collaboration in the form of patent and technology pools because other technologists can learn about the patented

[34] See, eg *RTE, ITV and BBC* (n 19); *Magill* and *Microsoft*, discussed in S Anderman and H Schmidt, *Intellectual Property Rights and EU Competition: The Regulation of Innovation*, 2nd edn (Oxford, Oxford University Press, 2011).

[35] Ibid.

[36] Case C-549/10 P *Tomra Systems ASA v European Commission* (19 April 2012) [68], [79].

technology. Moreover, patent laws limit the exclusivity granted to patentees to make, use and sell the protected product or process during the period of protection. In that sense, they offer a relative property right, subject to the internal rules of the patent system. The right is limited by defences to infringement, such as experimental use, and by the possibility of a compulsory licence under certain conditions.

These elements of patent law offer an internal system of dispute resolution and procedures which may in some cases prevent disputes reaching the stage of a competition concern. However, if a patentee's conduct amounts to an infringement of the competition rules, it is often too late to argue that the competition case should be suspended and left to be resolved by the procedures of patent law. In the first place, there may be no remedy available under patent law. In the second place, there may be a possible remedy, but one that will not be adequate to solve the competition dispute. In either case the conduct of the patentee will be tested under the competition law rules.

It is important to observe that the logic of the competition rules interpreting exceptional circumstances can impel them to give support for a second dimension of the patent rules, the balance between first inventors and 'follow on' or 'cumulative' innovation[37] at the expense of rewards and incentives to 'first inventors'.

VI. Understanding the Nature of the Relationship of the Competition Rules to Follow On Innovation

The support of the competition rules for follow on innovation can be seen at several levels in the analysis of abuse. In the first place, an important component of the test of abuse under TFEU, Article 102 is the EU courts' treatment of the innovative efficiency defence as an objective justification. A recent version of the innovative efficiency defence has been the argument that if competition rules provide compulsory licences of IPRs as a remedy, they will reduce the incentives of undertakings to innovate. For example, in the *Microsoft* case, Microsoft asserted that it would have less incentive to develop a given technology if it were required to make that technology available to its competitors. The Commission had attempted to tackle Microsoft's assertion by balancing the arguably negative impact on Microsoft's incentives to innovate against the positive effect of a compulsory licence improving innovative efficiency for the industry *as a whole* because interoperability would result in plural sources of innovation and avoid consumers being locked in to the innovation of a single firm.

The General Court took the view that what was called for under TFEU, Article 102 was not a balancing exercise of the two theories of innovation but a more legally structured assessment of Microsoft's arguments. It held that Microsoft's assertion

[37] See Kaseberg (n 13).

could only be raised under the head of objective justification if Microsoft came forward with sufficient evidence to show that it had a plausible claim. The Court stated that once the constituent elements of the abuse have been established, in this case that there were exceptional circumstances requiring an obligation to provide interface information, the burden shifts to the dominant firm to raise any plea of objective justification and support it with arguments and evidence. In the event, Microsoft did not meet its burden. Its arguments were too vague, general and theoretical.[38] The Court of Justice in *Post Danmark*[39] indicated that there was some life in the efficiencies defence, but only under strictly defined conditions, and not at the expense of eliminating effective competition.[40] Insofar as the burden rests on firms to make a plausible case for innovative efficiencies, there is a built in restriction on speculative claims based upon internal prospects for innovation.

Thus, arguments about incentives to innovate (and pro-consumer efficiencies) will be accepted as objective justifications only in so far as they are rooted in findings of fact about current conduct or information known at the time the conduct was engaged in. Predictions about the future are often viewed as too speculative to provide convincing legal evidence. The net effect of this for patent holders is that there will be little room to argue future innovative benefits as a justification for patent practices that break the competition rules.

Secondly, it is important to note that when the substantive competition rules are actually applied to limit the practices of IP owners, it often leads them to take the form of supporting 'follow on' innovation when support has not been offered by the IP laws. For example, in *Microsoft* the Court approved the Commission's interpretation of the exceptional circumstances rule to extend to all cases where the conduct of the dominant firm tends to *limit the technological development of markets to the detriment of consumers.* The case itself, as is perhaps well known, was one where Microsoft decided not to continue to share their interface codes for the Windows 2000 operating system with Sun after having done so in a previous version of their operating system. Sun was a maker of high-quality work servers that underpinned networks based on computers with Windows operating systems. If Microsoft had been successful in their refusal to supply the codes, it was likely that Sun's higher quality work server would have been unavailable to business users and that their product improvement innovation would have been stopped. By requiring Microsoft to continue to supply interface codes, the Commission ensured that that alternative source of innovation survived. In this way Article 102 can be used to strike a balance in favour of plural sources of innovation in an industry as opposed to individual sources of innovation where the protected IP owner attempts to use its market power to block other sources of innovation. It was significant that in *Microsoft*, the defendant argued that the

[38] *Microsoft* (n 1), [698].
[39] Case C-209/10 *Post Danmark v Konnkurrenceradet* (27 March 2012) [22].
[40] Ibid, [42].

Computer Programs Directive[41] offered an appropriate remedy consisting of a right to reverse engineer the codes. This argument was rejected in part because the right to reverse engineer the interface codes was clearly not an adequate remedy. In *Magill*[42] the competition rules were held to offer a remedy of compulsory licence for copyright program listings to a competitor producing a new comprehensive TV guide who had been enjoined by the TV companies wanting to preserve their monopoly in single TV guides. The Court's test of exceptional circumstances in this case emphasized, inter alia, that a dominant IP owner of an indispensible input should not refuse to supply or license that input for a novel product for which there is demonstrable unmet consumer demand. This created a competition remedy for a blocking IPR that was otherwise absent from the copyright legislation. The 'new product' test offers an alternative test which is narrower than the 'limiting technological development' test but both make it clear that in certain defined circumstances, the competition rules will make available a competition remedy of compulsory licence to address a case of a blocking IPR.

The competition rules have also been interpreted to supplement the IP laws when patentees engage in a misuse of their patent protection. As we have seen, in *AstraZeneca* the misuse of the process of Supplementary Protection Certificates for pharmaceuticals was held to be unlawful, under the competition rules, because the mistaken entries resulted in an unlawful extension of the period of exclusivity and thereby denied access to generic producers. The Court of Justice confirmed the analysis of the General Court regarding definition of relevant markets, dominance and abuse. As regards abuse, the Court repeated the General Court's observation that a strategy for protecting a firm's market position after expiration of the patents protecting its products is not in itself evidence of an anticompetitive scheme, unless it contemplates methods of competition that are anticompetitive.[43] In reviewing the arguments relating to misleading the licensing authorities, the Court emphasised the fact-specific nature of the abuse, observing that the case does not mean that any unsuccessful application for grant or extension of an IP right would be abusive. In reviewing the arguments related to the marketing authorisations, the Court rejected the defence argument that AstraZeneca's legal 'right' to withdraw the authorisations could be equated with a 'property right' that could only be limited in exceptional circumstances. The Court was protective of the discretion of competition law to determine the scope of an abuse under Article 102 and unwilling to extend the prerogatives of property rights in cases where they foreclosed the entry of competitors into markets. Again there was a possible alternative remedy if the validity of the Supplementary Protection Certificate was challenged in the courts. However, the existence of that possibility did not prevent the Commission from applying a competition law remedy.

[41] Now Directive 2009/24/EC of the European Parliament and of the Council of 23 April 2009 on the legal protection of computer programs, OJ L111/16 (5 May 2009).

[42] *RTE, ITV and BBC* (n 19).

[43] This represents an implicit critique of the Commission decision in *AstraZeneca*, which repeatedly referred to the company's overall anticompetitive plan.

Another recent example of patent misuse is offered by the EU Commission's inquiry into the pharmaceutical sector. After its investigations, the Commission found evidence that some blockbuster patent owners were entering into agreements designed to delay market entry of cheaper generic versions of the patented product after the patent had expired.[44]

Lundbeck owned a patent on Citalopram, a blockbuster antidepressant medicine. Its basic patent on the Citalopram molecule had expired, and the market had opened to generic competition by several competitors, one of which had started selling its own generic version of Citalopram. At that point, Lundbeck could expect its prices to drop drastically, by as much as 90 per cent on average, in the face of the widespread generic market entry.[45] Lundbeck's strategy was not to enforce its remaining process patents, which it would have been entitled to do as competition on the merits, but instead to reach an agreement with each generic whereby it would stay out of the market in return for a substantial payment and other inducements from Lundbeck[46] amounting to tens of millions of euros. This would have ensured that Lundbeck could maintain its high patent level prices for Citalopram even after the patents had expired. The Commission imposed a fine of €93.8 million on Lundbeck, and fines totalling €52.2 million on several generic producers.[47] In this case the Commission chose to treat the agreements as an anticompetitive cartel-like arrangement under Article 101. In principle, such agreements could also be viewed as exclusionary conduct and an abuse of dominance under Article 102. In the US, such 'pay for delay' agreements are treated as potentially exclusionary conduct violating Section 2 of the Sherman Act, which is the US counterpart to Article 102.

VII. Excessive Pricing by Standard Essential Patent Holders with FRAND Obligations

It is well established under Article 102 that a patent holder can legitimately price their IPRs at a supra competitive price ('what the market will bear') in order to obtain a return for their R&D in that and possibly other less successful products.

[44] In a second case, the Commission fined Johnson & Johnson and Novartis €16 million for agreeing to delay the sale of a generic version of Fentanyl. See European Commission Press Release, 'Antitrust: Commission fines Johnson & Johnson and Novartis €16 million for delaying market entry of generic pain-killer fentanyl', IP/13/1233 (10 December 2013).

[45] Eg prices of generic citalopram dropped on average by 90% in the UK compared to Lundbeck's previous price level once widespread generic market entry took place following the discontinuation of the agreements.

[46] Lundbeck paid significant lump sums, purchased generics' stock for the sole purpose of destroying it, and offered guaranteed profits in a distribution agreement.

[47] These generic companies were Alpharma (now part of Zoetis), Merck KGaA/Generics UK (Generics UK is now part of Mylan), Arrow (now part of Actavis) and Ranbaxy.

This is a quintessential recognition by competition law of the importance of rewards and incentives to first inventors. However, an exception to that principle has been introduced in the case of certain firms participating in technology pools and standard setting organisations in the interest of supporting cumulative forms of innovation. When firms enter into a technology pool for the purpose of setting up a standard, such as 3G, they generally agree to licence their patented technology on a FRAND basis if any of their patents become essential to the chosen technology for the standard (SEPs). In some recent cases, patent owners in that position have adopted strategies to obtain prices above FRAND levels. In some competition cases, these attempts to obtain higher than FRAND royalties have been viewed as abusive conduct under Article 102.

One of the early cases, *Rambus*, consisted of conduct labelled 'patent ambush'. In *Rambus*,[48] as we have seen, a SEP holder maintained that it was not bound by the FRAND obligation because it had not disclosed certain relevant patent applications to the patent pool although it had been party to a contractual disclosure obligation as part of the organisation of the pool. The Commission thought that this type of deceit was an infringement of Article 102. They held that Rambus enjoyed a dominant position once its patents were selected as essential to the chosen technology for the standard. They also held that the conduct was abusive unfair pricing under Article 102(a) and that the potential remedy was to offer the technology to the pool on FRAND terms. The basis of the anticompetitive conduct was the deception practiced by Rambus vis-à-vis the patent pool. Rambus settled with the Commission. The conduct could also have been viewed as abusive under Article 102(b) because it interfered with technological development.

Certainly, other cases placing limits on the attempt to obtain higher than FRAND returns in the face of a FRAND obligation have proceeded on the basis that an attempt by a holder of an SEP to extract a higher than FRAND rate could amount to an infringement of Article 102(b) because withholding the technology from a consumer demanded standard would amount to limiting technical progress to the detriment of consumers. In the latter case, a remedy could be a compulsory licence on FRAND terms.

For example, when IPCom, a patent owning entity, acquired a portfolio of more than a thousand Bosch patents, including 16 families of patents, it initially maintained that it was not bound by its predecessor's FRAND commitment for a patent that was a SEP for the 3G standard. After the European Commission's intervention, IPCom reaffirmed publically that it was bound by the FRAND commitment and the Commission terminated its antitrust investigation. The interest of competition law in a refusal to honour a contractual commitment to charge FRAND only royalties occurs because it causes a 'hold up' in bringing the technology to consumers and distorts the standard setting process.

48 *Rambus* (n 4).

A third type of patent misuse attracting the attention of the competition authorities and the courts are the cases where a patent holder of an SEP subject to a FRAND obligation attempts to enforce the patent by asking for a remedy of an injunction despite the potential licensee/infringer being willing to pay a licence fee on FRAND terms. An injunction would be an inappropriate remedy since the patent owner is only entitled to compensation on FRAND terms. The Commission has indicated that in a case of a licensee willing to pay a FRAND rate, a 'good faith potential licensee', an application for an injunction could be abusive conduct by a SEP holder under a FRAND obligation because it may force 'the potential licensee into agreeing to potentially onerous licensing terms which it would otherwise not have agreed to'. The Commission raised this issue in two statement of objections sent to Samsung and Motorola because of their attempts to enforce their SEPs against Apple in national courts.[49]

These cases make it clear that current strategies involving the commercial use of patents have the potential to infringe the competition rules. There seems to be little limit to the types of conduct that entrepreneurial imagination will give rise to. Insofar as any particular use or misuse of patents crosses the lines established by the competition rules, there is the possibility of a competition remedy. In that sense, the competition rules provide a potential form of external regulation of the patent system complementing the internal system of regulation provided by the patent rules themselves.[50]

VIII. Conclusions

The unitary patent and the new Unified Patent Court will create a new basis for obtaining a patent with a European wide territorial coverage but it is not likely to alter the existing relationship between patent practice and the EU competition laws. The competition rules will continue to provide an external level of regulation to the internal system of regulation provided by the provisions of patent law themselves. In the face of the recent competition cases concerning patent misuse, there has been some speculation that the patent system can rely on competition law to deal with the problems of patent misuse and excessive patenting. However, that is to over-estimate the potential role of competition law in relation to patents. The competition cases of necessity will be few and far between. They will be restricted to rare and somewhat random cases of exceptional circumstances. Insofar as an imbalance exists between first inventor and follow on protection in the patent rules, the competition rules offer no substitute for a realignment of the patent laws themselves. The optimum path to improvement lies with the powers of the patent legislator rather than the competition authority.

[49] See, eg *Samsung* IP/12/1448 (21 December 2012); *Motorola Mobility* IP/13/406 (6 May 2013).

[50] See I Rahnasto, *Intellectual Property Rights, External Effects and Antitrust Law-Leveraging IPRs in the Communications Industry* (Oxford, Oxford University Press, 2003).

9

An International Perspective I: A View from the United States

ROCHELLE C DREYFUSS*

To students of US patent law and procedure, the decision by members of the European Union to adopt a unitary patent system (UPS) is intriguing. Because the United States operates under an analogous regime, Americans are arguably in a better position than are Europeans to predict how the new system will work out. In this essay, I start by describing how the procedures used in the United States to protect inventions and to decide patent cases developed, detailing the many ways in which the concerns now expressed in Europe echo the reactions Americans voiced as the US system unfolded. I then summarize the US experience and ask whether drafters of the UPS have managed to capture its benefits and avoid its pitfalls. I suggest that the Europeans have in some ways perfected what I have called the American experiment.[1] At the same time, however, the EU may have made itself vulnerable to many of the problems with which the United States is currently coping. But I conclude that even if neither regime is perfect, together the two systems—along with similar developments elsewhere—can work in concert to improve both patent law and its global administration.

I. The US Experience

While the US patent system mirrors the UPS in many important ways, its evolution was significantly different. The American regime developed slowly, over a period of more than two centuries. As a result, it was able to respond to problems as they emerged. Moreover, the patent industries, the patent bar, and the public had time to acclimate to it and adjust their practices, albeit not without controversy.

* Pauline Newman Professor of Law, New York University School of Law. The author is grateful for the historical perspective provided by Christopher Beauchamp and to Michael J Crowley (NYU Class of 2015) for his research assistance.

[1] RC Dreyfuss, 'The Federal Circuit: A Case Study in Specialized Courts' (1989) 64 *New York University Law Review* 1; RC Dreyfuss, 'The Federal Circuit: A Continuing Experiment in Specialization' (2004) 54 *Case Western Reserve Law Review* 760, 793–96.

Roughly speaking, the US system unfolded in four stages. The first move was to centralize authority over intellectual property protection. In part, this was accomplished by the Framers of the Constitution, who, in 1789, gave Congress the authority (but interestingly, not the obligation) 'To promote the progress of science and useful arts, by securing for limited times to authors and inventors the exclusive right to their respective writings and discoveries'.[2] Despite its discretionary nature, the first Congress quickly used this power: in 1790, it adopted the first Patent Act, thereby creating a 'unitary' patent, good throughout the nation.[3] Although neither the Constitution nor that Act explicitly barred the states from adopting concurrent forms of intellectual property protection, the broad pre-emptive power of the federal government has generally been read as excluding the states from offering equivalent sorts of rights to comparable advances.[4] Nonetheless, some state laws promoting innovation endure, most prominently, trade secrecy protection.[5]

While the 1790 Act established a right of action for infringement, it did not specify which courts—states or federal—were competent to hear such claims. But because Congress had not granted federal courts general authority over federal causes, the necessary assumption was that patent actions would be litigated in state courts.[6] That soon changed. Starting in 1793, Congress made the second move. It revised the statute to permit recovery in the 'circuit court of the United States, or any other court having competent jurisdiction'[7] and in 1800, it ended patent litigants' prerogative under the 1793 Act to choose their forum: federal jurisdiction became near-exclusive.[8]

This system did not, however, fully mirror the UPS. For most of its history, the procedural law of the United States included a concept of mutuality of estoppel: a party could preclude re-litigation of an issue already decided in its favour only if the other side could have done the same had the earlier resolution gone the other way. Thus, judgments of invalidity were good only *inter se*: a patentee who had suffered a finding of invalidity could continue to assert the patent, so long as it refrained from suing the very same party that had earlier succeeded in its validity challenge. The third move—to a system of 'central attack'—took over a century to implement. In 1971, in *Blonder-Tongue Laboratories, Inc v University*

[2] US Constitution Art 1, § 8.

[3] Act of Apr 10, 1790, ch 7, 1 Stat 109–12.

[4] See, eg *Bonito Boats, Inc v Thunder Craft Boats, Inc* 489 US 141 (1989) (citing older case law). However, the move to centralize patent authority was, arguably, also subject to development. Thus some states continued to issue patents (or continued to believe they had concurrent authority to issue patents) for some time after the adoption of the Constitution, see CA Hrdy, 'State Patent Laws in the Age of Laissez-Faire (2013) 28 *Berkeley Journal of Law and Technology* 45.

[5] *Kewanee Oil Co v Bicron Corp* 416 US 470 (1974).

[6] DS Chisum, 'The Allocation of Jurisdiction between State and Federal Courts in Patent Litigation' (1970–71) 46 *Washington Law Review* 633.

[7] Act of Feb 21, 1793, ch 11, § 5, 1 Stat 318–23.

[8] Act of Apr 17, 1800, ch 25, § 3, 2 Stat 37. As explained below (n 78), there is some residual jurisdiction in both regional circuits and state courts.

of Illinois Foundation—which happened to be a patent case—the Supreme Court finally abolished the doctrine of mutuality.[9] Invalidity determinations became effective *erga omnes* (as were judgments that specific acts and embodiments were non-infringing).

Of course, due process requires that every litigant enjoy a full, fair opportunity to litigate its case.[10] Accordingly, if the patentee *wins* a validity challenge, the patent remains open for attack by strangers to the first litigation. And because the Evarts Act, which established the regional appellate courts in the US federal system, does not bind the appellate courts to each other's decisions,[11] multiple litigations over the same patents and the same infringements were possible, as was the potential for inconsistent outcomes.[12] Indeed, because review of the decisions of the Patent Office was in the hands of a special court (since 1929, the Court of Customs and Patent Appeals),[13] there were also 'notorious differences between the standards applied by the Patent Office and by the courts'.[14]

To solve that problem, a fourth change was necessary. In 1982, Congress established the United States Court of Appeals for the Federal Circuit to hear patent appeals from all of the trial courts in the nation, from the US Patent and Trademark Office (USPTO), from the Court of Federal Claims, and from the International Trade Commission.[15] In this way, nearly all common law rule-making, power over statutory interpretation, and authority over patent validity and claim interpretation now resides in a single court, with only discretionary review in the Supreme Court.

II. Relevance to the European Union

It may seem to Europeans that the US experience has little relevance for the EU and its members. After all, the United States is a single nation consisting of 50 fairly homogeneous states. It may thus appear obvious that a central authority should determine innovation policy and a unified system of national courts should implement it. However, a closer look at the history of the US system reveals that the reception of the patent regime has much in common with what is now occurring in Europe.

Unfortunately, the details of the debate over the first move—centralization of authority over intellectual property—are largely unknown. While the Federalist

9 *Blonder Tongue v University of Illinois* 402 US 313 (1971).

10 US Constitution Amendments V, XIV.

11 Act of Mar 3, 1891, 26 Stat 826.

12 See, eg *Graham v John Deere Co* 383 US 1 (1966) (*John Deere*), where a patent held valid in the 5th Circuit was invalidated in the 8th Circuit.

13 For a history of this court, see *Glidden Co v Zdanok* 470 US 530 (1962).

14 *John Deere*, 18.

15 Pub L No 97-164, 96 Stat 25 (codified at 28 USC § 1295(a) (1983)).

Papers and the materials written in connection with ratification chronicle most of the concerns raised by the Constitution, very little attention was apparently paid to the clause giving Congress authority over patents and copyrights. It is, however, clear that Thomas Jefferson was highly sceptical of monopolies and did not believe they were necessary to promote innovation. (As visitors to his home in Monticello know, Jefferson was a prodigious inventor).[16] He nonetheless went along with the inclusion of patent authority in the Constitution, most likely because he wanted to ensure that any monopoly created would be for 'limited times'.[17] With the disaster of the Articles of Confederation fresh in their memories, it is also probable that the Framers thought that if colonial powers over rights to intellectual property were perpetuated in the states, the grand objective of the Commerce Clause[18]—to create a genuinely integrated market—would be subverted.[19]

Reliance on federal adjudication was also remarkable for its day. Now, all federal questions can be litigated in a federal court. However, that competence began rather late in the nation's history: in 1875, more than 70 years after federal jurisdiction over patent cases was recognized.[20] And even today litigants in non-patent federal cases generally have a choice between a federal and a state forum.[21] In the eighteenth and nineteenth centuries, states jealously guarded their sovereign authority to adjudicate and had little interest in ceding it to the central government.[22] Federal courts mainly heard cases involving interests that were overwhelmingly federal—admiralty cases and federal crimes, such as treason, piracy, and the counterfeiting of currency.[23] In addition, the first Congress acted on its constitutional authority to recognize diversity jurisdiction.[24] That is, it created competence to hear cases between citizens of different states or between a citizen and an alien. History suggests that its goal was to assure creditors that they would be able to assert their claims in a neutral forum, rather than in the (potentially biased) tribunal of the state where the debtor resided.[25]

Why the 1793 and 1800 Congresses federalized the adjudication of patent cases is also lost in the mists of time.[26] But likely, Congress was concerned that states

[16] See *John Deere*, 7–8.

[17] EC Walterscheid, 'The Nature of the Intellectual Property Clause—A Study in Historical Perspective' (2002) 83 *Journal of the Patent and Trademark Office Society* 763.

[18] US Constitution Art 1, § 8.

[19] EC Walterscheid, 'To Promote the Progress of Science and Useful Arts: The Background and Origin of the Intellectual Property Clause of the Constitution' (1994) 2 *Journal of Intellectual Property Law* 1.

[20] Act of Mar 3, 1875, § 1, 18 Stat 470–73.

[21] 28 USC § 1331.

[22] A statement by Patrick Henry is illustrative: 'I see arising out of that paper [a proposal for diversity jurisdiction], a tribunal, that is to be recurred to in all cases, when the destruction of the state judiciaries shall happen; and from the extensive jurisdiction of these paramount courts, the state courts must soon be annihilated'. HJ Friendly, 'The Historic Basis of Diversity Jurisdiction' (1928) 41 *Harvard Law Review* 483, 489.

[23] See, eg Act of Mar 3, 1825, 4 Stat 115–23.

[24] US Constitution Art 3, § 2.

[25] Act of Sept 24, 1789, 1 Stat 73; Friendly (n 22) 494.

[26] See Chisum (n 6).

would be wary of federal rights in general (as intrusions on their sovereignty), or sceptical about patent rights in particular (because they would raise prices without producing compensatory benefits locally). By relying on federal courts, Congress could give patentees the same assurance it provided to creditors: a neutral forum receptive to their claims. Conversely, it could protect local technology users from the well-heeled elites that sometimes controlled state courts. However, even as late as the 1880s, this jurisdiction continued to cause considerable stir. As Christopher Beauchamp has documented in connection with litigation over the barbed wire patent,[27] 'agrarian hostility [was] aroused by ... inflammatory attempts to demand royalties for basic rural articles, and was channeled into a series of legislative attempts to weaken or abolish the federal patent law'.[28]

Similarly, even now, 40 years after *Blonder Tongue*, the *erga omnes* effect of invalidity determinations remains controversial. First, it forces the patentee to put all its eggs in one (litigation) basket. Second, while this system makes it less expensive to attack a US patent, it reduces the incentive to do so. One party absorbs all of the cost of challenging validity, only to have its competitors share in the benefit if its win.[29] But as with the exclusivity moves (first, to exclusive original jurisdiction in federal trial courts and then to exclusive appellate jurisdiction in the Federal Circuit), *Blonder Tongue* recognizes the importance of achieving uniform outcomes; that the option to litigate essentially the same case in multiple fora creates many problems.

Indeed, there was a time when certain appellate courts upheld patents almost 10 times as often as others (40 per cent in the Fourth and Fifth Circuits versus 4.8 per cent in the Second Circuit).[30] Under that system, forum shopping abounded, as did satellite litigation over when cases could be transferred from one court to another.[31] Without a system that promotes uniform outcomes, there is also the potential for redundant liability, inconsistent judgments—and, paradoxically, inadequate compensation in cross-border cases.[32] Further, the parties may

[27] *The Barbed Wire Patent* 143 US 275 (1892).

[28] C Beauchamp, 'Technology's Trials: Patent Litigation in the United States Courts, 1860–1910' (on file with the author). See also, 'The Wiring of America', *The Economist*, 17 December 1998 <www.economist.com/node/179803>.

[29] In the pharmaceutical context, the Hatch-Waxman Act creates an incentive to challenge patents, see Drug Price Competition and Patent Term Restoration Act of 1984, Pub L No 98-417, 98 Stat 1585 (codified as amended in scattered sections of 15, 21, 35, and 42 USC). In 2003, Congress amended this scheme in Title XI of the Medicare Prescription Drug, Improvement, and Modernization Act of 2003, Pub L No 108-173, tit XI, subtits A–B, 117 Stat 2066, 2448–64 (codified at 21 USC § 355 (2006)). However, patentees and generic manufacturers have colluded to use the incentive scheme to delay competitive entry, see *Federal Trade Comm'n v Actavis, Inc* 133 SCt 2223 (2013); CS Hemphill and MA Lemley, 'Earning Exclusivity: Generic Drug Incentives and the Hatch-Waxman Act' (2011) 77 *Antitrust Law Journal* 947.

[30] See, eg L Baum, 'The Federal Courts and Patent Validity: An Analysis of the Record' (1974) 56 *Journal of the Patent Office Society* 758.

[31] See, eg *Hoffman v Blaski* 363 US 335 (1960).

[32] See 'Introduction' in American Law Institute (ed), *Intellectual Property: Principles Governing Jurisdiction, Choice of Law, and Judgments in Transnational Cases* (St Paul Minnesota, American Law Institute, 2008) 1–8.

be forced to litigate such questions as whose law applies, which court can order preliminary relief, and the circumstances under which a foreign judgment should be enforced.[33] It is important to stress that the problem of multiple litigation is vexing not only for patentees, but also for accused infringers. If cases touching multiple jurisdictions can be litigated piecemeal, the accused infringer never fully wins; there is always another place where the patentee can sue. Eventually, the weaker party (usually the infringer) runs out of money and is forced to settle, possibly improvidently.[34]

It is no wonder then that similar systems would develop in the United States and in Europe. Both include a trans-jurisdictional patent, which can be litigated in a set of courts where validity can be centrally attacked and in which trans-jurisdiction enforcement can be obtained.[35] Even some of the minor features of the regimes are similar. Other supra-jurisdictional rules, such as competition/antitrust law, remain in effect and are considered primary (or in US lingo, supreme).[36] Conversely, certain local (or regional) laws continue to apply and to supplement the supra-jurisdictional right. Examples include constraints on the patentee's exercise of its rights[37] and rules on various aspects of ownership and transfer of ownership.[38]

III. Lessons

On many dimensions, Europeans worried about the UPS can draw comfort from the US experience. At the same time, however, there are several persistent (indeed, growing) problems in US patent practice; the issue for Europeans is whether the UPS avoids—or could be modified to avoid—those difficulties.

[33] For a similar problem in the EU, see R Romandini and A Klicznik, 'The Territoriality Principle and Transnational Use of Patented Inventions—the Wider Reach of a Unitary Patent the Role of the CJEU' (2013) 44 *International Review of Intellectual Property and Competition Law* 524.

[34] See RC Dreyfuss, 'Resolving Patent Disputes in a Global Economy' in T Takenaka and R Moufang (eds), *Patent Law and Theory: A Handbook of Contemporary Research* (Cheltenham, Edward Elgar, 2009) 610.

[35] Arts 34 and 82 Agreement on a Unified Patent Court, OJ C175/1 (20 June 2013) (UPC Agreement).

[36] Art 20 UPC Agreement; Art VI, cl 2 US Constitution. See, eg *Illinois Tool Works, Inc v Independent Ink, Inc* 547 US 28 (2006).

[37] In Europe, national compulsory licensing rules apply: Recital 10 Regulation (EU) No 1257/2012 of the European Parliament and of the Council of 17 December 2012 implementing enhanced cooperation in the area of the creation of unitary patent protection, OJ L361/1 (31 December 2012) (Regulation 1257/2012). In the United States, there is arguably an opening for the application of state antitrust laws, see DA Crane, 'A Neo-Chicago Perspective on Antitrust Institutions' (2012) 78 *Antitrust Law Journal* 43.

[38] Art 7 UP Regulation; *Stanford v Roche* 131 SCt 2188 (2011). See also n 5.

A. Benefits

Especially with the establishment of the Federal Circuit, the US patent bar and patent industries have been highly satisfied with the patent regime.[39] With a single court hearing all patent appeals, forum shopping at the appellate level is virtually impossible. (As described below, trials are a different matter).[40] Apart from claim construction, where there has been considerable debate over the efficacy of the Federal Circuit's jurisprudence,[41] on every other patent question it is clear that the law has been far more predictable and rights in patents far more certain since a 'unified' court was established.[42] Indeed, the Federal Circuit's expertise in technology transfer is such that other courts have deferred to its reasoning even on issues such as technology licensing, which remain matters of state law.[43]

Harmonization has led to impressive changes in practice. As economist Bill Landes and Judge Richard Posner wrote in a 2004 article, the current system has had a 'positive and significant impact on the number of patent applications, the number of patents issued, the success rate of patent applications, the amount of patent litigation, and, possibly, the level of research and development expenditures'.[44] Indeed, it may well be the success of the Federal Circuit that has spurred so many other countries to develop specialized intellectual property tribunals.[45]

[39] RC Dreyfuss, 'In Search of Institutional Identity: The Federal Circuit Comes of Age' (2008) 23 *Berkeley Technology Law Journal* 787.

[40] See n 48; 'Daily Report: Tech Industry Warns Europe of Concerns on Patent Trolls', *New York Times* Bits Blog, 26 September 2013 <bits.blogs.nytimes.com/2013/09/26/daily-report-tech-industry-warns-europe-of-concerns-on-patent-trolls/?_r=0&pagewanted=print>; D Hakim, 'Tech Giants Fear Spread of Patent Wars to Europe', *New York Times*, 25 September 2013 <www.nytimes.com/2013/09/26/technology/tech-giants-fear-spread-of-patent-wars-to-europe.html?pagewanted=all>.

[41] Compare RP Wagner and L Peterbridge, 'Is the Federal Circuit Succeeding? An Empirical Assessment of Judicial Performance' (2004) 152 *University of Pennsylvania Law Review* 1105 (documenting problems with claim construction jurisprudence) with JA Leftstin, 'Claim Construction, Appeal, and the Predictability of Interpretive Regimes' (2007) 61 *University of Miami Law Review* 1033 and JA Lefstin, 'The Measure of Doubt: Dissent, Indeterminacy, and Interpretation at the Federal Circuit' (2007) 58 *Hastings Law Journal* 1025 (showing that problems in claim construction are no different from problems in contract interpretation and suggesting that the court's jurisprudence is not causing significant uncertainty).

[42] See, eg MD Henry and JL Turner, 'The Court of Appeals for the Federal Circuit's Impact on Patent Litigation' (2006) 35 *Journal of Legal Studies* 85; CJ Katopis, 'The Federal Circuit's Forgotten Lessons?: Annealing New Forms of Intellectual Property through Consolidated Appellate Jurisdiction' (1999) 32 *John Marshall Law Review* 581; JF Merz and NM Pace, 'Trends in Patent Litigation: The Apparent Influence of Strengthened Patents Attributable to the Court of Appeals for the Federal Circuit' (1994) 76 *Journal of the Patent and Trademark Office Society* 579.

[43] RW Gomulkiewicz, 'The Federal Circuit's Licensing Law Jurisprudence: Its Nature and Influence' (2009) 854 *Washington Law Review* 199.

[44] WM Landes and RA Posner, 'An Empirical Analysis of the Patent Court' (2004) 71 *University of Chicago Law Review* 111, 112.

[45] 'Study on Specialized Intellectual Property Courts' (International Intellectual Property Institute and United States Patent and Trademark Office, 2012) 2 <iipi.org/wp-content/uploads/2012/05/Study-on-Specialized-IPR-Courts.pdf> (noting that over 90 countries have established some sort of specialized tribunal).

B. Costs

Uniform, predictable law is not, however, synonymous with good law—that is, law that encourages the optimal level of innovation. Patent protection that is too weak (which was arguably the case in the United States prior to the establishment of the Federal Circuit) provides insufficient incentives to innovate and can lead to a preference for trade secrecy, despite its attendant inefficiencies.[46] But there is also a problem if rights become too strong. If patents are too easy to obtain, then patent thickets can become dense, transaction costs mushroom and entry barriers become impenetrable. Weak defences reduce the ability of new generations of innovators to build on prior advances and push the frontiers of science forward. Broad, indefinite patents can make it hard to determine freedom to operate *ex ante*. Generous remedial measures, coupled with ready access to injunctive relief, encourage assertion entities ('trolls') to sue large, successful firms, especially in industries where combining multiple inventions is the norm, as well as marginal operations that are financially unable to mount effective defences.[47] Finally, centralized litigation at the appellate level can induce a false sense of security: forum shopping among trial courts can run rampant—and give birth to communities whose economies are heavily dependent on attracting patent litigants.[48]

Despite the satisfaction of the patent bar, there are several indications that the Federal Circuit is erring on the side of overly protective patent law. Aspects of current US patent law have been heavily criticized by those who represent consumer and research interests, including the Federal Trade Commission, the Secretary of Health and Human Services, and the National Academies of Science.[49] More important, the Supreme Court has begun to wonder—in Justice Breyer's words—whether the law might be 'imped[ing] rather than promot[ing] the Progress of Science and useful Arts'.[50] Thus, in the Federal Circuit's first

[46] See, eg Industrial Innovation and Patent and Copyright Law Amendments: Hearings Before the Subcomm on Courts, Civil Liberties, and the Admin of Justice of the H Comm on the Judiciary, 96th Cong 574–75 (1980) (statement of Sidney A Diamond, Commissioner of Patents and Trade Marks).

[47] J Bessen, 'Op-Ed: How Patent Trolls Doomed Themselves by Targeting Mainstreet', *ars technica*, 12 September 2013 <arstechnica.com/tech-policy/2013/09/op-ed-how-patent-trolls-doomed-themselves-by-targeting-main-street>.

[48] AK Taylor, 'What Does Forum Shopping in the Eastern District of Texas Mean for Patent Reform' (2007) 6 *John Marshall Review of Intellectual Property Law* 570.

[49] 'Gene Patents and Licensing Practices and their Impact on Patient Access to Genetic Tests' (Secretary's Advisory Committee on Genetics, Health and Society 2010) <oba.od.nih.gov/oba/sacghs/reports/SACGHS_patents_report_2010.pdf>; 'Antitrust Enforcement and Intellectual Property Rights: Promoting Innovation and Competition' (US Department of Justice and the Federal Trade Commission, 2007) <www.ftc.gov/reports/innovation/P040101PromotingInnovationandCompetitionrpt0704.pdf>; Committee on Intellectual Property Rights in Genomic and Protein Research and Innovation, National Research Council, *Reaping the Benefits of Genomic and Proteomic Research: Intellectual Property Rights, Innovation, and Public Health* (National Academies Press, 2006); SA Merrill (ed), *A Patent System for the 21st Century* (National Academies Press, 2004); 'To Promote Innovation: The Proper Balance of Competition and Patent Law and Policy' (Federal Trade Commission, October 2003).

[50] *Lab Corp v Metabolite* 548 US 124, 126 (2006) (Breyer J, dissenting from dismissal of *certiorari*).

15 years of operation, the Supreme Court heard only eight patent cases, half on procedural issues; in the second 15 years, it heard close to 30 cases, almost all on substantive matters. And it reversed, vacated, modified, or otherwise seriously questioned the Federal Circuit's approach in about 80 per cent of those cases. Currently, the Federal Circuit 'enjoys' the highest reversal rate in the nation.[51]

Among other things, the Supreme Court has criticized the Federal Circuit's test for non-obviousness, complaining it is too rigid and sets the bar on patentability too low;[52] three times, it has reined in the court's definition of what constitutes patentable subject matter (again, complaining about the court's rigidity);[53] it has questioned the Circuit's narrowing of the scope of the research exemption;[54] and it has admonished the court to be more receptive to validity challenges.[55] Nor has this vigilance abated. In October Term 2013, the Supreme Court heard six patent cases.[56] Since in other contexts Supreme Court review has declined, something untoward appears to be occurring. Significantly, Judge Posner, who we saw was a proponent of the Federal Circuit as recently as 2004, has now begun to question the effects of its jurisprudence.[57] And his colleague on the Seventh Circuit (and previously, on the faculty of the University of Chicago), Diane Wood, recently suggested that the time is ripe to end the Federal Circuit's exclusive control over patent cases; she would give appellants a choice between review in the Federal Circuit or the circuit court covering the region in which the trial court is located.[58]

The question, then, is whether the European system has been constructed in ways that avoid the propensity towards a pro-patent bias. To answer, it is helpful to ask why the problem has occurred in US patent law. To some observers, the issue is the asymmetric distribution of specialized knowledge. First, it is suggested that the Supreme Court is meddling in areas where it has very little expertise and—

[51] RC Dreyfuss, 'Percolation, Uniformity, and Coherent Adjudication: The Federal Circuit Experience' (2013) 66 *Southern Methodist University Law Review* 505.

[52] *KSR Intern Co v Teleflex Inc* 4550 US 398 (2007).

[53] *Bilski v Kappos* 130 SCt 3218 (2010); *Mayo Collaborative Services v Prometheus Laboratories, Inc* 132 SCt 1289 (2012); *Association for Molecular Pathology v Myriad Genetic, Inc* 133 SCt 2107 (2013).

[54] *Merck KGaA v Integra Lifesciences I, Ltd* 545 US 193 (2005).

[55] *Medimmune, Inc v Genentech* 459 US 118 (2007).

[56] *Alice Corp Pty Ltd v CLS Bank, Int'l* SCt (31 March 2014) (Federal Circuit decision affirmed); *Highmark, Inc v Allcare Health Management Sys* 134 SCt 1744 (2014) (Federal Circuit decision vacated and remanded); *Medtronic, Inc v Mirowski Family Ventures, LLC* 134 SCt 843 (2014) (Federal Circuit decision reversed); *Nautilus v Biosig Instruments* 134 SCt 2120 (2014) (Federal Circuit Decision vacated); *Octane Fitness, LLC v Icon Health & Fitness, Inc*, 134 SCt 1749 (2014) (Federal Circuit decision reversed); *Limelight Networks, Inc v Akamai Technologies, Inc*, 134 SCt 211 (2014) (Federal Circuit decision reversed; stating at 217 that 'the Federal Circuit's analysis fundamentally misunderstands what it means to infringe a method patent').

[57] RA Posner, 'Why Are There Too Many Patents in America', *The Atlantic*, Washington, 12 July 2012 <www.theatlantic.com/business/archive/2012/07/why-there-are-too-many-patents-in-america/259725>.

[58] DP Wood, 'Is it Time to Abolish the Federal Circuit's Exclusive Jurisdiction in Patent Cases?' (2013) 13 *Chicago Kent Law Journal* 1. Chief Judge Wood is not alone in taking the view that more appellate courts should handle patent cases, see CA Nard and JF Duffy, 'Rethinking Patent Law's Uniformity Principle' (2007) 101 *Northwestern University Law Review* 1619; PR Gugliuzza, 'Rethinking Federal Circuit Jurisdiction' (2012) 100 *Georgetown Law Journal* 1437.

improperly—reversing judges who understand more about both the law and the facts. As Judge Michel, formerly Chief Judge of the Federal Circuit put it, 'there's ... a certain amount of suspicion that there might be some deeper immersion, deeper familiarity, harder thinking and greater exposure [to patent law] at the Federal Circuit than the Supreme Court itself can offer'.[59] Or as then Chief Judge Rader made clear in connection with the subject matter cases, the Federal Circuit has 'no hope whatsoever' that the Supreme Court can clarify the rules.[60] Second, there is the problem of allowing patent cases to be tried in courts of general jurisdiction. Under this view, the Federal Circuit is caught between its mission to make patent law uniform and Congress's decision to leave patent trials in courts of general jurisdiction. To ensure uniform outcomes in these courts, the Federal Circuit is forced to classify many issues as questions of law so that they can be reviewed *de novo* on appeal. Furthermore, it must adopt rigid rules and 'dumb down' patent law to facilitate decision-making by judges who lack expertise in patent law and experience working with technological facts.[61]

If this is the explanation for the perceived deficiencies in the Federal Circuit's jurisprudence, then the UPS system may well avoid the problems the United States is experiencing. Provisions on substantive patent law were shifted from the UPS Regulation to the UPC Agreement,[62] thereby minimizing review by the generalist Court of Justice of the European Union (CJEU).[63] Furthermore, UPS trial courts are highly specialized. Training is envisioned and some judges will have both a technological education and substantial technical experience.[64] Accordingly, there will be no need for the Court of Appeal to sacrifice optimal law in order to make it easy for laymen to reach uniform and predictable results. In addition, the UPS will benefit from the separateness of the European Patent Office (EPO) which can bring its own independent judgment to bear on issues of patentability.[65]

It is, however, doubtful that asymmetries in expertise furnish a full explanation. There is a mismatch between the Supreme Court and lower tribunals in other areas as well. For example, the Supreme Court reviews tax cases decided by the United States Tax Court, employment law decisions made by the National Labor Relations Board, and administrative law cases, which are largely concentrated in

[59] R Zwhalen, 'Mayo v Prometheus: Thought Leaders Express Concern and Evaluate the Impact', *BIOtech NOW*, 21 May 2012 <http://www.biotech-now.org/public-policy/patently-biotech/2012/05/mayo-v-prometheus-thought-leaders-express-concern-evaluate-business-impact-and-discuss-the-future>.

[60] E McDermott, 'Rader: Help Me to Keep our Patent System Strong' *Managing Intellectual Property*, October 26, 2012, AIPLA Daily Report 11 <www.managingip.com/pdfs/02_AIPLA-DC2012-fri.pdf>.

[61] RC Dreyfuss, Lecture, 'What the Federal Circuit Can Learn from the Supreme Court—and Vice Versa' (2010) 59 *American University Law Review* 787; RP Wagner, 'The Two Federal Circuits' (2010) 43 *Loyola Law Review* 785.

[62] Compare Art 5 Regulation 1257/2012 with Arts 6–8 Commission Proposal for a Regulation of the European Parliament and of the Council implementing enhanced cooperation in the area of the creation of unitary patent protection, COM(2011) 215 final.

[63] But see below and the discussion by Angelos Dimopoulos in ch 5 of this volume.

[64] Arts 8, 9, 15 and 19 UPC Agreement.

[65] See the discussion by Stefan Luginbuehl in ch 4 of this volume.

the United States Court of Appeals for the District of Columbia.[66] Yet no one argues that the law in these fields has become distorted. Significantly, in these other situations, there is always more than one court involved in adjudicating substantive claims in the same area of law. Accordingly, there is reason to believe the problem in patent law stems from the decision to channel patent cases to just one appellate forum. As Sivaramjani Thambisetty suggested during the Oxford/East Anglia Unitary Patent System Workshop, the epistemic community may have become too small. Or as American scholars describe it, there are no longer opportunities for percolation—for dialogue among appellate courts as to which interpretation of the law works best or a chance to observe how different approaches work in practice.[67]

At the time the United States perfected its system, scholars and jurists were of the view that percolation is useless in the statutory context. For example, Dan Meador, one of the founders of the Federal Circuit considered '"percolation" [to be] a euphemism for incoherence';[68] to Paul Bator, 'percolation is not a purposeful project. It is just a way of postponing decision'.[69] Arguably, we have now learned that these scholars were wrong. Perhaps the problem is that patent law is less statutory than these observers supposed.[70] Or perhaps patent law does not have the political salience necessary to attract legislative attention when mistakes are made. More likely, there is real value in having more than one court think about an issue. As Fred Schauer noted in his aptly named article, 'Do Cases Make Bad Law' (a play on the expression 'hard cases make bad law'), any one court can be heavily influenced by the first case it hears on an open question of law. That case frames the debate; once the court chooses an approach, it compares the facts of subsequent cases to the original, and that anchoring effect then controls further evolution of the legal regime.[71] In contrast, when there are multiple courts hearing cases in the same field, Schauer's anchoring and framing effects can wash out. Each court starts with a different first case and can wind up at a different endpoint; ultimately the highest court or the legislature may harmonize the law, but when it does, it has empirical evidence from each of the different jurisdictions on how each rule works in practice.

Percolation is helpful in other respects as well. Judge Wood's description of her participation in the regional appellate system is telling: 'mistakes teach valuable lessons'; 'circuit splits and disagreements with colleagues force judges to sharpen

[66] See Wood (n 58).

[67] See, eg Dreyfuss (n 51).

[68] DJ Meador, 'A Challenge to Judicial Architecture: Modifying the Regional Design of the US Courts of Appeal' (1989) 56 *University of Chicago Law Review* 603, 633.

[69] PM Bator, 'What is Wrong with the Supreme Court' (1990) 51 *University of Pittsburg Law Review* 673, 689–90. See also EM Griswold, 'The Federal Courts Today and Tomorrow: A Summary and Survey' (1987) 38 *South Carolina Law Review* 393; HJ Friendly, *Federal Jurisdiction: A General View* (New York, Columbia University Press, 1973) 161–62 (as cited in PD Carrington and P Orchard, 'The Federal Circuit: A Model for Reform?' (2010) 78 *George Washington Law Review* 575, 583).

[70] CA Nard, 'Legal Forms and the Common Law of Patents' (2010) 90 *Boston University Law Review* 51.

[71] F Schauer, 'Do Cases Make Bad Law?' (2006) 73 *University of Chicago Law Review* 883.

their writing, push them to defend their positions, and from time to time persuade them that someone else's perspective is preferable'.[72] Each adjudication also spurs the litigants to build more creative arguments.[73] Perhaps most important, when the highest court or the legislature harmonizes on a new approach, the court that was overruled or reversed is not solely responsible for operationalizing the new rule. In contrast, when that responsibility falls on the court that was rebuffed, it may well resist implementation. For example, then Chief Judge Rader once promised that *KSR*, the Supreme Court's major revision of non-obviousness jurisprudence, would change nothing.[74]

If the absence of percolation is, indeed the source of the United States' difficulties, the European approach may be extremely vulnerable to equivalent problems, for the epistemic community the UPS creates is very small indeed and the pressures on it are quite extreme. First, the UPS system gives patentees, *but not other litigants*, the right to opt-out of the Unified Court system.[75] The effect is to put the UPS courts in competition for patent holders. To ensure filled dockets, the judges will inevitably be tempted to adopt interpretations of the law that will attract patentees into the system. And as the US experience with forum shopping suggests, that tendency may be exasperated by the desire of certain regional and local courts to bring new business to their territories.

Second, the compositions of the docket will tend to isolate the Court of Appeal in ways that are not possible in the United States. Although the Federal Circuit hears almost all patent appeals, only half its docket is patent-related. The remainder includes a diverse array of tort, contract, employment, energy law, and export control cases, as well as appeals of trade mark cases from the Patent and Trademark Office.[76] Furthermore, the court has *case* rather than *issue* jurisdiction: it hears every issue in every case in which the complaint includes a patent claim. For example, the court reviewed *Oracle America, Inc v Google, Inc*,[77] even though only copyright issues were preserved for appeal. In addition, the exclusiveness of federal authority—and Federal Circuit authority—over patent cases is not total. As described in the margin, the degree of exclusivity has varied over time.[78] Under current law, if a patent issue first surfaces in a permissive counterclaim in a federal

[72] Wood (n 58).

[73] Nard and Duffy (n 58) 1634.

[74] G Quinn, 'Chief Judge Rader Says KSR Didn't Change Anything, I Disagree', *IP Watchdog*, 6 October 2011 <www.ipwatchdog.com/2011/10/06/chief-judge-rader-says-ksr-didnt-change-anything-i-disagree/id=19603>.

[75] Art 83 UPC Agreement.

[76] 28 USC § 1295(a).

[77] *Oracle America, Inc v Google, Inc* _ F3d _, 2014 WL 1855277 (Fed Cir 9 May 2014).

[78] The 1800 Act gave patentees the right to bring actions in a federal court; it said nothing about patent claims that arose in defences. Indeed, in 1908, the Supreme Court made clear that federal power depended on the nature of the 'well pleaded complaint', and not on the issues first raised in the answer, *Louisville & Nashville Railroad Co v Mottley* 211 US 149 (1908). That state of affairs persisted until 2011, when the Leahy-Smith America Invents Act, Pub L No 112-29, § 19(b)(1), 125 Stat 284, 331–32 (2011) (AIA) (codified at 28 USC § 1295(a)(1)), enlarged the competence of federal courts to include compulsory (but not permissive) patent counterclaims.

case, the appeal will be to a regional circuit. And if the claim arises in a defence, or in a permissive or compulsory counterclaim in a state case, the case will stay in state court (though appeal from the state Supreme Court to the US Supreme Court may be possible).[79] As a result, the Federal Circuit is required to stay abreast of legal developments outside patent law and it is in a dialogic relationship with other circuits and state courts, even if only rarely and on highly selective matters. The UPS system appears to contain none of these avenues for keeping patent law in the mainstream of EU jurisprudence.

Third, the emphasis in the UPS on experienced patent trial judges, technology experts, and training may have an extremely deleterious effect on the court's ability to consider patent issues in the context of other important EU and national values, such as competition, free movement, health, and welfare.[80] It is not clear how much exposure to these issues the experienced patent judges will have had before ascending the UPS bench. For example, at the Workshop it was suggested that some may come from the EPO, where countervailing issues arise very rarely. The technology experts are even more unlikely to have non-patent legal experience. And if the EPO provides most of the envisioned training, the isolation of the jurists from other values will be near complete. In contrast, some Federal Circuit judges are chosen for patent experience, but others are picked for their knowledge of the other fields within the court's jurisdiction. As noted earlier, US patent cases are tried in courts of general jurisdiction. A few of the trial judges have patent experience and some will gain it by participating in a new initiative, the Patent Cases Pilot Program.[81] However, all the trial judges hear non-patent cases and these controversies sensitize them to competition issues and other matters that serve as counterweights to the interests of the patent industries.

Given the isolation of the Unified Court, the decision to minimize review by the CJEU appears particularly problematic. The US Supreme Court may not provide sufficient guidance on patent law matters, but its decisions do force the Federal Circuit to stop, think, and (occasionally) alter course.[82] If the UPS drafters succeed in avoiding the CJEU, the UPS will have nothing comparable to reverse any pro-patent momentum that builds in the Court of Appeal. The situation may be even worse. Thus, Angelos Dimopoulos suggests in chapter five that the CJEU will retain the right to review decisions for compatibility with the TRIPS Agreement. If he is correct, the system is extraordinarily stacked in favour of patent holders: because

[79] See *Gunn v Minton* 133 SCt 1059 (2013) (holding that state malpractice claims predicated on mishandling a patent suit belong in a state court); *Lear, Inc v Adkins* 395 US 653 (1969) (appeal of a patent issue decided in a state court to the US Supreme Court). See also TB Lee, 'How Vermont could Save the Nation from Patent Trolls', *The Switch*, 1 August 2013 (describing actions by Attorney Generals in Vermont and Nebraska to curb patent trolling) <www.washingtonpost.com/blogs/the-switch/wp/2013/08/01/how-vermont-could-save-the-nation-from-patent-trolls>.

[80] Arts 8, 9, 15 and 19 UPC Agreement.

[81] Pub L No 111–349, 124 Stat 3674 (2011) <www.gpo.gov/fdsys/pkg/PLAW-111publ349/pdf/PLAW-111publ349.pdf>.

[82] JM Golden, 'The Supreme Court as "Prime Percolator": A Prescription for Appellate Review of Questions in Patent Law' (2009) 56 *UCLA Law Review* 657.

TRIPS sets out minimum standards of protection and mainly defers to Member States on defences to infringement, only patentees will have grounds to seek CJEU consideration. When coupled with the facts that only patentees have a right to choose the judicial system in which to litigate, and the likelihood that judges drawn from the EPO will be inhospitable to challenges to the Office's decisions, the system as a whole treads rather heavily on fundamental concepts of fairness and due process.[83]

Of course it is possible that the European Court of Human Rights (ECtHR) will step in—either on the fairness issue or on questions involving the rights of those needing access to the fruits of innovation.[84] But human rights violations tend to be found in extreme situations; the ECtHR is unlikely to take on the full task of structuring a balanced system that ensures that patents are not impairing progress. Furthermore, if the Court of Appeal takes the Federal Circuit's 'they just don't understand us' attitude, it is questionable whether the decisions of the ECtHR (or, for that matter, the CJEU) will have a significant impact on its jurisprudence.

C. Benefits Revisited

While neither the United States nor the European Union have developed a perfect system, together, they could improve patent law and its global administration. As noted earlier, specialized courts have been established in many countries. Accordingly, a new type of percolation is possible. The size of the epistemic community may continue to be somewhat limited. Nevertheless, because courts in different parts of the world struggle with different countervailing considerations, dialogue among them could be highly productive. As with the US regional circuits, this dialogue should also spur thoughtful, persuasive, and transparent decision-making and help litigants sharpen their arguments. If the courts put different policies into effect, their efforts will create an empirical basis for higher courts, legislators, and international negotiators to determine the best approach.

Dialogue among courts of different nations could have other salutary effects. As global trade increases, the problems the United States grappled with in the eighteenth and nineteenth centuries and the EU is dealing with now are increasingly multinational problems. While it is unlikely that there will ever be a unitary global patent, as judges come to understand one another, they may begin to converge on best practices or choose among equally plausible rules on the ground that the choice would lead to a more harmonized global system.[85] The cost of multinational litigation might also decline, for judges who respect each other may take a

[83] Art 6(1) Convention for the Protection of Human Rights and Fundamental Freedoms (European Convention on Human Rights, as amended).

[84] Cf *Ashby Donald v France* (10 January 2013, ECtHR (5th section)).

[85] RC Dreyfuss, 'The Leahy-Smith America Invents Act: A New Paradigm for International Harmonisation?' (2013) 24 *Singapore Academy of Law Journal* 669.

chapter from transnational bankruptcy practice and cooperate on transnational patent cases.[86] Furthermore, as they become more acquainted with each other's decisions and more confident about each other's procedures, they may become more willing to enforce each other's judgments.

IV. Conclusion

A comparison of the US and EU approaches to specialization suggests that the UPS is likely to provide many of the same benefits that have accrued to the United States by reason of its unitary patent and unified method of patent adjudication. However, the US system appears to be producing law that entrenches incumbents, facilitates sharp practice, and is insufficiently attentive to user interests, to competition policy, or even to sound innovation policy. Whether the same fate awaits Europeans remains to be seen. The European courts and their dockets are likely to be more specialized—that has some advantages, but it also produces an environment conducive to the creation of law aimed at pleasing patent holders. From an American perspective, however, the European development is very welcome indeed. US practitioners are comfortable with a unified system. More important, the establishment of a specialized judiciary provides the Federal Circuit with a much needed opportunity for dialogue and experimentation.

[86] See, eg JL Westbrook, 'An Empirical Study of the Implementation in the United States of the Model Law on Cross Border Insolvency' (2013) 87 *American Bankruptcy Law Journal* 247; JL Westbrook, 'International Judicial Negotiation' (2003) 38 *Texas International Law Journal* 567.

10

An International Perspective II: A View from Private International Law

PAUL LC TORREMANS*

I. Introduction

Looking at the international aspects of the unitary patent[1] from inside the European Union can be a short-lived exercise. One is not comparing the new unitary patent with a system that is in operation in another state or regional organisation and, as the applications remain in the safe hands of the European Patent Organisation and its procedural rules, nothing will change for foreign applicants. The exercise becomes, however, anything but short-lived if one turns to the private international law aspects of the unitary patent and the Unified Patent Court,[2] with which it is inextricably linked. Then one enters uncharted waters, especially from a patent law perspective.

The European Union is quite used to deal with the jurisdiction of courts in civil and commercial matters,[3] but in essence all that experience refers to national courts of single Member States. The Benelux Court[4] has been in existence for quite a number of years as a court that is common to Belgium, the Netherlands and Luxembourg, but at least until now it has never operated at first instance

* Prof Dr Paul LC Torremans, Professor of Intellectual Property Law, School of Law, University of Nottingham.

[1] Regulation (EU) No 1257/2012 of the European Parliament and of the Council of 17 December 2012 implementing enhanced cooperation in the area of the creation of unitary patent protection, OJ L361/1 (31 December 2012) (Regulation 1257/2012).

[2] Agreement on a Unified Patent Court, OJ C175/1 (20 June 2013) (UPC Agreement).

[3] See the various versions of the Brussels Convention and the Brussels I Regulation that eventually resulted in Regulation (EU) No 1215/2012 of the European Parliament and of the EU Council of 12 December 2012 on jurisdiction and the recognition and enforcement of judgments in civil and commercial matters, OJ L351 (20 December 2012) (Regulation 1215/2012).

[4] Verdrag betreffende de instelling en het statuut van een Benelux-gerechtshof (Treaty establishing a Benelux Court and its Statute) 31 March 1965, [1973] *Belgisch Staatsblad—Moniteur Belge* 14062. The Court has been operational since 1974.

level.[5] That removed the need to include it in the jurisdiction rules. Hence, even if that picture may change for the Benelux Court, the Unified Patent Court is the one that does not fit the mould. The Unified Patent Court will be a first instance court that is common to a large number of Member States. In addition, the Unified Patent Court will have local and regional divisions, which again at least potentially raises issues of jurisdiction, or at least of a division of labour.

It was not entirely clear from the outset how this would fit in with the European legal framework on jurisdiction. At least arguably, nothing needed to be done. A common court which a Member State shares with other Member States is, or at least fulfils the role of, a national court of the Member State concerned and if it deals with civil and commercial matters it comes within the scope of the Brussels I Regulation.[6] That gives one a set of international jurisdiction rules to play with and the rest is a matter to be dealt with in patent law and therefore with the Regulation and the UPC Agreement. But that would have created some uncertainty and also the need to establish jurisdiction rules for defendants that are not domiciled in a Member State, as a common court cannot rely on various national rules in this respect.[7] The way forward that was chosen was therefore to have explicit rules and to amend the Brussels I Regulation.[8] That should have provided for legal certainty. But maybe one needs to emphasise the word 'should' here...

II. The Starting Point(s)

The UPC Agreement provides a first obvious starting point in its Article 31:

> Article 31: International jurisdiction
>
> The international jurisdiction of the Court shall be established in accordance with Regulation (EU) No 1215/2012 or, where applicable, on the basis of the Convention on jurisdiction and the recognition and enforcement of judgments in civil and commercial matters (Lugano Convention[9]).[10]

[5] The Benelux Court issues preliminary rulings at the request of national courts, eg concerning the Benelux trade mark. Negotiations are ongoing to allow the public direct access to the court in trade mark matters. See the enabling Protocol, Protocol tot wijziging van het Verdrag van 31 maart 1965 betreffende de instelling en het statuut van een Benelux-Gerechtshof, ondertekend te Luxemburg op 15 oktober 2012, Tractatenblad 2013, nr 12. Further changes to the relevant Benelux texts on intellectual property are still required before the system can be put into action.

[6] Regulation 1215/2012.

[7] The Brussels I Regulation does not deal with these cases. A proposal to change that was rejected when the Regulation was recast in 2012.

[8] Art 89(1) UPC Agreement.

[9] Convention on jurisdiction and the recognition and enforcement of judgments in civil and commercial matters, OJ L339/3, signed between the EU on the one hand and Norway, Iceland and Switzerland on the other hand in Lugano in 2007.

[10] Art 31 UPC Agreement.

Article 31 is the first Article in Chapter VI of the UPC Agreement that is entitled 'International jurisdiction and competence'. Article 31 deals with the international jurisdiction, whilst the remainder of the Chapter deals with competence issues. The international jurisdiction of the Unified Patent Court is therefore governed by the Brussels I Regulation. The court should fit in with the existing system for civil and commercial matters, despite the fact that it is not a national court, but a court common to Member States, and despite other aspects that do not fit straightforwardly into the mould of the Brussels I Regulation.

For a private international lawyer every court needs to establish its international jurisdiction first. This is where it all starts and without international jurisdiction a court cannot hear the case. Before the Unified Patent Court can hear a case it has to establish that it has international jurisdiction to hear the case. Article 31 of the UPC Agreement imposes the Brussels I Regulation rules as the only rules by which the Unified Patent Court can establish its jurisdiction. That was also made clear by the change of the word 'jurisdiction' to the word 'competence' for the other elements contained in Chapter VI. From Article 32 onwards one finds provisions on the internal distribution of labour inside the Unified Patent Court and its various local and regional divisions and aspects of subject matter jurisdiction. International jurisdiction is a separate matter and one that comes first. Only once international jurisdiction has been established can one turn to the competence of the court, which means on the one hand the subject matter jurisdiction of the court, as a common patent court that will deal roughly speaking with the infringement and validity issues surrounding European Patents and European patents with unitary effect, and on the other hand the division of labour inside the Unitary Patent Court, its central, local and regional divisions.

A second starting point is found in Article 89(1) of the UPC Agreement:

> Article 89
>
> Entry into force
>
> 1. This Agreement shall enter into force on 1 January 2014 or on the first day of the fourth month after the deposit of the thirteenth instrument of ratification or accession in accordance with Article 84, including the three Member States in which the highest number of European patents had effect in the year preceding the year in which the signature of the Agreement takes place *or on the first day of the fourth month after the date of entry into force of the amendments to Regulation (EU) No 1215/2012 concerning its relationship with this Agreement, whichever is the latest.* (Emphasis added).

Once more it is clear that the international jurisdiction of the Unified Patent Court will be governed by the Brussels I Regulation. But the Unified Patent Court does not fit the mould and therefore the Brussels I Regulation will be amended.[11]

[11] There is also the view that Art 89(1) is a clerical error. The negotiators had the idea that the unitary patent negotiations would be concluded first and then there would have been no point in starting the operations of the court with the 'old' Brussels I Regulation. One would wait for the recast that was also supposed to extend its rules to defendants that were not domiciled in a Member State, which is

When putting both these starting points together a clear approach emerges. The UPC Agreement itself contains no rules on the international jurisdiction of the common court. It refers the issue entirely to the Brussels I Regulation, as amended in due course. The Unitary Patent Regulation also offers no provisions on private international law. The Unified Patent Court will therefore only be able to deal with those cases for which the Brussels I Regulation, as amended in due course, grants it jurisdiction. If such jurisdiction is forthcoming the other provisions in Chapter VI of the UPC Agreement, those on competence, will become relevant and will decide whether the subject matter of the case forms part of the subject matter for which the court has competence and which division of the court can deal with the matter.[12] But this is a second stage that merely comes into play once the jurisdiction issue is dealt with in favour of the Unified Patent Court.

For our current purposes this implies that we should look first of all at the Brussels I Regulation, and the amendments to it, before we turn to the competence rules in the UPC Agreement.

III. Amending the Brussels I Regulation

The European Commission set the process to implement Article 89(1) of the UPC Agreement and to amend the Brussels I Regulation in motion on 26 July 2013, with a proposal for a Regulation. Or to put it in the words of the Commission:

> Article 89(1) of the UPC Agreement provides that the Agreement cannot enter into force prior to the entry into force of the amendments to the Brussels I Regulation (recast) regulating the relationship between both instruments. The aim of these amendments is twofold. First, the amendments aim at ensuring compliance between the UPC Agreement and Brussels I Regulation (recast), and second, at addressing the particular issue of jurisdiction rules vis-à-vis defendants in non-European Union States.[13]

Ensuring compliance is of course vital if the Brussels I Regulation is supposed to provide the international jurisdiction rules for the UPC Agreement. Both

a crucial point for the Unified Patent Court. As it happens, the Brussels I recast went ahead (in a different form) before the negotiations on the European patent with unitary effect were concluded and that should have meant that the requirement that the Brussels I Regulation be amended first should have been dropped. See MD Real, 'Hay que modificar el Reglamento Bruselas I bis de 12 de diciembre de 2012 para que pueda entrar en vigor el Acuerdo sobre un Tribunal Unificado de Patentes de 19 de febrero de 2013?' <http://conflictuslegum.blogspot.be/2013/03/manuel-desantes-el-acuerdo-tup-no-exige.html>.

[12] Along the lines of the civil procedure rules in a civil law jurisdiction that decide whether the subject matter at hand is one for the civil courts or for the commercial courts to deal with and whether the civil or commercial court of judicial district X or Y will deal with the case.

[13] Proposal for a Regulation of the European Parliament and of the Council amending Regulation (EU) No 1215/2012 on jurisdiction and the recognition and enforcement of judgments in civil and commercial matters, COM(2013) 554 final, 2.

instruments have to cooperate seamlessly and a perfect fit is required. Since the Brussels I Regulation does not contain uniform jurisdiction rules for defendants that are not domiciled in a Member State, and instead relies on the national law of the Member States, that point has to be addressed head-on, as the common court cannot apply several different national laws on this point.

The proposal seems to suggest that the compliance exercise is a minor one. Several elements point in that direction. The Commission constantly uses the term 'to clarify', which seems to hint at minor amendments that provide clarifications rather than changes of a fundamental nature. And no modification at all is proposed to the core of the Brussels I Regulation which is formed by its jurisdiction rules. Instead, the 'clarifications' are almost to be buried at the end of the Regulation in new Articles 71a–71d, amongst the provisions that deal with other private international law agreements concluded by the Member States. This is hardly a place to which the attention of most readers is drawn and one does not expect to find there changes to the main jurisdiction rules of the Regulation, let alone changes that are of a fundamental nature. Nevertheless, the compliance operation is anything but a minor one and some of the changes are rather fundamental in nature!

The proposal was eventually adopted in a slightly modified version on 15 May 2014 as Regulation 542/2014.[14]

A. The Insertion of a Common Court: A Mere Clarification

But let us start with what is indeed little more than a mere clarification. A court common to several Member States does, for each of the Member States concerned, the work of a national court, so it makes sense to treat it as such for the purposes of the Brussels I Regulation. If the common court is a court of the Member State then the Brussels I Regulation determines the international jurisdiction of such a court when it deals with civil and commercial matters, as defined in the Regulation. The Regulation clarifies this point for two common courts, the Benelux Court of Justice[15] and the one that concerns us at present, the Unified Patent Court:

In Chapter VII of Regulation (EU) No 1215/2012, the following Articles are inserted:

> Article 71a
>
> 1. For the purposes of this Regulation, a court common to several Member States (a 'common court') shall be a court of a Member State when, pursuing to the

[14] Regulation EU No 542/2014 of the European Parliament and of the Council of 15 May 2014 amending Regulation (EU) No 1215/2012 as regards the rules to be applied with respect to the Unified Patent Court and the Benelux Court of Justice, OJ L163/1 (29 May 2014).

[15] For Belgium, the Netherlands and Luxembourg, of which the Benelux consists.

agreement establishing it, it exercises jurisdiction in civil and commercial matters within the meaning of this Regulation.

2. For the purposes of this Regulation, each of the following shall be a common court:
   (a) the Unified Patent Court established by the Agreement on a Unified Patent Court signed on 19 February 2013 (the 'UPC Agreement'); and
   (b) the Benelux Court of Justice established by the Treaty of 31 March 1965 concerning the establishment and statute of a Benelux Court of Justice (the 'Benelux Court of Justice Treaty').[16]

B. Uniform Jurisdiction Rules Regardless of the Domicile of the Defendant: Anything but a Mere Clarification

This is entirely uncontroversial, as one merely declares the Unified Patent Court a court of a Member State, or at least the equivalent of one. But the controversy is not far away. Indeed, in the very first paragraph of the same Article of the draft Regulation one finds an addendum to Recital 14 of the Brussels I Regulation. At first glance it brings a mere reference to the concept of the common court into the Recitals of the Brussels I Regulation by stating that uniform jurisdiction rules are also required for the common court. Nothing is more logical and straightforward if the common court de facto operates for each of the Member States concerned as a national court for that Member State. The same need for uniform jurisdiction rules that gave birth to the whole Brussels I system arises if one integrates the common court into the landscape of national courts dealing with civil and commercial matters. But almost inadvertently, a little phrase that refers to the second aim of the amendments to the Brussels I Regulation is slipped in. Article 1(1) therefore reads as follows:

> Uniform jurisdiction rules should also apply *regardless of the defendant's domicile* in cases where courts common to several Member States exercise jurisdiction in matters coming within the scope of application of this Regulation.[17] (Emphasis added.)

It is indeed obvious that we need uniform jurisdiction rules that apply regardless of the defendant's domicile. This was referred to above and the proposal that resulted eventually in the 2012 recast of the Brussels I Regulation contained an extension of the existing common jurisdiction rules that rely on the cornerstone of the defendant being domiciled in a Member State, unless one is concerned with exclusive jurisdiction, to defendants that are not domiciled in a Member State. That extension would therefore have replaced, on that point, the national private international rules of the Member State on jurisdiction. Suffice it to say that that extension did not make it into the final recast. The Brussels I regime is therefore still based on, and limited to, defendants that are domiciled in a Member State. Doing for patents what was turned down for all other cases is anything

[16] Art 1(*partim*) (n 4).
[17] Art 1(1) (n 13).

but a clarification of the application of the Brussels I Regulation. Burying the change at the end of the Regulation is potentially misleading and at least mildly controversial. In fact, what is introduced is a form of subject matter jurisdiction, irrespective almost of personal jurisdiction, and that remains a concept that is alien to the Brussels I system. The fact that the national jurisdiction rules tended to provide that solution and that patent lawyers are at ease with the concept does not change that. One is paying lip service to Brussels I to do exactly the opposite of what the system stands for, which is an unusual type of clarification.

Article 1(1) did not survive in the Regulation, as adopted. But the principle has been retained and has instead been slipped in as part of Recital 6 to the amending Regulation:

> As courts common to several Member States, the Unified Patent Court and the Benelux Court of Justice cannot, unlike a court of one Member State, exercise jurisdiction on the basis of national law with respect to defendants not domiciled in a Member State. To allow those two Courts to exercise jurisdiction with respect to such defendants, the rules of Regulation (EU) No 1215/2012 should therefore, with regard to matters falling within the jurisdiction of, respectively, the Unified Patent Court and the Benelux Court of Justice, also apply to defendants domiciled in third States. The existing rules of jurisdiction of Regulation (EU) No 1215/2012 ensure a close connection between proceedings to which that Regulation applies and the territory of the Member States. *It is therefore appropriate to extend those rules to proceedings against all defendants regardless of their domicile.* When applying the rules of jurisdiction of Regulation (EU) No 1215/2012, the Unified Patent Court and the Benelux Court of Justice (hereinafter individually referred to as a 'common court') should apply only those rules which are appropriate for the subject-matter for which jurisdiction has been conferred on them. (Emphasis added.)

This does not address the lack of clarity; on the contrary it aggravates it, as it will not be part of the amended version of Brussels I. The reader will barely notice that part of the new jurisdiction rules in Article 71b are de facto based on the principle and the non-expert reader is likely to overlook this point.

C. The New Rules on International Jurisdiction: Article 71b

i. Paragraph 1

Let us start with the straightforward element in the new international jurisdiction rules. In a situation where the Brussels I Regulation gives jurisdiction to the courts of a Member State that is party to the UPC Agreement, and where the subject matter of the case comes inside the scope of the subject matter covered by the UPC Agreement,[18] that jurisdiction is transferred from the national court to the Unified Patent Court. This works well if the Brussels I jurisdiction is based on the domicile of the defendant in the Member State concerned, in application

[18] What we will discuss below as the 'competence' of the court.

of what has now become Article 4 of the Brussels I Regulation.[19] Persons so domiciled can also be sued in the courts of the place where the harmful event occurred, or may occur, in application of Article 7(2) Brussels I Regulation.[20] A domicile in a Member State remains the *conditio sine qua non*, unless the ground for exclusive jurisdiction in Article 24(4) applies, that is, in cases dealing with the validity of the patent. Article 24(4) does not create problems at this stage and neither does Article 8(1) that allows the claimant to bring multiple defendants before a single court if certain circumstances are met.[21]

By using the words 'a common court shall have jurisdiction', Article 71b seems to suggest that the common court will merely also have jurisdiction. This is not the case. The UPC Agreement clearly works on the basis that the jurisdiction of the national courts will be transferred to the Unified Patent Court and that the national courts lose their jurisdiction. It might have been better to spell this out *expressis verbis*; especially in relation to Article 24(4) there can only be one court with exclusive validity jurisdiction and the UPC Agreement clearly sees the Unified Patent Court in that role. But that can only happen if the Brussels I Regulation grants it exclusive jurisdiction. This is clearly intended, but it would have been clearer to spell it out at the level of the Brussels I Regulation.

This is even more so in as far as the seven-year transition period is concerned. During that period Article 83(1) of the UPC Agreement accepts that parties will be able to bring cases both before the national courts and before the Unified Patent Court. This concurrent jurisdiction should ideally be spelled out in the Brussels I Regulation. Admittedly the current wording of Article 71b leaves this possibility open, but this is clearly not intended. The plan was not to leave it open and to again amend the Brussels I Regulation at the end of the seven-year transition period. Even worse, at least during the transition period there will be two courts with exclusive jurisdiction under Article 24(4). That means that the jurisdiction of the court excludes the jurisdiction of any other court. But how is that to work vis-à-vis another court with exclusive jurisdiction? Simply leaving Article 24(4) as it is provides no solution. One can only assume that the idea might have been to leave this matter to the *lis pendens* rules and to operate on the basis that the court first seised has priority, but that is not clear from the text. If a national court deals with the validity of a single designation of a European patent the Unified Patent Court should be able to deal (at least) with the validity of the other designations of the same patent, but its judgment covers by definition

[19] The old Art 2.

[20] For a detailed analysis of the application to intellectual property cases of the jurisdiction rules of the Brussels I Regulation, see JJ Fawcett and P Torremans, *Intellectual Property and Private International Law*, 2nd edn (Oxford, Oxford University Press, 2011) ch 5.

[21] Compare the evolution between Case C-539/03 *Roche Nederland BV et al v Frederick Primus and Milton Goldenberg* [2006] ECR I-6535, Case C-145/10 *Eva-Maria Painer v Standard Verlags GmbH et al* [2011] ECDR 6 and Case C-616/10 *Solvay SA/Honeywell et al* (12 July 2012). See also P Torremans, *Intellectual Property puts Article 6(1) Brussels I Regulation to the Test*, CREATe Working Paper No 8 <http://www.create.ac.uk/wp-content/uploads/2013/09/CREATe-Working-Paper-No-8-v1.0.pdf>.

all designations.[22] Contradictory judgments which invalidate the patent in one designation, and validate it for all designations, or vice versa, then become an option. This cannot be intended and is entirely undesirable and unacceptable, even during the seven-year transition period.

Far less controversial, but maybe unexpected, is the fact that Article 25 of the Brussels I Regulation may also apply. Parties to a licence agreement may agree that any infringement case amongst them will be brought before the Unified Patent Court.[23] This may be particularly useful during the seven-year transition period, as it provides predictability and certainty.

ii. Paragraph 2

The drafters of the proposed Article 71b clearly thought that paragraph 1 dealt in the most complete possible way with cases involving defendants that are domiciled in a Member State. As the 2012 Brussels I Regulation recast had rejected the extension of these jurisdiction rules to defendants that are not domiciled in a Member State, the problem that remained was to deal with those defendants, as they may be the ones infringing European Patents (with or without unitary effect) or as they may want to invalidate such patents or, on the contrary, be called upon to defend the validity of such patents. The solution that was retained in the proposal is exactly what was rejected in the recast. Let us do to patent cases what was not acceptable for all other cases and act as if the defendant was domiciled in a Member State even if this is not the case. The jurisdiction rules shall apply as if the defendant was domiciled in a Member State.

Admittedly, paragraph 2 needs to deal with pure subject matter jurisdiction to implement the 'regardless of the defendant's domicile' phrase. The language of the provision is shocking though: one cannot apply the solution to Article 4, as one cannot create a fake domicile and there is no impact on Article 24(4) either, but the language of the new provision clearly refers to them as they are cornerstones of Chapter II of the Brussels I Regulation. Effectively what one does is to remove the requirement that the domicile requirement in Article 4 is met before one can apply Article 7 in infringement cases, or for that purpose Article 8(1) in multiple defendant cases. The non-expert reader might find it very hard to extract that simple message from the text and applying both Articles as mere subject matter jurisdiction is not without its risks. They have been designed to apply with the added safeguard that the defendant is domiciled in a Member State, which guaranteed a strong link between the case and the Brussels I territory. Removing that safeguard without replacing it can give the Unified Patent Court jurisdiction over defendants whose links with the Brussels I territory are extremely weak. Territorial patents are ideally suited to locate some damage in the jurisdiction and

[22] Art 37 UPC Agreement leaves no doubt on this point.

[23] Parties are free not to treat the case as contractual for example when the licensee allegedly goes beyond what is allowed in the licence contract.

it is relatively easy to blame, for example, a foreign (parent) company for it. One may not succeed in substantive law, but harassing defendants by obliging them to defend the case becomes relatively easy.

It would be far clearer for the user of the system, and from a legal perspective much more elegant, clear and safe to provide Article 7 specific language. Hence the proposal to replace the current language by the following text:

> In disputes concerned with the infringements of intellectual property rights over which a court common to several Member States exercises subject matter jurisdiction, a person may be sued in the common court if the alleged infringement occurs or may occur in any of the Member States concerned, unless the alleged infringer has not acted in any of the Member States concerned and his or her activity cannot reasonably be seen as having been directed to that state.
>
> In disputes concerned with a contractual obligation that comes within the subject matter jurisdiction of a court common to several Member States, a person may be sued in the common court if the obligation in question is to be performed in any of the Member States concerned.[24]

The second paragraph is irrelevant for the Unified Patent Court, but is there to cover any other common court, since the proposal also covers the Benelux Court. Paragraph 1 clearly states what the mechanism is, place of infringement without domicile, but also builds in a safeguard mechanism. One does not want the common court to have jurisdiction over a foreign defendant that did not act or direct action in or towards the jurisdiction, such as a manufacturer of a patented product based in a country where there is no patent protecting the product whose independent distributor imports the product in the Member States (where a patent is in force). But as the safeguard applies cumulatively, any foreign parent company that directs the operations of subsidiaries, etc will be caught without the need to rely on Article 8(1).[25]

For reasons of clarity it is advisable to add a paragraph to Article 24(4):[26]

> In disputes having as their object a judgment on the validity or revocation of intellectual property rights over which a court common to several Member States exercises subject matter jurisdiction the common court will have exclusive jurisdiction.
>
> During the transition period provided for by Article 83(1) Agreement on a Unitary Patent Court the exclusive jurisdiction of the common court and the national court will be exercised concurrently. The relationship between the common court and the national court will be determined by Article 31.

[24] Based on Arts 2:201 and 2:202 of the CLIP Principles; see European Max Planck Group on Conflict of Laws in Intellectual Property (CLIP), *Conflict of Laws in Intellectual Property: The CLIP Principles and Commentary* (Oxford, Oxford University Press, 2013) ('CLIP Principles') 69–84. (The author is a member of CLIP).

[25] For a complete explanation of the approach that is proposed and of the safeguard mechanism, see CLIP Principles.

[26] For a full background on the current version of Art 24(4), and the problems associated with it, see Fawcett and Torremans (n 20) ch 7.

Inside the common court the division before which validity is raised during infringement proceedings has the option to continue with the infringement case and to rule on validity too.[27] This effectively reverses the position taken by the CJEU in *GAT v Luk*.[28] As a result, it no longer makes sense to keep the strict current version of Article 24(4) Brussels I Regulation, as interpreted in *GAT v Luk*, for other registered intellectual property rights[29] and for national patents. Not allowing the infringement court to rule *erga omnes* and to instruct a foreign patent office to change the register is sufficient. Hence the idea to add the following paragraph to Article 24(4):

> Paragraph 1 does not apply where validity arises in a context other than by principal claim or counterclaim. The decisions resulting from such disputes do not affect the validity of those rights against third parties.

It would allow the defendant in an infringement case to raise the invalidity of the right as a defence, that is, one cannot infringe an invalid right, without the infringement court having to stay the case. But it then remains an infringement case and the decision of the court will simply determine between the parties whether the defendant infringes the right of the claimant. Any decision on invalidity proper, that is one with effect *erga omnes* that will find its way onto the register, will still have to be brought in the court that has exclusive jurisdiction.[30]

Article 8(1) Brussels I Regulation allows multiple defendants to be brought before a single court and can of course also be extended to defendants that are not domiciled in a Member State, but its application in patent cases (and in intellectual property cases in general) is a mess.[31] *Roche Nederland*[32] was unduly strict and without stating so the CJEU has been backtracking ever since. There was the *Freeport* case[33] and then *Painer*[34] and *Solvay*.[35] The latter two cases are simply incompatible with the strict *Roche Nederland* approach. One can leave it to the CJEU to sort out the confusion and hope the Court will continue with the de facto more flexible approach in *Solvay* and *Painer*. However, Article 33(1)(b) UPC Agreement has very different language to offer:

> An action may be brought against multiple defendants only where the defendants have a commercial relationship and where the action relates to the same alleged infringement.

Admittedly, this provision cannot operate at international jurisdiction level, where Article 31 refers uniquely to the Brussels I Regulation and its Article 8(1), and it therefore only operates at the competence level, that is once the Unified

[27] Art 33(3) UPC Agreement.
[28] Case C-4/03 *GAT v Luk* [2006] ECR I-6509.
[29] Since the rule was essentially there for (European) patents.
[30] For a complete explanation of the approach that is proposed, see CLIP Principles 138–52.
[31] A detailed analysis would lead too far here; see instead Torremans (n 21).
[32] Case C-539/03 *Roche Nederland BV et al v Frederick Primus and Milton Goldenberg* [2006] ECR I-6535.
[33] Case C-98/06 *Freeport Plc v Arnoldsson* [2007] ECR I-8319.
[34] Case C-145/10 *Eva-Maria Painer v Standard Verlags GmbH et al* [2011] ECDR 6.
[35] Case C-616/10 *Solvay SA/Honeywell et al* (12 July 2012).

Patent Court already has jurisdiction over each of the defendants. But it may not be wise to leave both versions in existence side by side, without any clarification for the non-private international law expert as to which one applies when. Be that as it may, there will be little scope for Article 8(1) if the defendant is not domiciled in a Member State. It will be very hard to find a defendant that one would nevertheless want to join to the case before the Unified Patent Court, but that cannot be brought before the court on the basis of Article 7(2) if the domicile safeguard no longer applies. Any defendant against whom one has a realistic chance of success will at least contribute to the act causing the damage or be at least partially responsible for the damage. Once the jurisdiction point has been handled by Article 7(2) of the Brussels I Regulation the competence provision in Article 33(1)(b) will enable the claimant to centralize the claim against multiple defendants before a single division of the court.[36]

Finally, the proposal makes Article 35 of the Brussels I Regulation applicable even if the courts of other Member States have jurisdiction as to the substance of the case. This gives the Unified Patent Court an appropriately wide power to issue provisional measures.

iii. Paragraph 3

Paragraph 3 was always intended to add to the basis on which jurisdiction can be taken, but what was proposed in the draft Regulation was very different from what made it into the Regulation that was in the end adopted. Let us look in turn at both versions.

Paragraph 3 of the proposal was intended to offer a further ground of jurisdiction over a defendant that is not domiciled in a Member State. The idea was simple: an additional ground of jurisdiction was provided as a safety net for those cases for which no other provision of the Regulation gives jurisdiction to a Brussels I court. Whilst this may not only appear to be simple, but also reasonable if one considers the recast of the Brussels I Regulation, it is hard to see how this remains simple and reasonable if the massive expansion that results from paragraph 2 of Article 71b is also taken on board. Be that as it may, paragraph 3 did set out to grant the Unitary Patent Court jurisdiction over a defendant that is not domiciled in a Member State and that is not subject to the jurisdiction of the court on the basis of any other Brussels I provision if:

a) property belonging to the defendant is located in a Member State party to the agreement establishing the common court;
b) the value of the property is not insignificant compared to the value of the claim;

[36] Art 33(1) does not expressly extend the application of its para (b) to defendants that are not domiciled in a Member State, but this is clearly intended. The paragraph on defendants that are not domiciled in a Member State merely adds the option to sue them before the central division, without excluding anything.

c) the dispute has a sufficient connection with any Member State party to the agreement establishing the common court.[37]

The explanatory memorandum referred to the fact that various Member States have an asset-based ground of jurisdiction in their national jurisdiction rules, but that does not mean it is needed or useful in a patent context where paragraph 2 is already in place. The explanatory memorandum gave the example of a Turkish defendant (with assets in the EU one assumes) who infringes a European patent covering several Member States and Turkey.[38] There is a slight problem with the example though: it is not covered by paragraph 3. Paragraph 2 does the job as Article 7(2) without the domicile requirement will grant jurisdiction in respect of any of the Member States concerned, as the infringement takes place there, and Article 34 Unified Patent Court makes sure that the judgment covers any designation of the European patent. One never gets to paragraph 3, as there is a ground of jurisdiction in the Regulation that applies.

The version of the proposed paragraph 3 of Article 71(b) is the ultimate power grab! It could make sense as a limitation or check and balance on paragraph 2, but that is clearly not what it is. It is however very hard to see which case, that would not already be covered by paragraph 2 would be covered by paragraph 3, and would be reasonable in terms of the jurisdiction of the common court. One can only assume that this is supposed to cover the foreign parent or holding company in a multiple defendants case in the absence of a working multiple defendants provision at international jurisdiction stage. As shown above, a properly worded paragraph 2 will do the job and a properly worded Article 8(1) provision can only help. Paragraph 3 is thus redundant and will only serve to (rightfully) infuriate foreign countries. It also undermines the criticism always made when, for example, the Texas courts seize jurisdiction on such a basis.[39] In its proposed version, paragraph 3 is also entirely out of line with the very principles of the Brussels I jurisdiction.

As these criticisms were conveyed to the draftsmen, it is satisfying to see that the final version of paragraph 3 looks radically different. The starting point is now very clearly not an independent ground of jurisdiction, but a case where the common court does already have jurisdiction on the basis of paragraph 2. In such a case damage inside the EU may be coupled with damage outside the EU in a third state. It may make sense for the common court to also deal with that latter damage and to avoid the need for there to be additional litigation in the third state. Article 7(2) of the Brussels I Regulation, even if applied without the domicile requirement as a result of paragraph 2, may not have covered damage in a third state and paragraph 3

[37] Art 1(2) (n 13).

[38] Above n 13, 6–7.

[39] *Rhapsody Solutions, LLC v Cryogenic Vessel Alternatives, Inc* (US District Court, SD Tex, 5 March 2013), a foreign company accessing software on a server in the US, with the foreign company having a subsidiary and assets in the US is subject to the jurisdiction of the court in Texas. Even in the US this case and the District Court for the Southern District of Texas' approach to jurisdiction is controversial.

serves a useful purpose on this point. Once that starting point has been established two of the factors that were also retained in the proposal return, but this time they operate as additional safeguards:

> Such jurisdiction may only be established if property belonging to the defendant is located in any Member State party to the instrument establishing the common court and the dispute has a sufficient connection with any such Member State.

iv. Lis Pendens

The issue of *lis pendens* arises if we leave jurisdiction rules in the strict sense to one side. The idea of several courts that deal with the same or a related issue between the same parties has never found favour, for obvious reasons, in private international law. The proposal has a simple solution to offer: the existing Brussels I Regulation rules on *lis pendens* is expanded to cover two additional situations. On a permanent basis there is the situation where proceedings are brought in the Unified Patent Court and in the national courts of an EU Member State that is not a party to the UPC Agreement and on a temporary bases there is the situation where proceedings are brought in the Unified Patent Court and in the national courts of a Member State that is a party to the UPC Agreement during the transition period that is referred to in Article 83(1) of the Unified Court Agreement.

Complications

One has to ask the question, though, whether matters can be that simple. The Brussels I approach can be abbreviated to the concept that the court first seized is given preference. But that assumes that there is a single cause of action, that is, the same (or a very related) case is brought in two or more courts. Patent cases fit badly with that idea. There are infringement cases, claims for a negative declaration and (in-)validity claims or counterclaims. They can arise in the same case or in separate cases, but the link between them is very strong. And until we are merely left with European patents with unitary effect there are the various national designations of a European patent. Not all claims relate to all designations and the various claims do not necessarily refer to the same designations, even though there may (or may not) be an overlap on this point. Perhaps the easiest way forward is to look at a number of practical examples and it will become clear very quickly that these complicating factors cause significant problems for the simple solution proposed by the Commission.

v. Some Examples

It is quite common for a competitor who wants to clear the way to commence one or more national revocation actions in respect of one or more designations of a European patent. The rightholder can react with an infringement action before the Unified Patent Court (between the same parties). Let us assume that the infringement action before the Unified Patent Court relates to all designations of the European patent. The defendant to that infringement action then attempts to counterclaim to revoke all designations of the European patent. At least in so far as the Unified Patent Court counterclaim relates to the revocation of those designations of the European patent seized by national courts, Article 71c(2) would prevent this UPC counterclaim.

The infringement action is not the problem in such a scenario, as Article 83(1) UPC Agreement explicitly provides for parallel proceedings. It is the counterclaim that is hit by the *lis pendens* rules and as that is brought by the same party as the validity action, they can drop the latter in the national court and raise the same issue by way of counterclaim in the common court. This is not an elegant solution, but it is a workable solution, and arguably it provides an acceptable balance between the interests of the parties, with respect for Article 83(1) UPC Agreement. In general there is something to be said for an option that requires a party that wants to raise the same point in both courts to choose between the courts and to drop the action in the other court if it wishes to change courts. That also applies to a party that wants to make an infringement claim in both courts. However, disaster would strike if a final judgment had been given in the national court. As that one designation is necessarily also before the Unified Patent Court, and as the judgment of that court necessarily covers all designations, the defendant would be estopped from raising the invalidity argument by way of counterclaim in the Unified Patent Court and there is no obvious way out. The proposal offers no solution. Similarly, it may be hard to ask the defendant to drop an appeal in the national court after the invalidity claim has been rejected at first instance, as again estoppel would follow.

One always accepts, as this is most likely in current practice, that invalidity is raised by claim or counterclaim. But would it not be possible to refrain from counterclaiming and merely raise the validity point as a defence to the infringement claim? If this is an option, the cause of action in both courts would be different and the hard *lis pendens* rule would not operate. All that is open to the judge then is that he 'may' stay proceedings. The infringement court would then merely decide the infringement claim (ie succeeds or fails) if that option is not taken and the validity court would deal with validity. No irreconcilable judgments in the strict sense would emerge, but at least *inter partes* the infringement court would deal with the validity issue. Private international *lis pendens* rules are not good at dealing with such claims that almost inevitably involve two issues, hence the best solution would be to make sure that invalidity has to be raised as a counterclaim in infringement proceedings.

In a second example the patentee starts infringement proceedings in the Unified Patent Court. The defendant first responds with a series of national revocation actions, before counterclaiming for revocation in the Unified Patent Court. Article 71c(2) would prevent this counterclaim. The defendant cannot stop the Unified Patent Court proceedings in such a scenario, but as he first seised the national courts of the invalidity claims, he is himself estopped from raising it in the Unified Patent Court proceedings on the basis of *lis pendens*. He would have to drop the national claims if he wants to counterclaim in the Unified Patent Court proceedings. However, he is not obliged to do so as a result of Article 83(1) of the UPC Agreement. This can lead to the undesirable situation in which the common court can award damages and injunctions in a mere infringement case, only for the various designations of the European patent to be revoked in the national courts during the transition period. At least it is now possible to reclaim damages paid for the infringement of an invalid patent[40] and injunctions can, of course, also be lifted.

Let us now look as a third example to the scenario where there is no overlap between the designations of the European patent. A single national revocation action is then, for example, followed by an infringement action before the Unified Patent Court, but we assume here that the latter relates to another designation of the European patent and only to infringing acts in another state. The defendant to the infringement action then counterclaims to that designation of the European patent. In this scenario, the Unified Patent Court and the national court are dealing with different subject matters, being infringement of different designations of a European patent. One could argue that at best these are related actions where a stay 'may' follow. But one can also convincingly argue that, by virtue of Article 34 UPC Agreement, the decision of the Unified Patent Court will have effect in respect of all designations of the European patent and that that creates an overlap and a same cause of action. Matters are not clear and the situation where a 'competence' rule has to come to the rescue of the *lis pendens* private international law rule is not ideal. Be that as it may, it makes no sense that it will necessarily be the court first seized (the national court in our example) that will continue with the case if the *lis pendens* rules apply one way or another. Here the court that should continue is the common court, as it is the one that can rely on the broad coverage of Article 34. And to make things worse, different parties can own different designations of a single European patent. The proposed system has no mechanism for all owners to be represented before the court, even though Article 34 necessarily leads to a decision that affects all designations of the European patent. The patent can be revoked in proceedings to which the owner is not even a party. But that is strictly speaking not a *lis pendens* issue. Rather, Article 34 makes perfect sense for a European patent with unitary effect, but less for a mere European patent if its designations are owned by different parties.

In a fourth scenario the problem arises from the fact that negative declarations and infringement actions are seen to involve the same cause of action.[41] This allows the potential defendant in a (common court) infringement case to bring

[40] *Virgin Atlantic Airways Ltd v Zodiac Seats UK Ltd* [2013] UKSC 46. Previously the UK was out of step with the legal position in most Member States.

[41] See, eg *Société Belt Buckle v Guenoun* [2006] IL Pr 43 (French Supreme Court/Cour de Cassation); *Mölnlycke Health Care v BSN Medical* [2009] EWHC 3370 (Pat) per Floyd J.

a national negative declaration case (potentially in combination with a validity claim, potentially in a torpedo jurisdiction). Article 29 Brussels I Regulation does then prevent the rightholder from bringing an infringement case in the common court because the rule is imported by the proposal. Does it then make sense to rely on the court first seized? Does one not, by paying lip service to Article 83(1) UPC Agreement, deny the rightholder the option to enforce its rights effectively by means of a single action? The defendant can effectively force the rightholder down the national country by country enforcement route as the holder of a supposedly valid right cannot sue on validity grounds. The question that needs to be asked here is whether a preference for the common court instead of the court first seized does not make more sense.

vi. Outcome

It needs to be clarified what the private international law role is of Article 34 of the UPC Agreement. How and when does it lead to a same cause of action? The systematic preference for the court first seised in the Brussels I Regulation is not always the way forward in the patent related cases. Maybe one ought to give preference to the Unified Patent Court in a (large) number of circumstances. But can that be reconciled with the political compromise that underpins Article 83(1) of the Agreement? This is clearly an area where the proposal, as adopted, is anything but satisfactory and where a lot of clarifying work remains to be done.[42]

D. Recognition and Enforcement

Not all EU Member States will become parties to the UPC Agreement. There will therefore in practice be judgments from those Member States that did not join and judgments from the Unified Patent Court. Each of these may require recognition and enforcement in the other area. The proposed Article 71d deals with this problem and applies the standard Brussels I Regulation mechanism. This does not give rise to major problems and is acceptable as a workable solution.

The focus changes, of course, if one is merely dealing with the recognition and enforcement of a judgment given by a common court in a Member State that is party to the instrument establishing the common court. The proposal did not address this issue, but the Regulation, as adopted, now adds the obvious solution, which is to apply any rules on recognition and enforcement in that instrument instead of the Brussels I rules.[43]

[42] A Johnson and R Pinckney, 'Proposed Amendment to the Brussels 1 Regulation: Some Potential Issues' <http://www.bristows.co.uk/articles/proposed-amendment-to-the-brussels-1-regulation-some-potential-issues-by-richard-pinckney-and-alan-johnson>.

[43] Art 1 (*in fine*), which will become the final paragraph of Art 71d Brussels I Regulation (n 14).

E. Competence

Once the international jurisdiction of the Unified Patent Court has been established the second part of Chapter VI of the UPC Agreement comes into play.

Article 32 deals with the competence of the court and establishes the subject matter with which the court will deal. Article 33 follows up with the internal distribution of cases between the various divisions of the court. Here one finds elements such as the flexible multiple defendant rule that was referred to above and rules on *lis pendens* and priority. There is also a rule that allows a case that really covers most the territory of the court to be transferred from the regional divisions to the central division if the infringement has occurred at least in the territories of three regional divisions, as well as further procedural rules.

What follows then in the scheme of things is of course the by now well-rehearsed rule in Article 34 that was already referred to above. Its role as a competence rule is uncontroversial and clear, but its wider implications in relation to jurisdiction are less clear and less uncontroversial. It would, however, lead too far to offer here a complete in-depth analysis of the competence rules. Suffice it to repeat that they are to be distinguished from the jurisdiction rules and that they play a different role.

IV. Conclusion

The least one can say is that the questions surrounding the jurisdiction and competence of the Unified Patent Court raise interesting issues. These issues also involve the interaction between the Brussels I Regulation and the UPC Agreement. That interaction is not straightforward and has maybe not been thought through carefully enough when the Agreement was drafted. The solution which the Commission proposed to sort out the compliance between both instruments suffers from the same defect, even in the amended version that was adopted. Simply expanding the scope of the Brussels I Regulation to the Unified Patent Court, and to defendants that are not domiciled in a Member State, does not lead to a workable solution. In the course of the analysis above I have tried to offer some alternative suggestions, but the maze that arises from the UPC Agreement is a complex one and one that is not easily solved merely by rules of private international law.

11

Looking Forward: A User Perspective

ALAN JOHNSON*

In view of the numerous uncertainties about the proposed unitary patent (UP) system, it is no surprise that there are concerns among users. The concerns go further than merely the procedural uncertainties identified, however: the fundamental issue is that until the system is tried and tested it will lack predictability. As one user from the pharmaceutical industry said: 'even if I could design the system, I still wouldn't use it'. He, like many others, would prefer to wait and see how the new system evolves before risking his patents (which will inevitably be very valuable) in an untested court. That concern is exacerbated by the fact that we will have a new group of judges from different traditions operating in the numerous different divisions, central, local and regional. Present indications are that there will be over a dozen of these divisions. Although multi-national in composition, the panels in all regional divisions and most local divisions will include two local judges. Human nature suggests a tendency to interpret rules of procedure in a way consistent with existing local traditions. One may look to the interpretation of the Enforcement Directive[1] as a parallel example of this. It resulted in very little procedural harmonization because the attitude of many states, despite their widely differing procedures, was simply: 'we already do that'.

In some sectors, the concerns also include that so-called 'troll' litigation will become prevalent in the new system. Businesses making investment decisions hate uncertainty, and the inability to counter-sue a non-practising entity (NPE) makes negotiation far more difficult than with a traditional industrial competitor. There are, of course, important features of the US litigation system which make 'troll' activity so prevalent there,[2] and which are absent from the Unified Patent Court (UPC) system. These are notably the inability to recover costs against unsuccessful claimants, and the huge cost of litigation. Essentially, upon finding contingency fee lawyers to act, any NPE may take risk-free action. This will not be so in the UPC. The legal costs in the UPC should be much lower than in the US and there are provisions for costs recovery. Nonetheless it is very likely that NPEs will start

* Partner, Bristows LLP.

[1] Directive 2004/48/EC of the European Parliament and of the Council of 29 April 2004 on the enforcement of intellectual property rights, OJ L157 (30 April 2004).

[2] See the discussion by Rochelle Dreyfuss in ch 9 of this volume.

proceedings in a number of different UPC divisions throughout Europe to see what can be achieved. The result is that in the opening few months of the UPC's existence, the majority of litigants are likely to be either those seeking to revoke patents centrally, or NPEs trying out the new system in the hope that they will persuade defendants to settle rather than face an uncertain outcome.

I. Opt-out Provisions

A large number of patentees, on the other hand, who use their patent assets to protect a business, will be nervous of risking central revocation of their patents in the new system, and will wish to take advantage of the transitional provisions which allow an opt-out. Before looking at how the opt-out system works (or may work) it is necessary to go back into the history to understand the basis for the arrangement.

A political decision was taken many years ago that the new unitary patent (at the time termed the Community patent) should be litigated in a common court rather than by giving individual national courts jurisdiction over the unitary right. However, the difficulty and expense of setting up a court for such patents could not be justified on its own. Instead, therefore, it was necessary to extend the system to conventional European patents. At the same time, it was thought positively beneficial that the existing method of litigating centrally obtained European patents in national litigation systems should be reformed by having a common court in which to litigate those European patents. Indeed such a centralised litigation system had been promulgated following the 1997 review of the European Patent Convention when an optional protocol (variously termed the European Patent Litigation Protocol or European Patent Litigation Agreement[3]) was proposed. The difficulty, however, was that this amounted to a change in the goalposts for patent owners who, when applying for European patents, had 'signed up' to a national litigation regime for enforcement. The solution to this problem was a transitional arrangement whereby existing European patents would be subject to the new court's exclusive competence, but with the possibility of the patentee being able to opt-out during a seven-year period. These last words are carefully chosen for their ambiguity as will now be explained.

When one looks at the Article from the UPC Agreement[4] which deals with this provision, namely Article 83, the two main provisions are in sub-articles 1 and 3. These read as follows:

> (1) During a transitional period of seven years after the date of entry into force of this agreement, an action for infringement or for revocation of a European patent, or an

[3] See the discussion by Christopher Wadlow in ch 3 of this volume.

[4] Agreement on a Unified Patent Court, OJ C175/1 (20 June 2013) (UPC Agreement).

action for infringement or for declaration of invalidity of a supplementary protection certificate issued for a product protected by a European patent, may still be brought before national courts or other competent national authorities.

…

(3) Unless an action has already been brought before the court, a proprietor of or an applicant for a European patent granted or applied for prior to the end of the transitional period under paragraph 1 and, where applicable, paragraph 5, as well as the holder of the supplementary protection certificate issued for a product protected by a European patent, shall have the possibility to opt out from the exclusive competence of the Court. To this end they should notify their opt-out to the Registry by the latest one month before expiry of the transitional period. The opt-out shall take effect upon its entry into the register.

There are also relevant provisions in Articles 83(4) and (5) which are to the effect that the opt-out may be withdrawn and that the transitional period may be extended by up to seven years.

The widely accepted meaning of these provisions can be summarised as follows:

— The transitional period lasts seven years;
— If you do nothing within seven years, your patent is in the UPC system;
— However, during the transitional period, national infringement and national revocation actions remain possible, even if you have not opted out (Article 83(1));
— Patentees can opt the European patent (EP) out of the UPC system for the life of the patent (Article 83(3));
— The opting out regime applies to new patent applications as well as existing patents and applications and supplementary protection certificates (SPCs);
— It is possible to opt back in to enforce separately under Article 83(4); and
— The transitional period might be extended to up to 14 years (Article 83(5)).

This conventional view is reflected in the Commission's questions and answers posted on 19 February 2013, which reads as follows:[5]

During a transitional period of seven years, actions for infringement or for revocation concerning 'classical' European patents without unitary effect can still be brought before national courts. A proprietor of or an applicant for a European patent granted or applied for prior to the end of the transitional period will also have the possibility to opt out from the exclusive competence of the Court (unless an action has already been brought before the Court).

The first sentence quoted above appears to be a reflection of Article 83(1), whilst the second sentence appears to be a reflection of Article 83(3).

There is, however, an alternative interpretation possible of these provisions, which may be termed 'holistic', and hence rather European in its character.

[5] <http://ec.europa.eu/internal_market/indprop/patent/faqs/index_en.htm>.

Article 83(1) may be read as an introduction or recital to the remainder of the Article. It may be read merely to state that despite the foregoing provisions of the Agreement assigning exclusive competence to the UPC over litigation of European patents, there remains the possibility of national actions. Then Article 83(3) informs the reader how this is to be achieved, namely by opting-out. What then would the effect be of such an interpretation?

The first effect would be that European patents not opted-out could *only* be litigated in the UPC. As we shall see later, this removes the possibility of a nonsensical situation of competing revocation actions existing in national and UPC courts. More importantly, however, it would mean that the opt-out would apply for seven years only, because Article 83(1) says that this is how long the transitional period lasts. This would mean that not only would existing European patents be forced back into the UPC regime after seven years, but that so too would new European patent applications lodged with the European Patent Office (EPO) after start up of the UPC system. Currently many patentees seem intent upon continuing their existing filing practice in the belief that they will be able to opt-out for the life of that patent. Under this interpretation, that would be a false premise.

How realistic then is this 'holistic' interpretation? This question may first be answered by noting that the Commission's questions and answers have not always read as quoted above. On the contrary, when the relevant page was launched on 11 December 2012, it read as follows:[6]

> During a transitional period of 7 years, actions concerning 'classical' European patents without unitary effect can still be brought before the national court *if those patents have been opted-out* before an action has been brought before the UPC. (Emphasis added).

Clearly whoever at the Commission wrote and approved that summary believed the alternative interpretation postulated to be the correct one. Why then was it changed on 19 February 2013? The answer to that is that upon the prompting of several individuals in the UK (the author included), the UK Intellectual Property Office (IPO) informed the Commission that its interpretation was inconsistent with the apparent literal meaning of the provisions.

Another way of addressing the question is to note that in Rule 5 of the 16th draft Rules of Procedure,[7] the following note was included:

> The Drafting Committee would like to note, in response to certain written comments received, that the provisions of Article 83 of the Agreement for opting out are clear and provide for:
>
> (i) a complete ousting of the jurisdiction of the UPC;

[6] See 'Patent Reform Package—Frequently Asked Questions', European Commission Memo/12/970 (11 December 2012) <http://europa.eu/rapid/press-release_MEMO-12-970_en.htm?locale=FR>.

[7] Preliminary set of provisions for the Rules of Procedure ('Rules') of the Unified Patent Court, 16th draft of 31 January 2014 <http://www.unified-patent-court.org/images/documents/revised-draft-rules-of-procedure.pdf>.

(ii) such ouster is, subject to Rule 5.8, for the life of the relevant patent/application including the time after the patent has expired, has lapsed or has been withdrawn; and
(iii) covers all designations owned by the proprietor(s) in question.

The third point raises a separate issue which is outside the scope of this discussion, but the first and second plainly support the conventional view.

Given that the Rules Committee is made up of individuals who are pre-eminent in their field, and also include at least some who may in due course be judges of the UPC, their views are of great importance, but they are in no way definitive. Indeed *any* current views are irrelevant because it is only at a later stage that the provisions will be interpreted, and it is only the views of those individuals (judges) which will matter. Moreover, it will not, in the author's view be the judges of the UPC who will decide, but the judges of the Court of Justice of the European Union (CJEU). Why is this? The following examples are illustrative:

— Company A owns a European patent with several designations;
— Company A does not opt-out;
— Company B brings a national revocation action, assuming Article 83(1) permits this;
— Company A counter-sues in the UPC for infringement;
— Company B counterclaims for revocation in the UPC, resulting in both national and UPC revocation proceedings.

It is not possible under normal Brussels Convention Regulation (1215/2012)[8] principles for two sets of revocation proceedings concerning the same national designation to coexist. In this scenario, the patentee would inevitably say that the counterclaim in the UPC either could not be brought at all, or at least not in respect of the designation already the subject of the national action. How would the UPC decide this? It would have to interpret Article 83, and consider the impact of Regulation 1215/2012. In short, it would surely have to refer the case to the CJEU unless it regarded the point as *acte claire* (which it surely is not).

Even were the UPC in this instance to decide the matter to be *acte claire*, the matter could reach the CJEU another way through a national route. Consider the second example:

— Company A owns a European patent with several designations;
— Company A does not opt-out;
— Company B brings a national revocation action, assuming Article 83(1) permits this;

[8] Regulation (EU) No 1215/2012 of the European Parliament and of the EU Council of 12 December 2012 on jurisdiction and the recognition and enforcement of judgments in civil and commercial matters, OJ L351 (20 December 2012) (Regulation 1215/2012). Between the writing and publication of this chapter, Regulation 1215/2012 was amended: see Regulation EU No 542/2014 of the European Parliament and of the Council of 15 May 2014 amending Regulation (EU) No 1215/2012 as regards the rules to be applied with respect to the Unified Patent Court and the Benelux Court of Justice, OJ L163/1 (29 May 2014).

— Company A says that it has not opted-out and the national case cannot therefore be heard in the national court, since Article 83 has to be read holistically.

In these circumstances, the national court will have to determine the meaning of Article 83(1) and whether it has jurisdiction. Again, ultimately, however, that is a question of jurisdiction under Regulation 1215/2012.[9]

Plainly, it would be entirely justifiable for the CJEU to come to either conclusion as to the correct interpretation of the Article 83 provisions, either 'conventional' or 'holistic'.

II. Forum Shopping

A feature of the UPC system is that it gives great scope to patentees to decide upon the division in which it may bring infringement proceedings. Indeed, it is true to say that in most cases, an action will probably be capable of being brought in any division under the broad rules of Article 33(1) UPC Agreement. This is because it is often, and indeed usually possible to arrange for a 'trap purchase' to be made anywhere, and even in cases where this is not possible, joinder of co-defendants who have a 'commercial relationship' widens options, together with the lack of any requirement to choose the most appropriate or natural forum for the dispute. (Challenges under Rule 19 are only possible to the jurisdiction and competence of the Court and the competence of the division). Although normally local and regional divisions should be selected for infringement actions, the central division has competence where infringing acts are committed (or defendants are found) in states who do not host a local division or share a regional division. There will surely be at least some of these, including Malta, Luxembourg, and possibly Eire and Portugal. Only in cases brought in regional divisions where there is infringement in the territories of three or more regional divisions may actions be mandatorily transferred upon the request of the defendant, and it remains to be seen whether there will be three or more divisions, with currently only two looking relatively certain.[10]

Why then in a unified court should a choice of division make any difference? Again one goes back to the possibility of different divisions behaving differently according to local traditions, be it procedural or substantive. If a patentee–claimant perceives any possible advantage in a particular case, it will surely seize this perceived advantage. It is true that in due course differences both procedural

[9] See further the discussion by Paul Torremans in ch 10 of this volume.

[10] These are the Swedish and Baltic division, and the south-east Europe (Romania, Bulgaria, Greece, Cyprus and Slovenia) division. Rumours of other divisions have circulated, for a Czech–Slovak division, in particular.

and substantive will be ironed out by the Court of Appeal, but the question of whether the Court of Appeal itself can grant leave to appeal in procedural cases remains unclear at present, and if only the first instance division can grant leave, the process of harmonization will be slow. As to substantive law, again it will take time to resolve differences of opinion, with 'jury' questions on issues of obviousness being a classic instance where harmonization of thinking is very difficult to achieve quickly. Taken together, one can see obvious cases which would preferably (to the perception of a patentee) be brought in one division, or most definitely not. Bearing in mind the present national laws and procedure, what patentee in the early days of the UPC would wish to bring a dosing regimen patent case before the French division? Which patentee requiring disclosure, would bring an action before one of the German divisions? If there is any doubt at all, one only has to look at the position in the US and the popularity of the Eastern District of Texas to put the matter beyond doubt. Despite the control exercised by the Court of Appeals for the Federal Circuit, this remains the district of choice for many patentees.

In the UPC there may be many factors in the mind of patentees. Foremost among them is 'where will I be most likely to win?', but others include:

— Language—what will favour me or cause problems for the defendant?;
— Speed—where will I get the fastest result?;
— Attitude to preliminary injunctions if at all justifiable;
— Attitude to what constitutes infringement/threat to infringe if a defendant is in the pre-launch phase;
— Attitude to pre-action discovery/saisies (orders permitting seizure of documents from premises);
— Attitude to common law features (discovery, evidence and cross-examination);
— Likelihood of bifurcation if the patent is of questionable validity.

III. Litigation Strategies: Use of Opt-out Provisions

As well as being able to select a division of choice within the UPC, a patentee may, of course, use its opt-out option to avoid the system altogether, or, more interestingly, potentially have the best of both worlds. The premise to this is that in some countries, the litigation systems are efficient (or as importantly, perceived to be), whilst others are less so. For example, the UK is an excellent place to litigate pharmaceutical patents and obtain interim relief to prevent generic launches, whilst in Portugal, it is near-impossible to take effective action in pharmaceutical cases. In an ideal world, therefore, why would a pharmaceutical company not wish to retain

UK national jurisdiction, but use the UPC to enforce in Portugal? There are four ways in which this might be achieved.

First, one could adopt an Article 83(1) approach and leave patents in the system whilst suing nationally if preferred. The problem with this is central revocation by way of countersuit or pre-emptive strike.

The second is in the existing portfolio, to opt some patents relating to a particular product out, whilst leaving others in the system. In this way, only some patents could be revoked centrally.

The third is an extension of the second in that one could use divisional cases in the EPO to increase the number of related patents and have some of those opted-out, with others remaining in the system.

Fourth is a more contentious idea of attempting to opt-out some designations, but not others of individual European patents. This, according to the third point of the note of the Rules Committee quoted above, is not possible, but that remains to be seen, at least when different entities own different designations, which raises the possibility of different group companies owning different national designations if internal tax policies permit. There could, however, be issues of competition law if ownership is manipulated in a way seen to be improper (though what could actually be improper is difficult to see from a litigator's perspective), and a more serious problem with the partial opt-out strategy is the effect of Article 34 which says decision of the UPC shall cover the territory of all contracting Member States for which the European patent has effect. However, can this really mean that if, for whatever reason, one patentee owns some designations and opts-out, but another patentee owns other designations and does not opt-out, then a decision in the UPC against the second owner results in the revocation also of the first owner's patents?

A related question is whether the effect of an-opt out is fixed in time in the sense that as more countries accede to the UPC, does one have to update the opt-out? What if a revocation action is pending in the UPC and the day before the decision is handed down a new state accedes?

These and many other issues remain unclear. Nonetheless, and despite these complications, it is patentees who have the choices. As ever, a defendant can do nothing to stop itself being sued. In the UPC if it 'clears the way' with central division revocation or declaratory non-infringement proceedings, it can still find itself counter-sued in a local or regional division with the central division action being stayed.

IV. Patenting Strategies

A different area in which patentees have new options is in their patenting strategy. Since the European Patent Convention (EPC)[11] patentees have had the choice of either or both of national or European patents. In practice most patentees use

[11] Convention on the Grant of European Patents of 5 October 1973 (EPC).

the EPO route, although national routes remain popular with many small and medium-sized enterprises (SMEs) where only local protection is really necessary. These routes both remain open, but now the additional possibility arises of the unitary patent. It is not a truly new genus of patent, since one cannot have both a European patent covering for example the UK, France and Germany, and also a unitary patent. But neither is a unitary patent merely a designation. It is a new legal species of sorts. But will it be popular? How will the new species of patent and the new court system impact upon the popularity of conventional European patents and national patents?

The short answer is probably that in the short term little will change, and that few patentees will use the unitary patent, and not many will move away to using national patent offices to obtain purely national patents. Why is this?

The main advantages of unitary patents are their broad geographic coverage and the ability to enforce centrally. However, these options are available also with conventional European patents not opted-out. The real question is cost as between these two options and flexibility.

At the stage of prosecution there can be no difference in cost, since the process is identical at the EPO. On grant, however, the unitary patent option is cheap in that there is proposed to be no unitary patent designation fee, and the only additional translation cost is to put the specification into another language (English for German and French language cases, and into another EU language in the case of English language cases). This compares with the costs of designation and translation as required by the different states. If very broad (geographic) protection is required then the costs savings at this stage will be substantial. However, not many patentees designate very widely. Even the average of six or seven states is deceptive, because this number will usually include Spain, which the unitary patent will not cover, and the average is distorted by the small number of patentees who designate virtually everywhere. Excluding Spain, many patentees may designate in only two or three states. For them the cost savings are minimal or non-existent. But surely, one would think they will be attracted by getting something for nothing? Sadly not: there is no such thing as a free lunch in this context. The sting is in the tail of renewal fees and the lack of flexibility.

The renewal fees have yet to be set, but need to be seen by reference to what patentees now pay and how they behave to save money in less important cases later in the life of a patent. The author attended a conference in Brussels on the eve of the signing of the UPC on 19 February 2013. There, Dr Margot Fröhlinger, Principal Director of Patent Law and Multilateral Affairs at the EPO, asked rhetorically: 'how much more will patentee pay [in renewal fees] for the extra coverage?' She speculated it may be the equivalent of 6–8, 8–10 or even 10–12 countries.[12] She was wrong. All patentees have budgets and new pressures on costs in Europe have arisen in recent years as China and other Far Eastern countries

[12] Cf G Edmonson, 'Europe's Unitary Patent to Launch in 2015—but will Companies Embrace It?' in *Science/Business* (16 October 2013) <http://www.sciencebusiness.net/news/76292/Europe's-unitary-patent-to-launch-in-2015—but-will-companies-embrace-it> (reporting Dr Fröhlinger as saying that 'no one is prepared to pay the equivalent fees of 25 member states or even 12').

markets have increased in importance. They balance their European 'need' according to how much they can afford. Unless the extra coverage is truly free, then it is simply never going to be the case that patentees will pay more overall for something which they might like, but do not need.

But the situation is worse again for Dr Fröhlinger. Her question ignores the flexibility which comes with the existing European patent system. Almost all patentees 'prune' their portfolio of patents every year or even less. They review whether whole families or individual designations are still required. If not, they are allowed to lapse. This is a business decision based on cost and value. If a designation is not earning its keep, it is dropped. What frequently happens is that some, but not all designations are dropped. Only a few, or even one may remain even if there was wide initial designation. This saves renewal fees. With a unitary patent, this is impossible. It is an all or nothing game, and hence unattractive for any forward-thinking patentee: relatively few will only think as far as the next budget cycle.

Of course after the end of the transitional period, all European patents will be subject to the UPC jurisdiction. It is to be hoped that by that time all wrinkles in the new system will have been ironed out. But if not, will then national patents make a revival (in the mid-2020s)? Indeed, if patentees are concerned at the ambiguity over the opt-out regime, might patentees begin even now to turn to this option?

The answer to this probably again is governed largely by cost, both of external fees and management time. The practical difficulty and cost of obtaining wide-ranging coverage via the national route is considerable, and indeed it is this fact which has (in part at least) made the EPO so successful. It is hard to imagine many patentees wanting wide geographic coverage going down the national route. There is a further problem too. The route from the Patent Cooperation Treaty 1970 (PCT) to national offices is now closed in a number of countries including France and Italy for example. The effect of this is to require a decision to apply to be made at 12 months after priority, which is far too soon for many patentees. This alone makes wide-ranging national filing unrealistic for many.

However, it is a different story for patentees interested in only one or two countries such as Germany and the UK. For such patentees it is very realistic to abandon the EPO altogether. This includes many UK and German SMEs who want protection only in their home state, plus perhaps one other. It also includes many companies in the ICT sector who operate on a pan-European basis with identical products such that the threat of being able to interrupt a competitor in one or both of two main parts of the European market is quite sufficient. For both these classes of patentees, the national route has significant attractions.

V. Conclusion

In summary, the whole concept that industry needs unitary patent protection is flawed. Many patentees operate a business model which means that adequate protection is obtained by a minimal number of designations in such countries as the UK and Germany, and perhaps one or two others. To them the unitary patent is never going to be of real interest. The only companies which routinely currently seek pan-European protection are pharmaceutical companies. They are currently unimpressed by the possibility of valuable assets being revoked centrally by an untested forum. When in due course, the transitional period ends such that new applications, whether maturing into traditional European patents or unitary patent will all compulsorily be litigated in the UPC, then unitary patents will become more attractive for such companies. Even then, however, the possibility of wanting to save costs by portfolio pruning will remain in mind, since one cannot often predict at the time of grant whether a pharmaceutical will be sold throughout the EU: one may hope so, but will likely be unsure. The superficial attraction of unitary patents is just that. They promise a free lunch, but will simply deliver a large service charge.

On the other hand, one can see that the new litigation system will give patentees the whip hand. In the initial phase they can choose whether to opt-out or stay in the system. They may even be able to have the best of both worlds through judicious use of opt-outs and divisional cases. Within the system they can choose the division that most suits their case for procedural or substantive law reasons, despite the unified nature of the Court. Whether 'troll' litigation becomes a problem remains to be seen. The author is optimistic. The UPC system does not suffer the 'no risk' attractions to patentees of the US. Further, if an NPE has a good patent which is being infringed, and seeks to enforce it, then what is the problem? The system should permit enforcement. Lest it be forgotten, many industrial companies use their patent portfolios to extract licence fees as well as to protect their sales. Universities do too. Companies who purchase patents and enforce them are providing a service to those from whom they buy: the vendors recoup on research by virtue of the sale. Provided the new system does not allow invalid patents to be enforced—which means by permitting bifurcation, or by taking too broad a view of what is a valid patent—then there is no problem.

The EPO has an impossible task in filtering out invalid patents. It could do better and must aim to do so. However, the real guardians of industry both as claimants and defendants are the courts. The UPC will in due course be the main forum and simply must be a success. More is needed than just a set of uniform procedural rules: one thing also required is an agreed practice guide made available *before* the system goes live, which, in particular, makes it clear that practice will not deviate from division to division. Setting up a system with divisions which compete was a political compromise. Competition would drive pro-patentee behaviour. The judges need to be strong and uniform in their approach, and happily there is every chance they will be just that.

12

Concluding Remarks

ALISON BRIMELOW CBE

'How is this going to work?': a good question to address when considering the likely effects of a new policy or administrative development. However, a useful answer is not only contingent on legible small print, but also prophetic accuracy in the matter of behaviour responding to new circumstances and, I suggest, on a clear understanding of what you are trying to achieve.

Of course the future is rarely clear, or at the very least views of what it will be are likely to conflict. It is therefore unsurprising that participants in the two-day conference organized by Justine Pila and Christopher Wadlow (the Oxford/East Anglia Unitary Patent System Workshop) in September 2013 had one clear point of agreement: uncertainty about exactly how the unitary patent package (UPP) will work. This was complemented by a recognition that what is currently on offer as a patent system to European inventors is 'unfinished', though serviceable and well understood.

'Evidence based policy' is a much touted concept, but writing in the *Financial Times* in January 2014, John Kay commented that 'policy drives evidence in modern political debate'.[1] And on the basis of the contributions to this book, the same may be true of the UPP. The premises underpinning the negotiations which produced the package now being implemented were, broadly, that Europe needs a unitary right and that patenting costs in Europe are excessive when compared to other jurisdictions, and as such are a competitive disadvantage for Europe.

The creation (or should I say development) of the unitary right has a 50-year history. In the course of that half century the European Patent Office (EPO) has established itself as a major global player with a sound reputation for competence (not perfection), and patenting activity in Europe has grown steadily. Points of anxiety have been whether 'propensity to patent' has been weaker in Europe than elsewhere, and whether cost has been an inhibitor of growth in patenting. The idea that patents should be cheap has enjoyed a long shelf life, though in fact the contents of that particular tin may well be unhealthy. And of course, the idea that the European system is in some sense 'incomplete' has also lingered in the

[1] J Kay, 'For truth on immigration, look to the Bard not politicians', *Financial Times*, 22 January 2014 <http://www.johnkay.com/2014/01/22/for-truth-on-immigration-look-to-the-bard-not-politicians>.

antechambers of power for half a century or so. Lingered, but until now failed to provoke a deliverable response.

Since its inception, the EPO has consistently offered world class examination to its applicants, but once possessed of their patent, patentees have had to consider their options for validation, in terms of how much cover they need and what it will cost. Responses have been varied, shaped both by sectorial needs and by cost implications. The failure to 'complete' the European system by giving pan-European effect to an EPO granted patent (EP) seems to have been influenced by assumptions about the role of language in intellectual property (IP) ('local inventors need to know what is being protected on their territory': discuss). As a result translation has been a major factor in the costs of patenting in Europe. But as importantly, Member States enjoy the local benefits of sharing patent renewal fees with the EPO, an income stream for which remarkably little work has to be done. And whether fortuitously or not, patentees have found that the current incomplete system offers many of them a useful spread of approaches to managing a patent, or patent portfolio. So the expectation must be that what is being implemented now by way of a unitary right will address this incomplete system in a fashion which improves the patent landscape in Europe, especially for innovators (both patentees and potential opponents, I suggest, since a patent is a powerful tool).

A further issue which is relevant is predictability. Predictability is a sort of Holy Grail in IP, and that is why traditionally 'a good presumption of validity' has been the hallmark of the decisions of a respected patent examining authority. Indeed the British inventor, James Dyson, has long argued that patent granting authorities should carry the cost of litigation, at least in respect of validity. Patent offices might blench, but his reasoning is understandable. Why should the inventor pay the costs of defending a right which is said to be sound? We could have a lot of fun with that idea, but not here. However the fact remains, embarking on the quest for a patent is a serious and expensive business, and a lengthy one. The current regime in Europe offers various paths to protection, and the decision tree is complex. Will the UPP regime simplify it? I have to interject a comment on predictability at this point. I used the term 'Grail' deliberately. If the process were to be completely predictable, it would impoverish large swathes of the patent profession, leave courts with endless time on their hands and make patent examination a much less serious task than it is now. I think 'predictability' belongs in Housman's 'blue remembered hills'.[2] But the existence of strategic options (which vary by sector) in pursuit of patent protection makes professional advice pretty much essential for any serious innovator looking for protection beyond the backyard, and by and large tips the balance in favour of those with deep pockets or a lot of IP to trade. It is not SME, or even more 'lone inventor', friendly. So will the UPP offer simplification

[2] AE Housman, *The Land of Lost Content* in AE Housman, *A Shropshire Lad* (London, K Paul, Trench, Treubner, 1896).

which makes using the system more comfortable and affordable for those who currently struggle with it?

Reflecting on the thoughtful contributions to this book, I think my answer has to be a cautious 'not overnight'. Transitional arrangements, incomplete participation by all Member States, the simple fact that the European Patent Organisation has an extensive non-EU membership, all add to the range of options available to those pursuing patent protection and its defence. At least in its early years, predictability is unlikely to improve and that means that the position of the SME in the patent game is also unlikely to improve. The need to develop consistency of practice comes through clearly.

I was also struck by the recurring view of contributors that the outcome was likely to favour the patentee. 'What's wrong with that?' you may ask. An inventor deserves all the security for his/her rights that s/he can get. Two points are worth noting: a patent is a potentially powerful instrument, and can be (and sometimes is) deployed in ways that are anticompetitive. Secondly, 'a good presumption of validity' does not mean that patent examination is infallible. Challenge has to be effective and affordable. This is particularly so now that patent volumes, both pending and granted, are so great that certainty about what space is unoccupied by a competitor is elusive.

Which brings me to my sense of regret as I reflect on what contributors have to say about the UPP. There is a saying that armies always plan for the last war, and indeed looking backwards for how to plan for the future is fairly normal in human activity. The package on offer assumes that 'as things have been, they remain', in the context of how patents protect and sustain innovation. And indeed Georg von Graevenitz gave the Workshop a sound and confident economist's statement of how patents do pretty much what they say they do. So one should conclude that 'completing' the European system will enhance or sustain its benefits. But this probably fails to take adequate account of the effectiveness of adaptation to the deficiencies of the current system. Alan Johnson's well-grounded contribution signals that clearly. Useful flexibility is being lost and complexity of choice increased. Rochelle Dreyfuss suggests that on balance what is on offer will work, citing US experience, but also signals areas of uncertainty and risk.

I think we have to remind ourselves that offshore rumbling (or wailing) is often heard from the UK, where our linguistic strength (by which I mean the ubiquity of the English language) and our distinctively 'other' legal tradition make us sceptical of much that is seen as both normal and effective elsewhere in the EU/European Patent Convention states. We have a strong IP profession, are seen as offering a good service to those who litigate here (albeit expensively) and are also seen as particularly attuned to the needs of the pharmaceutical sector when it comes to litigation. And, of course, part of the doubtful rumbling concerns the importation of the 'German' approach to handling validity and infringement separately. The disadvantages and risks are clearly and authoritatively set out by Sir David Kitchin. On the other hand Chris Wadlow suggests that the proposals for the UPC reflect 'pragmatism and compromise', which may bode well for its future. I certainly hope so, but note that pragmatism is often seen as a 'nasty British concept' elsewhere within Europe. Which is of course why compromise is so essential to making Europe work.

But if the doubts are essentially those of the 'arms length' Europeans, and those well-adapted to working effectively within the constraints of the current system, does that mean that Europe can sigh with relief now that a long existent gap is being filled? Well, sigh perhaps. My great regret is that something which I see as desirable in the context of the single market, and indeed the realisation of benefits of working together within Europe, is in fact not as good as it could have been. The system will still be incomplete, the transitional provisions will favour the fleet of foot and deep in pocket (and their advisers), the small may enjoy the idea of a pan-European right but their larger opponents will work the system in ways which may well be daunting (or worse) for the small, delays will not disappear, and we shall yet again have ducked the challenge of getting the patent system in Europe into optimal order. But as we know from our experience to date, markets adapt to the imperfect, and what is being implemented will offer plenty of positives as well as doubts and regrets. I just hope that the patent system finds better ways (probably globally) of handling the huge volume of patent applications which now oppress it.

INDEX